Logos
Messiah

Resurrection
& the Life

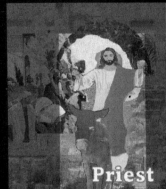

Priest
Prophet
King

Suffering
Servant

The meaning of John's gospel

For personal or group reflection

The Meaning of St John's Gospel
– for personal or group reflection

This set of reflections attempts to shine a light on perhaps the most mystical book ever written. It attempts to do it no more than a page at a time. Inevitably, then, particularly in the first five chapters, you will feel like you are hacking your way through dense jungle.

Keep going. The jungle will not get any easier first time through, but you might find some nice bananas. John intends that we should then read it again, fuelled by the nutrition we found on the first journey. Then a third time; and so on. Hopefully, you like bananas.

By the way, I had planned to be calling God 'Her'. 'Him' would be just as wrong. Eventually, when trying to tell St. John's story, it did not quite work to go with God's maternal side.

Jesus makes up for it by so often challenging the misogynism of his day.

Laurence Wood 2021

Dedication:
To my lovely daughters, Jenny, Madeleine, Mollie and Katey.
This is my faith!

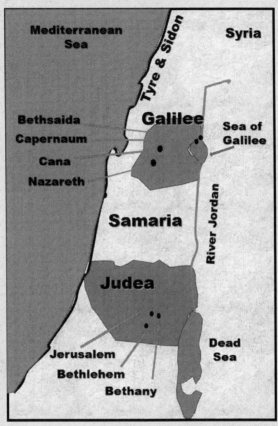

The Holy Land 33AD

Reflections on St John
Prelude: St John's Gospel – an unfolding of the Truth
Prologue: God or nothing?

Part 1: Logos – Messiah

Part 2: Priest Prophet King

Part 3: Lamb of God – Suffering Servant

Part 4: Resurrection and the Life

Prelude: St John's Gospel – an unfolding of the Truth.

In the first three decades after Jesus died, his message had spread to much of the known civilised world – but with little written down. Perhaps this was in part because some disciples might have expected that the world would end in their lifetime – or perhaps it was simply that the oral tradition was the recognised way to pass things on.

However, this spoken means of spreading the news of Jesus, which had disseminated at least as far as Spain, Greece, Persia, and Africa, understandably led to some inconsistencies in the message. Not surprisingly, then, around 70AD, the first 'canonical' – ie church-approved – gospel was written. Two more canonical gospels followed over the next couple of decades. Between them, these three gave deep insight into what Jesus said and did.

However, John must have felt that one message had still not percolated widely enough – the inside story as to who Jesus actually <u>was</u> – the manifestation of God on Earth. As the last canonical gospel to be written, then, John's gospel spoke to the identity of this amazing man. At the end of his Gospel, John says: "Now Jesus did many other signs in the presence of his disciples, which are not written in this book. But these are written so that you may come to believe that Jesus is the Messiah, the Son of God, and that through believing, you may have life in his name."

In particular, for a sympathetic and educated Jew at the time, reading John's gospel would have spoken volumes as to Jesus being the Promised One of Israel, the fulfilment of Moses. John therefore omits many of the actions of Jesus, and picks out moments of immense symbolic importance. Whether or not the chronology is correct, (we do not know), the sequence in which John presents us with signs and discourses, and the circumstances in which these happened, are powerfully significant.

In short, I had not realised until writing these reflections, that John's gospel works best when read from start to finish, because each episode builds on the previous one. The evocative arrangement drives home not just the extraordinary power of the revelation of Jesus as the Messiah, but the harmony of the way in which he fulfilled the Messianic promise.

For that reason, the reflections are short, and they pick out the aspects of the story that underpin John's unfolding of the message. In doing so, they also encapsulate my faith in Jesus as our Redeemer.

(By the way, in some of the reflections I add references at the end for completion. They are just additions for those with plenty of time and an insatiable appetite for cross-referencing. Please do not read them unless you feel the urge!)

1. Prologue: God or nothing?

This exploration of St John's Gospel is not for scholars or saints. Scholars already know all this, and saints no longer need to. These reflections are aimed at people who would like to be good but sometimes aren't; who would like heaven to exist but sometimes doubt it; and who would like to make sense of a religion that sometimes feels improbable or out of touch.

Why St. John's gospel? Well although it was the last written of the four gospels, in a way, it was written <u>as if</u> to be the first book of the New Testament, (the part of the Bible from Jesus onwards). It even starts with the same words as the Old Testament, but then takes us to its fulfilment. It goes on to deal with, not so much the nuts and bolts of Christianity, (like the other three gospels), but rather with what comes before all that – faith. Faith in God, and faith in Jesus, 'the Word of God'.

One more thing to say before we start, and a provocative one, at that: In a sense, there is no such faith as 'atheism'. Let me explain: Atheism is a verbal short-cut for 'not believing in God', but it does not say what the person actually <u>does</u> believe in. Were an atheist to have to come up with a non-God alternative explanation for existence, it might sound equally unlikely. For instance: "I'm an atheist. I think that before the Beginning, there was non-existence of everything. This nothing-ness built up and built up, until finally there was a Big Bang so mind-blowingly awesome, that fourteen billion years later, the unimaginably vast universe is still expanding ... into ... whatever is beyond it ..."

Doesn't really work as an explanation, does it? Despite being vastly preferable to hypocrisy, then, atheism of itself is not a creed; not an explanation. By contrast, as a Christian, I have an explanation: I believe that there <u>was</u> a Big Bang, and that God caused it. I recognise that this is monumentally improbable, but I contest that any other explanation is even more unlikely.

This is particularly important in one way that might have crept under your radar: If there is nothing else shaping us other than the forces of Nature and Evolution; if any seeming benevolence or nastiness of humans is just a function of DNA and Natural

Selection; if God does not exist ... then neither does evil exist. Nor love. We are just fooling ourselves in order to maintain a society that survives.

However, the very fact that you are thinking about the choice between love and evil suggests that there is a part of you – call it your soul if you like – that is capable of stepping outside of the turmoil of human experience, and making moral choices that influence your relationships and experiences.

To put it another way, either morality exists, or it is an illusion. If it is an illusion, then you are never truly being either moral or immoral when you choose your actions, and nothing makes sense. If, instead, morality does exist, then it exists <u>outside</u> of our natural world. Supernatural.

This set of reflections on John's gospel will try to explain why I believe that, ultimately, the supernatural does indeed exist ...

that Love does indeed exist ...

and that this Love is God, the Author and Purpose of the universe.

2. Who is Jesus?

1 In the beginning was the Word, and the Word was with God, and the Word was God. 2 He was in the beginning with God. 3 All things came into being through him, and without him not one thing came into being. What has come into being 4 in him was life, and the life was the light of all people. 5 The light shines in the darkness, and the darkness did not overcome it.

(Verses 6 – 9 are dealt with later)

10 He was in the world, and the world came into being through him; yet the world did not know him. 11 He came to what was his own, and his own people did not accept him. 12 But to all who received him, who believed in his name, he gave power to become children of God, 13 who were born, not of blood or of the will of the flesh or of the will of man, but of God.

14 And the Word became flesh and lived among us, and we have seen his glory, the glory as of a father's only son, full of grace and truth. 15 (John testified to him and cried out, "This was he of whom I said, 'He who comes after me ranks ahead of me because he was before me.'")

16 From his fullness we have all received, grace upon grace. 17 The law indeed was given through Moses; grace and truth came through Jesus Christ. 18 No one has ever seen God. It is God the only Son, who is close to the Father's heart, who has made him known.

2. Who is Jesus?

In the beginning was the Word ... and for me, that metaphor remains the most profound and most helpful way of understanding the infinitely indescribable relationship between God and Jesus.

John's original text used the Greek word 'Logos', which we translate as 'Word'. However, for the people of his day, Logos had a far greater meaning. It signified not just power, but the making real of what otherwise would just be a thought. God thinks, and Logos makes it an external reality. God conceives: Logos manifests: Life; Light.

I think that for many of us, (including those who put Jesus to death), the mistake is to begin our thinking about Jesus with Jesus the man; the person whose existence seemed to have begun on Christmas Day, who went on to be an amazing prophet. John puts that right: Start thinking not of the man, but of the Logos; the manifestor of Life. Fast forward a few billion years from the beginning of time, and, amazingly, the Logos becomes a 'son of man'. Then it starts making sense that Jesus called himself 'Son of Man'. When people asked him if he were the 'Messiah', or the 'Son of God', or 'King of the Jews', he would say that these were <u>our</u> terms for him – terms stacked with so much human nuance that they lost something of the infinite reality.

But is this believable, that God manifests by means of an intermediary? Why not just do the job Himself? For that matter – what IS the job? What is the meaning of Life? Well, if God is the infinite being, and if we recognise His existence by feeling, deep within ourselves, a pull towards either good or evil, then we can infer that God is Love, and that the purpose of life is love. (If not, then, as we have seen, there is no love. No good, no bad.)

And for us, our love can only be truly love when we have chosen it. When we have decided against evil, and decided it ourselves, without being in the unveiled presence of the blindingly obvious Light. By this argument, Creation is a device for us to have the opportunity to choose which side we are on.

The only difficulty is that an infinite God must surely also be infinitely just – which creates a problem for anyone who might not have lived a squeaky-clean life. (Like me.) (And you?) If, in His mercy, He were simply to forgive everything with no more said, then Creation loses its meaning – it no longer is a place where we learn to choose or reject Him.

But, without any manifestation of Him on earth, how do we know enough to make a fair choice? With the Logos being born as a human on that first, amazing Christmas day, the stage was set for humanity to have the chance to choose to be on his team. Or not.

That still leaves the problem of how an infinitely just God might forgive one person their white lies and another their serial killing, (etc), but more of this as we go on.

Pause for reflection: Have a look inside yourself. Do you perceive that inexplicable pull towards love that so often conflicts with what might be convenient or pleasurable? That is who you truly are.

3. Who is John the Baptist?

⁶ There was a man sent from God, whose name was John. ⁷ He came as a witness to testify to the light, so that all might believe through him. ⁸ He himself was not the light, but he came to testify to the light. ⁹ The true light, which enlightens everyone, was coming into the world.

¹⁹ This is the testimony given by John when the Jews sent priests and Levites from Jerusalem to ask him, "Who are you?" ²⁰ He confessed and did not deny it, but confessed, "I am not the Messiah." ²¹ And they asked him, "What then? Are you Elijah?" He said, "I am not." "Are you the prophet?" He answered, "No." ²² Then they said to him, "Who are you? Let us have an answer for those who sent us. What do you say about yourself?"

²³ He said, "I am the voice of one crying out in the wilderness, 'Make straight the way of the Lord,'" as the prophet Isaiah said. ²⁴ Now they had been sent from the Pharisees. ²⁵ They asked him, "Why then are you baptizing if you are neither the Messiah, nor Elijah, nor the prophet?"

²⁶ John answered them, "I baptize with water. Among you stands one whom you do not know, ²⁷ the one who is coming after me; I am not worthy to untie the thong of his sandal." ²⁸ This took place in Bethany across the Jordan where John was baptizing.

²⁹ The next day he saw Jesus coming toward him and declared, "Here is the Lamb of God who takes away the sin of the world!

³⁰ This is he of whom I said, 'After me comes a man who ranks ahead of me because he was before me.' ³¹ I myself did not know him; but I came baptizing with water for this reason, that he might be revealed to Israel."

³² And John testified, "I saw the Spirit descending from heaven like a dove, and it remained on him. ³³ I myself did not know him, but the one who sent me to baptize with water said to me,

'He on whom you see the Spirit descend and remain is the one who baptizes with the Holy Spirit.'

34 And I myself have seen and have testified that this is the Son of God."

3. Who is John the Baptist? – The end of the Old Testament

The Old Testament starts at 'the beginning of time', touches on the creation of souls, then fast-forwards to 1900BC, whence Abraham is chosen by God to be the Messiah's ancestor. From Abraham, many tribes arise, from whom the twelve tribes of Israel become the ones to take forward faith in one God. By the time of David, (1,000BC), in the South, there are only two main tribes left, and some remnants – collected under the tribe of Judah – and to its north a motley collection of other Israelites, (which later became Samaria).

To these peoples, many messengers from God appeared over time, some of them prophesying about the coming Lord who will bring salvation to God's people. The last piece of this Old Testament jigsaw to be put in place is the arrival of John the Baptist. John's gospel introduces the Baptist, and, importantly, deals not just with what John said and did, but of who he actually was. In this way, this exact chapter of John's gospel says goodbye to the Old Testament, and turns the page into the next chapter of salvation.

So who was the Baptist? Ancient prophesies[1,2,3] predicted that before the Messiah would come, there would be a prophet with the Spirit of Elijah, (who never died, but was taken to heaven in a fiery chariot). John declared himself[4] to be the fulfilment of Isaiah's "voice of one crying out in the wilderness". Jesus[5] affirmed John's greatness, saying that the Spirit of Elijah truly was on him[5,6]. This confirmed the angel's prediction to John's father[7].

You might ask what was the point God was making with this elaborate preparation for the first coming of Jesus at the end of the Old Covenant? (A covenant is a solemn promise, in this case God's promise of salvation to His people – a promise which had responsibilities on both sides.) One answer is perhaps that John's preparation was not just a message, nor an ancient version of a Facebook status. It was someone bravely getting out there into the rough world, and doing stuff, (baptising), to turn people's hearts to the coming of the Lord. (Ritual cleansing with water, to symbolise the forgiving of sins. More of this, and of 'The Lamb who takes away the sins of the World' – in due course.)

What, then, if part of the rationale for John is that he is an example? He was preparing for the first coming of Jesus, and we are supposed to be preparing the second coming. The Spirit, not of Elijah, but of God Himself is on us.

John the Baptist is perhaps asking us even today what are we doing to turn hearts to the coming of Jesus?

Fortunately, we are not all called to be evangelistic locust-eaters plunging people into rivers. That was John's identity – indeed, (so Malachi and Isaiah tell us), that was who he was even many centuries before he was born. And he was true to himself.

However, across two millennia, we can still hear the Baptist's voice, asking us, "Who are you? Whose side are you on? What are you doing about it?"

Pause for reflection: So who am I? If there had been a prophecy about me, what would it have said?: 'Thus says the Lord: "Behold! I will send before Me a curmudgeonly old codger, who does a lot of emails"'. Or maybe, each day, I have to be more true to the part I am supposed to be playing in preparing for the coming of the Lord ... True to myself ...

References: 1. Deuteronomy 18:18;   2. Malachi 3:1 & 4:5;
3. Isaiah 40:3-5;   4. John1:21-23;   5. Matthew 11:7-14;
6. Matthew 17:10-12;   7. Luke 1:13-17

4. Andy, Phil, Pete and Natt

35 *The next day John again was standing with two of his disciples,* 36 *and as he watched Jesus walk by, he exclaimed, "Look, here is the Lamb of God!"* 37 *The two disciples heard him say this, and they followed Jesus.*

38 *When Jesus turned and saw them following, he said to them, "What are you looking for?" They said to him, "Rabbi" (which translated means Teacher), "where are you staying?"* 39 *He said to them, "Come and see."*

They came and saw where he was staying, and they remained with him that day. It was about four o'clock in the afternoon. 40 *One of the two who heard John speak and followed him was Andrew, Simon Peter's brother.* 41 *He first found his brother Simon and said to him, "We have found the Messiah" (which is translated Anointed).* 42 *He brought Simon to Jesus, who looked at him and said, "You are Simon son of John. You are to be called Cephas" (which is translated Peter).*

43 *The next day Jesus decided to go to Galilee. He found Philip and said to him, "Follow me."* 44 *Now Philip was from Bethsaida, the city of Andrew and Peter.* 45 *Philip found Nathanael and said to him, "We have found him about whom Moses in the law and also the prophets wrote, Jesus son of Joseph from Nazareth."* 46 *Nathanael said to him, "Can anything good come out of Nazareth?" Philip said to him, "Come and see."*

47 *When Jesus saw Nathanael coming toward him, he said of him, "Here is truly an Israelite in whom there is no deceit!"* 48 *Nathanael asked him, "Where did you get to know me?" Jesus answered, "I saw you under the fig tree before Philip called you."*

49 *Nathanael replied, "Rabbi, you are the Son of God! You are the King of Israel!"*

50 *Jesus answered, "Do you believe because I told you that I saw you under the fig tree? You will see greater things than these."*

51 *And he said to him, "Very truly, I tell you, you will see heaven opened and the angels of God ascending and descending upon the Son of Man."*

4. Andy, Phil, Pete and Natt

The build up is an important part of any story. In the film, 'The Shawshank Redemption', it would not have been much of a story if it began as the wrongly imprisoned hero escapes from prison 10 minutes before the end of the film. Even when you go on holiday, it is human nature not to want a taxi to suddenly arrive, pluck you from home, and thrust some unexpected tickets to Bali in your hand.

So it is with the unfolding of God's redemption plan for mankind. The Messiah did not just pitch up, but had instead been prophesied about many times, in many ways. More importantly, however, an entire story had unfolded over many generations with Abraham's descendants, which turned out to be part of the build up to the Messiah.

The Israelites were being persecuted by evil. A leader arose – Moses. He led them to redemption. The defining moment was the Passover, when the blood of an unblemished lamb was sprinkled on the houses of the Israelites. As Retribution-For-Evil passed through, wreaking death on the Egyptians, the blood of the lamb saved God's people.

The Baptist recognised Jesus as the fulfilment of Moses – the one who would rescue not just the Israelites, but all of mankind. The Lamb of God. But just as in all good stories the final plot twist is a surprise, so it was with the Lamb of God. Not a King. Not an adopted son of the Pharaoh. But a carpenter.

(Actually, for all we know, he was the legitimate earthly king. Throughout the history of Judah, the king always managed to have his own son succeed him, up to the last known, in 586BC. We simply do not know who was the hereditary King of Judah in Jesus's day, except that it was a direct descendant of David. Someone maybe like Joseph, Jesus's adopted father, who was indeed a direct descendant? And Jesus was born in David's town ...)

The surprises did not stop with John naming the local carpenter as the Messiah. Jesus then began to pick his right-hand men, for which he went to ... a fishing village. He found first Andrew, Philip and Peter, (and John, the narrator, who even tells us the time of day it happened).

We do not know what names these men used to call each other, but it is safe to assume that the Greek translations of the name which later appeared in the Gospels, were not what their mums called them. The Logos, after a multi-billion year wait, picked – let's call them Andy, Phil, Pete and Natt – the uneducated; the unlikely; the awkward – to help spread his message of Salvation throughout the rest of time.

Two aspects of this occur to me: Firstly, Jesus does not judge by human standards, by human expectations, by preconceptions, by appearance. He sees what matters – in this case, he sees their heart. Honesty. Integrity. No deceit; no hypocrisy; but instead raw goodness mixed with a normal portion of human frailty.

Secondly, here's the crazy thing: According to the end of this same story, Jesus loves me no less than he loves Peter!

Peter himself famously came to realise that God has no favourites. (Acts 10: 34-35) Not Jews; not fishermen; not the educated; nor the uneducated. Simply no favourites, except those who feel drawn to goodness and love.

Pause for reflection: Jesus has also picked you.

because I picked him ?

5. Chapter 2 Water, wine and the Spirit

[1] On the third day there was a wedding in Cana of Galilee, and the mother of Jesus was there. [2] Jesus and his disciples had also been invited to the wedding. [3] When the wine gave out, the mother of Jesus said to him, "They have no wine." [4] And Jesus said to her, "Woman, what concern is that to you and to me? My hour has not yet come."

[5] His mother said to the servants, "Do whatever he tells you." [6] Now standing there were six stone water jars for the Jewish rites of purification, each holding twenty or thirty gallons.

[7] Jesus said to them, "Fill the jars with water." And they filled them up to the brim. [8] He said to them, "Now draw some out, and take it to the chief steward." So they took it. [9]

When the steward tasted the water that had become wine, and did not know where it came from (though the servants who had drawn the water knew), the steward called the bridegroom [10] and said to him, "Everyone serves the good wine first, and then the inferior wine after the guests have become drunk. But you have kept the good wine until now."

[11] Jesus did this, the first of his signs, in Cana of Galilee, and revealed his glory; and his disciples believed in him.

[12] After this he went down to Capernaum with his mother, his brothers, and his disciples; and they remained there a few days.

5. Water, wine and the Spirit

There are four 'gospels' – ie accounts of Jesus's life. Three of them view things from much the same perspective, ('synoptic'), and the fourth is John's gospel. The three synoptic gospel-writers, ('evangelists'), were educated men of whose identity we are fairly sure. (A tax collector; a disciple who teamed up with the apostles; and a doctor who was interested in the Jesus story.) But who was 'John', and why was his gospel so different?

The traditional understanding is that John was a fisherman, son of the boat-owner, and the younger brother of James. (In fact, not just the younger brother, but he was the youngest apostle, which is why in many stained-glass windows, he looks like beardless Leonardo di Caprio, whilst the others look like Brian Blessed.) He might even have been a sort of cousin of Jesus, and he refers to himself in his gospel as 'the disciple whom Jesus loved'.

John was the only one of the eleven apostles who stayed with Jesus during the crucifixion; and the only one not to be martyred. He died on the island of Patmos after having written the final version of his gospel maybe even 60 years or more after the death of Jesus.

Of course, generations of scholars have picked all sorts of holes in this traditional version of events, but the fact remains that this gospel seems to have authentic eyewitness accounts, from what, (so it seems), can only be John's eyes – for instance of the Transfiguration or the Crucifixion.

True, it is strange that a Galilean fisherman wrote such a sophisticated symbolic structure, and did it in good Greek, but for me, this is not a task beyond the Holy Spirit; given six decades, a burning desire, a clever man, and a deeply spiritual close friend of Jesus.

What, then, is this mystical structure that John's gospel has which does not appear elsewhere?

Well, it begins with this wedding feast. Having recruited disciples, the synoptic gospels open Jesus's ministry with him just getting out there on his mission; preaching and healing. In

John's account, by contrast, the ministry starts as it ends – with a party, and it is a party where deep significance is given to the wine.

Importantly, John does not refer to this water-into-wine as a 'miracle', but as a 'Sign'. In fact, it is the first of seven Signs, (seven being a number which symbolised completion or perfection). The miraculous nature of the event was a sign that here was the Logos, the Messiah.

More than that, however, the more clear-headed partygoers at Cana would have understood that wine, in the Old Testament, was used to signify two things. One of them was blessing, and they had been just prodigiously blessed with 600 to 900 litres of premier cru.

The other ancient Jewish significance of wine was judgement. At the other end of Jesus's ministry, wine was to be the sign that Jesus had taken the judgement of this world's sins on himself ...

Pause for reflection: Mary was there at the beginning and at the end. John says that it was she who sparked off Jesus's ministry with her request for help – help that was not earned nor even deserved, but just something to make the Divine Plan and the human one happily coincide.

John might even have been a sort of nephew to Mary – and indeed lived with her like her son, after Jesus's death and resurrection. I expect that they would have talked about that first day in Cana ...

6.. The end of the old Temple

¹³ The Passover of the Jews was near, and Jesus went up to Jerusalem. ¹⁴ In the temple he found people selling cattle, sheep, and doves, and the money changers seated at their tables.

¹⁵ Making a whip of cords, he drove all of them out of the temple, both the sheep and the cattle. He also poured out the coins of the money changers and overturned their tables. ¹⁶ He told those who were selling the doves, "Take these things out of here! Stop making my Father's house a marketplace!"

¹⁷ His disciples remembered that it was written, "Zeal for your house will consume me."

¹⁸ The Jews then said to him, "What sign can you show us for doing this?" ¹⁹ Jesus answered them, "Destroy this temple, and in three days I will raise it up." ²⁰ The Jews then said, "This temple has been under construction for forty-six years, and will you raise it up in three days?" ²¹ But he was speaking of the temple of his body.

²² After he was raised from the dead, his disciples remembered that he had said this; and they believed the scripture and the word that Jesus had spoken.

²³ When he was in Jerusalem during the Passover festival, many believed in his name because they saw the signs that he was doing. ²⁴ But Jesus on his part would not entrust himself to them, because he knew all people ²⁵ and needed no one to testify about anyone; for he himself knew what was in everyone.

6. The end of the old Temple

When my daughters were teenagers, I was frequently told, "My friends are coming round, Dad, so PROMISE you won't tell any of your stupid jokes!" Of course I would promise, but then I would tell jokes anyway. Maybe 'promise' was overstating it. In modern times, we even use the word 'promise' to imply that something only <u>might</u> happen – 'it has promise'.

This slackness in interpretation of giving one's word is utterly at odds with the Biblical understanding of promising. In Jewish Law, if two witnesses testified that something was true, then it was true – giving false testimony was a scandalous crime, even punishable by the same sentence as would have been received by the person falsely accused.

We have seen that 'signs' are vitally significant for John, but 'testimony' is also a remarkably powerful recurring feature of John's gospel – a version of the word being used 47 times.

Indeed, we even refer to the gospel as being part of the New Testament; the new witness; the new promise. However, when giving one's solemn word as part of an agreement, then a better word is 'covenant'. John's gospel is part of the New Covenant.

What, then, was the <u>Old</u> Covenant? Amongst other promises, God made a solemn contract with Moses and the Israelites in the desert, as they fled the Egyptians. If the people were to obey the Law given by God to Moses, then they would be richly blessed.

The Covenant was represented by the stone tablets on which God had written the Ten Commandments. These were most reverentially stored in 'The Ark of the Covenant', which itself came to be placed eventually in the 'Holy of Holies' of Solomon's temple.

The temple, then, was the dwelling place of the Word of God, and the centre-point of Jewish culture and fervent reverence in the Old Covenant. Then along comes a mad carpenter with his fisherman friends, and wrecks the place.

Except that he was not mad, but was in fact the Logos – the Word of God, coming to the one place in the world which represented his own presence. His violent expulsion of swindlers was a forerunner of his subsequent intolerance of the hypocrisy of the Pharisees, who tried to turn God's solemn Word, God's Covenant, into a travesty of itself.

"The time has come for a New Covenant", Jesus was saying by this highly symbolic episode, "and a new Temple for the Word of God – this human body". When Jesus said, "Destroy this temple, and in three days I will raise it up", he was talking in the voice of God, hinting that the new contract would involve the temporary death of the dwelling-place of the Logos – Jesus.

Thereafter, in some mysterious way, we would not need to make pilgrimages to Jerusalem to be in the presence of the Word of God.

Jeremiah had already prophesied about this new Covenant, under which God said that his Word would not be written on tablets of stone – but on our hearts[1].

Pause for reflection: If you have sometimes considered that a church building has limited relevance for you; if you, like me, have sometimes felt uncomfortable with all the rituals and customs in church services; then remember that Jesus more than understands where you are coming from.

Check what is written on your heart.

Reference: 1. Jeremiah 31:33

7. Chapter 3 Water and the Spirit again

[1] *Now there was a Pharisee named Nicodemus, a leader of the Jews.* [2] *He came to Jesus by night and said to him, "Rabbi, we know that you are a teacher who has come from God; for no one can do these signs that you do apart from the presence of God."*

[3] *Jesus answered him, "Very truly, I tell you, no one can see the kingdom of God without being born from above."* [4] *Nicodemus said to him, "How can anyone be born after having grown old? Can one enter a second time into the mother's womb and be born?"*

[5] *Jesus answered, "Very truly, I tell you, no one can enter the kingdom of God without being born of water and Spirit.* [6] *What is born of the flesh is flesh, and what is born of the Spirit is spirit.* [7] *Do not be astonished that I said to you, 'You must be born from above.'* [8] *The wind blows where it chooses, and you hear the sound of it, but you do not know where it comes from or where it goes. So it is with everyone who is born of the Spirit."*

[9] *Nicodemus said to him, "How can these things be?"*

[10] *Jesus answered him, "Are you a teacher of Israel, and yet you do not understand these things?* [11] *"Very truly, I tell you, we speak of what we know and testify to what we have seen; yet you do not receive our testimony.* [12] *If I have told you about earthly things and you do not believe, how can you believe if I tell you about heavenly things?*

[13] *No one has ascended into heaven except the one who descended from heaven, the Son of Man.* [14] *And just as Moses lifted up the serpent in the wilderness, so must the Son of Man be lifted up,* [15] *that whoever believes in him may have eternal life.*

[16] *"For God so loved the world that he gave his only Son, so that everyone who believes in him may not perish but may have eternal life.*

[17] *"Indeed, God did not send the Son into the world to condemn the world, but in order that the world might be saved through him. [18] Those who believe in him are not condemned; but those who do not believe are condemned already, because they have not believed in the name of the only Son of God.*

[19] *And this is the judgement, that the light has come into the world, and people loved darkness rather than light because their deeds were evil.*

[20] *For all who do evil hate the light and do not come to the light, so that their deeds may not be exposed.*

[21] *But those who do what is true come to the light, so that it may be clearly seen that their deeds have been done in God."*

7. Water and the Spirit again

Did you notice how John shifts the action from a stupendous sign in Cana in Galilee, suddenly to Jerusalem, four or five days walk away, without a mention of what happened in between?

One potential reason for this might have been that John's timeline might not actually reflect the chronology of Jesus's ministry, but instead is arranged symbolically.

Certainly, there are major differences between the synoptics and John. Matthew, Mark and Luke all agree on Jesus only visiting Jerusalem once as an adult, where John has Jesus attending on four different occasions. The jury is out as to which is right, but in favour of John's version, a devout Jew in those days – even one living four days' walk away – would have expected to visit Jerusalem for a number of the major feasts.

Furthermore, an important pointer to the authenticity of John's version is that it gives more time and more occasions for all of the ministry which occurred in Jerusalem – and more time to upset the High Priest enough to be condemned.

The fact remains however, that in John's unfolding of the Logos story, it was important for him to follow up the Cana event, first with the purging of the Temple, then with this puzzling passage.

Why?

Given the importance John places on the Logos and the New Covenant, perhaps therein lies an answer. In the Old Covenant, of which Nicodemus was a devout proponent, to find oneself in God's favour, the prerequisite was to be born a Jew. To have Jewish blood.

However, even in the days of Moses, thirteen centuries or more before, God prepared the ground for the understanding that a new blood was needed for salvation. Being an Israelite was not enough.

At the first Passover, the blood of a spotless lamb was sprinkled on the houses of those Israelites to be saved from death. In the New Covenant, Jesus recognised that he was the new Passover Lamb, and it would be his blood which would be sprinkled – not just for the Jews, but for all who were willing to accept him. The Lamb of God; the Messiah; the Son of Man; would shed the new Passover blood.

However, without Moses to sprinkle Nicodemus with the Blood of the Lamb, how might he access it?

The answer, Jesus cryptically tells Nicodemus, is 'to be born again', 'By faith in the Son of God'. What could this perplexing metaphor mean? One beautiful aspect of the arrangement of John's gospel, is that the answer to such profound metaphysical mysteries is likely to be found either in what just happened, or in what happened next.

In this case, the Baptist-Cana-Jerusalem sequence began with John the Baptist. When his disciples found that John's words spoke to their hearts, they showed it by being immersed in the Jordan. Thereafter, lifted out of their old selves, dripping with water, they were almost like babies coming from a womb. That outward sign of water signified an inward moving of the Spirit, to liven that person's soul with God's mark – if you like, to turn their watery humanity into the rich blood of eternity.

Water and the Spirit ... this continues in the next reflection.

Pause for reflection: At the start of his ministry – a celebratory meal, and water becomes wine – in abundance for all.

At the end of his ministry – a celebratory meal, and wine 'becomes' his blood – in abundance for all.

8. The one who is from above

22 After this Jesus and his disciples went into the Judean countryside, and he spent some time there with them and baptised. 23 John also was baptising at Aenon near Salim because water was abundant there; and people kept coming and were being baptised 24 — John, of course, had not yet been thrown into prison.

25 Now a discussion about purification arose between John's disciples and a Jew. 26 They came to John and said to him, "Rabbi, the one who was with you across the Jordan, to whom you testified, here he is baptising, and all are going to him."

27 John answered, "No one can receive anything except what has been given from heaven. 28 You yourselves are my witnesses that I said, 'I am not the Messiah, but I have been sent ahead of him.' 29 He who has the bride is the bridegroom. The friend of the bridegroom, who stands and hears him, rejoices greatly at the bridegroom's voice. For this reason, my joy has been fulfilled. 30 He must increase, but I must decrease."

31 The one who comes from above is above all; the one who is of the earth belongs to the earth and speaks about earthly things. The one who comes from heaven is above all. 32 He testifies to what he has seen and heard, yet no one accepts his testimony. 33 Whoever has accepted his testimony has certified this, that God is true.

34 He whom God has sent speaks the words of God, for he gives the Spirit without measure. 35 The Father loves the Son and has placed all things in his hands. 36 Whoever believes in the Son has eternal life; whoever disobeys the Son will not see life, but must endure God's wrath.

8. The one who is from above

... Water and the Spirit – and thus John's gospel neatly rounds up the Baptist-Cana-Jerusalem sequence with a return to the Baptist, witnessing that Jesus truly is the Logos.

With this in mind, returning to the conversation with Nicodemus, things begin to make more sense. In talking of 'being born again', Jesus is summing up John's gospel thus far: a new Covenant; the Logos made man; the water of baptism signifying the Spirit 'being written in our hearts'; the water-into-wine of Cana signifying that this produces rich blessing – and unearned justification; and the wine of Cana and the Blood of the Lamb, signifying God's judgement now being taken on himself by the Logos.

Phew. That's an entire library of religion right there in that one paragraph.

Jesus does not leave it at that, however. To complete the picture, and to hint at how this blessing of the Logos also becomes payment for our sins, Jesus foretells of his crucifixion.

He points out how, even in the detail of the way he will die, he is fulfilling the Old Covenant, as represented by Moses in the desert: When in the midst of their forty-year trek, fleeing from the Egyptians across the desert to the Promised Land, the Israelites had times of rebellion against trusting in the one God. In one such time, a plague of snakes caused havoc amongst the people and they pleaded with Moses to ask God's help.

Moses was told to fix a snake to a pole, and those who gazed on it with faith would be saved. Not so much that they had to gaze on the snake itself, however, but on the whole thing, a snake nailed to a tree branch, raised up.

Just as in the Adam and Eve story, the snake represents the sins of the people, and the tree, the Tree of Life. The promised Saviour of Israel would be hung on a tree, in some mysterious way carrying with him the sins of the world, (of which more later). Those who gazed on him with faith would be healed.

In the Old Covenant, to be favoured by God, you needed Israelite blood. To escape from the evil Pharaoh, you needed the blood of the Passover lamb.

In the New Covenant, you did not need to be an Israelite, but you did need a blood-sacrifice to atone for your misdeeds: not the blood of a perfect young sheep, but the Blood of the Lamb ... as represented by wine, and the cross.

Pause for reflection: It no longer matters what blood you were born with. What matters now is whose side you are on.

Do you gaze on Jesus with faith, or with contempt? John is trying to show us that being on Jesus's team, far from being self-delusion, is the one thing that gives proper meaning to life.

Some references for prophesies concerning the one who would come to save Israel: Deuteronomy 30:1-6, Jeremiah 23:1-8, Jeremiah 31:31-34, Jeremiah 32:37-41, Ezekiel 11:16-20, Ezekiel 36:16-28, Ezekiel 37:11-14, 37:21-28

Deut 30:4 Even if you are exiled to the ends of the world the Lord will gather you and bring you back

9. Chapter 4 *The first to be told: a foreigner, a sinner, a woman*

1 Now when Jesus learned that the Pharisees had heard, "Jesus is making and baptizing more disciples than John" 2 — although it was not Jesus himself but his disciples who baptized — 3 he left Judea and started back to Galilee. 4 But he had to go through Samaria.

5 So he came to a Samaritan city called Sychar, near the plot of ground that Jacob had given to his son Joseph. 6 Jacob's well was there, and Jesus, tired out by his journey, was sitting by the well. It was about noon.

7 A Samaritan woman came to draw water, and Jesus said to her, "Give me a drink." 8 (His disciples had gone to the city to buy food.) 9 The Samaritan woman said to him, "How is it that you, a Jew, ask a drink of me, a woman of Samaria?" (Jews do not share things in common with Samaritans.)

10 Jesus answered her, "If you knew the gift of God, and who it is that is saying to you, 'Give me a drink,' you would have asked him, and he would have given you living water."

11 The woman said to him, "Sir, you have no bucket, and the well is deep. Where do you get that living water? 12 Are you greater than our ancestor Jacob, who gave us the well, and with his sons and his flocks drank from it?"

13 Jesus said to her, "Everyone who drinks of this water will be thirsty again, 14 but those who drink of the water that I will give them will never be thirsty. The water that I will give will become in them a spring of water gushing up to eternal life."

15 The woman said to him, "Sir, give me this water, so that I may never be thirsty or have to keep coming here to draw water."

16 Jesus said to her, "Go, call your husband, and come back." 17 The woman answered him, "I have no husband." Jesus said to her, "You are right in saying, 'I have no husband'; 18 for you have had five husbands, and the one you have now is not your husband. What you have said is true!" 19 The woman said to him, "Sir, I see that you are a prophet. ²⁰ Our ancestors worshiped on this mountain, but you say that the place where people must worship is in Jerusalem."

²¹ Jesus said to her, "Woman, believe me, the hour is coming when you will worship the Father neither on this mountain nor in Jerusalem. ²² You worship what you do not know; we worship what we know, for salvation is from the Jews.

²³ But the hour is coming, and is now here, when the true worshipers will worship the Father in spirit and truth, for the Father seeks such as these to worship him. ²⁴ God is spirit, and those who worship him must worship in spirit and truth."

²⁵ The woman said to him, "I know that Messiah is coming" (who is called Christ). "When he comes, he will proclaim all things to us." ²⁶ Jesus said to her, "I am he, the one who is speaking to you."

9. The first to be told: a foreigner, a sinner, a woman

Nicodemus is portrayed as being a Jewish rabbi of exemplary righteousness. I imagine, then, that he was more than nonplussed to have visited the man that he hoped was the Messiah, only to be told, in cryptic cross-references to Scriptures, that righteousness was no longer the deal. Not even being of the Chosen Race mattered any more. The new arrangement depended on water, the Spirit, rebirth, and faith in the Son of Man.

If Nicodemus had been shaken by that encounter, how much more would his world have come tumbling down if he saw what Jesus did next, to make the point more strongly.

He found the polar opposite of righteous Jewish-Elder Nicodemus – a Samaritan, a woman and an outcast sinner, any one of which would mean that even noticing her would be seen as almost blasphemy – and he told her directly that he was the Messiah. Then went for a spot of lunch at her house.

The background to the reviling of Samaritans went back to more than a millennium before Jesus. When the Israelites reached the Promised Land, there were twelve tribes, but by the time of King David, (around 1000 BC), there was just the tribe of (mainly) Judah in the South, and the Kingdom of Israel in the north.

Whereas in Judah, starting with David, the King's son always succeeded the King; in the hotchpotch of tribes to the north, there were endless coups.

Eventually, Israel was conquered by the Assyrians, and the land became even more racially diverse, with their own home-grown version of an Israelite religion. By the time of Jesus, this land was called Samaria, and there was mutual revulsion between Samaritans and Jews.

And it was a Samaritan, a woman, and a social outcast even amongst her own people, to whom Jesus revealed his identity. He had not even told his own apostles directly that he was the

Messiah, and they must have been utterly perplexed by this behaviour.

They must have found the offer of 'living water' even more puzzling. Indeed, even today, this dialogue provokes more than a bit of reflection. Fortunately, in John's gospel, we get to see this Samaritan episode juxtaposed to the Nicodemus conversation.

We have just heard Jesus talking in Jerusalem, the Holy City, about being born of water and the Spirit. Now, sat down next to the water discovered by their mutual ancestor Jacob, (also known as Israel), Jesus expands on the water theme. He tells the woman – this polar opposite of righteousness – not only that he, the Logos, is the source of the Water of Life, but that in those that receive this 'baptism', the Water will become like a spring gushing up in them.

In other words, once again, we are talking about Water and the Spirit. When we receive the Spirit of God, we ourselves become vessels for the Spirit – presumably so that God's work might be multiplied through us. Through literally any of us.

Pause for reflection: In John's telling of the Jesus story, the nature of the New Covenant, being so far beyond our understanding, is introduced to us a little at a time, spiralling upward in increasing richness. We had heard about water; about blood; and about the Spirit.

Now, next to the Samaritan well, we hear about Truth. The Samaritan woman, who should not even have looked at Jesus, humbly confessed the truth about her love life – and this seemed to unlock the flow from Jesus. Humility. Truth. These are the way in.

10. A spiritual harvest

27 Just then his disciples came. They were astonished that he was speaking with a woman, but no one said, "What do you want?" or, "Why are you speaking with her?" 28 Then the woman left her water jar and went back to the city. She said to the people, 29 "Come and see a man who told me everything I have ever done! He cannot be the Messiah, can he?" 30 They left the city and were on their way to him.

31 Meanwhile the disciples were urging him, "Rabbi, eat something." 32 But he said to them, "I have food to eat that you do not know about." 33 So the disciples said to one another, "Surely no one has brought him something to eat?"

34 Jesus said to them, "My food is to do the will of him who sent me and to complete his work. 35 Do you not say, 'Four months more, then comes the harvest'?

But I tell you, look around you, and see how the fields are ripe for harvesting. 36 The reaper is already receiving wages and is gathering fruit for eternal life, so that sower and reaper may rejoice together. 37 For here the saying holds true, 'One sows and another reaps.' 38 I sent you to reap that for which you did not labour. Others have laboured, and you have entered into their labour."

39 Many Samaritans from that city believed in him because of the woman's testimony, "He told me everything I have ever done." 40 So when the Samaritans came to him, they asked him to stay with them; and he stayed there two days. 41 And many more believed because of his word. 42 They said to the woman, "It is no longer because of what you said that we believe, for we have heard for ourselves, and we know that this is truly the Saviour of the world."

10. A spiritual harvest

The last commentary ended with humility, and this section begins with it: the humility of the disciples in deferring to Jesus's lead, even when it was seemingly as outrageous as taking a drink from a Samaritan woman, and talking to her about being the Messiah.

Before they have a chance to draw their breath from this astonishing scenario, Jesus launches straight into a new theme. Here we have another example of the upward spiral of understanding that John uses to such good effect. As we will see as the gospel unfolds, John introduces a theme, then comes back to it again at just the right moment, to add complexity, richness – and, often, more mystery.

In this case, we had already been introduced to the idea of linking the manifestation of the Spirit of God in us, with water, then with wine, then with blood. To this recipe is now added the final element – bread.

In the agrarian world in which Jesus lived, although fish, milk and meat might have sparsely supplemented the diet for the fortunate, the mainstay of keeping food in one's stomach was bread. A principal purpose of reaping the harvest was to gather wheat for making bread. 'Food' and 'bread' were almost synonyms.

Jesus, however, talked of a bread, a food, 'that you do not know about'. Just as with Nicodemus, he is talking about the nurturing of the soul given by the Spirit of God. The Bread of Life.

In the Nicodemus conversation, he had alluded to the water of baptism as the outward sign of the manifestation of the Spirit. With the Samaritan woman, he continues with the water analogy, but then builds on it by suggesting that not only is the Water (i.e. the Spirit) the inexhaustible refreshment to his soul, but also that the Spirit is the Food that truly nourishes him.

As with water, wine, and blood, John places profound importance on this bread metaphor, and only when we reach the Last Supper, do we get to appreciate the full significance of some of Jesus's cryptic words.

Jesus goes on to suggest that if he is to minister not just to Jews but to all those who listen to his voice; and if they are to receive Water gushing up in them; and spiritual Food; then he, Jesus, is going to need help.

The help of an unlikely bunch of normal people who trust him enough to go where he leads, and to do unexpected things.

The harvest is now.

Pause for reflection: Give us this day our daily bread ...

11. Witnesses, signs and faith

43 *When the two days were over, he went from that place to Galilee* **44** *(for Jesus himself had testified that a prophet has no honour in the prophet's own country).* **45** *When he came to Galilee, the Galileans welcomed him, since they had seen all that he had done in Jerusalem at the festival; for they too had gone to the festival.*

46 *Then he came again to Cana in Galilee where he had changed the water into wine.*

Now there was a royal official whose son lay ill in Capernaum. **47** *When he heard that Jesus had come from Judea to Galilee, he went and begged him to come down and heal his son, for he was at the point of death.*

48 *Then Jesus said to him, "Unless you see signs and wonders you will not believe."* **49** *The official said to him, "Sir, come down before my little boy dies."*

50 *Jesus said to him, "Go; your son will live." The man believed the word that Jesus spoke to him and started on his way.* **51** *As he was going down, his slaves met him and told him that his child was alive.* **52** *So he asked them the hour when he began to recover, and they said to him, "Yesterday at one in the afternoon the fever left him."* **53** *The father realized that this was the hour when Jesus had said to him, "Your son will live." So he himself believed, along with his whole household.*

54 *Now this was the second sign that Jesus did after coming from Judea to Galilee.*

11. Witnesses, signs and faith

I think that by now we get the idea that John's gospel follows a carefully thought-through sequence. Although this Galilee trip was the natural end of the journey from Jerusalem via Samaria, John has nevertheless omitted any other minor bits and bobs of the road trip, to go straight into this story of healing.

We must therefore ask 'Why?' Why does John follow up Jesus's claim to be the Messiah; the Living Water; the Living Bread; with a miraculous healing? And why does he call it a 'sign'?

Before unpacking the idea of Signs in more detail, we need to have another look at the recurring idea of testimony in John's Gospel.

Testimony was (still is) a vital part of Jewish life. In ancient Jewish Law, a person could even be put to death if two witnesses of good standing agreed that he had confessed to the crime*. Jews in the time of Jesus would have been brought up on the importance of witnesses to any claim.

However, when Moses was giving final instructions to the Israelites before his death, he had received the instructions directly from God, with no human witness. How could they know that what Moses said was true?

The answer is that, in such momentous circumstances, it was deemed acceptable that something other than human could be a witness. Something lasting; something that could later support the person's story – a song; a book; even 'the heavens and earth'[1].

The criterion for these rare instances of witnesses being things rather than people, was that they 'spoke' to the truth[2].

Jesus's two non-human witnesses are the Spirit; and the Signs.

The Spirit, because it could 'well up like living water' within you, and let you know for sure that it was the Truth.

Signs, because they indisputably demonstrated the supernatural power of the Logos.

This story, then, uses the Sign as a witness to the fundamental truth he explained to both Nicodemus and the Samaritan woman. It is not your blood nor your righteousness that will save you, but rather it is faith that gets you the results.

Pause for reflection: It was 2am in University Hospital on the dark, lonely COVID ICU. The nurse came to my friend and asked whether he wanted to phone anyone, before they put him on the ventilator. A 60 year old businessman brought up as agnostic, he was terrified. All he could do was to call on some ill-defined belief, and surrender himself to his idea of God. He got better. Now, he says that his life has been turned on its head. "I have four businesses, dozens of staff, and no income. But I just can't bring myself to worry."

In the same way, the royal official in this story subjected himself humbly to Jesus. Suddenly, life was turned on its head. When the slave was healed, I wonder if the official also found it hard to worry about the same things ever again.

If, in these tough times, you find yourself worrying too much about things that do not last, how about sending a humble and faithful message to the Lord? As it says in another version of this story, (with the centurion instead of a royal official), Jesus needs only speak the Word ...

*References: 1. Deut 19:6&15 Deut 31:19 2. 26-28 Genesis 31:48-50 Psalm 89:37

12. Chapter 5 *Sooo missing the point*

1 After this there was a festival of the Jews, and Jesus went up to Jerusalem. 2 Now in Jerusalem by the Sheep Gate there is a pool, called in Hebrew Bethesda, (Bethzatha), which has five porticoes. 3 In these lay many invalids — blind, lame, and paralyzed. 5 One man was there who had been ill for thirty-eight years.

6 When Jesus saw him lying there and knew that he had been there a long time, he said to him, "Do you want to be made well?" 7 The sick man answered him, "Sir, I have no one to put me into the pool when the water is stirred up; and while I am making my way, someone else steps down ahead of me." 8 Jesus said to him, "Stand up, take your mat and walk." 9 At once the man was made well, and he took up his mat and began to walk.

Now that day was a sabbath. 10 So the Jews said to the man who had been cured, "It is the sabbath; it is not lawful for you to carry your mat." 11 But he answered them, "The man who made me well said to me, 'Take up your mat and walk.'" 12 They asked him, "Who is the man who said to you, 'Take it up and walk'?" 13 Now the man who had been healed did not know who it was, for Jesus had disappeared in the crowd that was there.

14 Later Jesus found him in the temple and said to him, "See, you have been made well! Do not sin any more, so that nothing worse happens to you." 15 The man went away and told the Jews that it was Jesus who had made him well. 16 Therefore the Jews started persecuting Jesus, because he was doing such things on the sabbath.

17 But Jesus answered them, "My Father is still working, and I also am working." 18 For this reason the Jews were seeking all the more to kill him, because he was not only breaking the sabbath, but was also calling God his own Father, thereby making himself equal to God.

12. Sooo missing the point

From Galilee, John reports that Jesus returns to Jerusalem, where the next Sign is performed. Again we need to search for meaning not just in the event itself, but in why Jesus chose to do this Sign at this moment.

(By the way, although we have noted that the sequence of events in John is different from the sequence in the synoptics, and that many scholars believe this to be attributable to John's symbolic unfolding of layers of understanding about the Logos, that does not preclude historical accuracy! As the Logos, Jesus would have been well aware of the importance of the timing of his actions and might therefore have chosen with great care the time and place of the two healings we have just seen – the second and third of the seven Signs.)

This healing at Bethesda stirs up in me a tempest of indignation against the Jewish authorities, at their pompous, smug, self-righteous intolerance. (We Baby Boomers saw all authority as being that way back in the 60s, and therefore maybe have a particular empathy with Jesus in this event! Certainly, if Bob Dylan had lived in Jesus's time, he would have written 'The Ballad of Bethesda Pool'.)

But how could they be so wrong! Given that this was a miracle, therefore it must have come from God! How could the Jewish authorities not get this? Or even just be perplexed rather than vindictive?!

It happened on the Sabbath, a day made especially holy in the Ten Commandments given to Moses[1]. The Commandment was: 'Do no work ... rest'. Many centuries of Scribes had converted this into: 'Obey an impenetrably complex (and at times hypocritical) set of tough restrictions', converting what had supposed to be a blessing into a pain. How could they not see that Jesus was shining a light on the true nature of the gift of the Sabbath?!

Jesus called God 'Father' – a title God Himself had claimed through Hosea[2]: 'They will be called children of the living God'. Many other Old Testament texts reflected the true nature of God as the Father[3]. How could the Scribes and Pharisees not know this?

And their response to the miracle – was it to get together to have a bit of a think about this cure, and a reappraisal of their understanding? No. It was ... that Jesus must be killed!

So, to sum up the two Signs: A healing in Galilee to show that it was no longer Jewish blood that saved you, but instead it was now the Word of God.

Then a healing in Jerusalem to show that the New Covenant was challenging not only Jewish blood, but also the Jewish tradition that had slowly evolved since Moses.

This Bethesda healing was designed to reveal the real Spirit of God's Word to Moses. Spirit. Word. ... Logos.

Pause for reflection: Kill or Cure? Which of these: kill, or cure, (metaphorically speaking), do we choose when we are confronted with a challenge to our authority and identity:

"Thanks. I must think about what you have said."

Or

"On your bike!"

*References: 1. Exodus: 20:8-11   2. Hosea 1:10
3. Deut 14:1 & 32:6 Psalms 82:6 Isaiah 63:16 & 64:8 Jer 3:19 & 31:9 Malachi 2:10*

13. Logos. Fulfilment. Spirit. Eternal Life

19 Jesus said to them, "Very truly, I tell you, the Son can do nothing on his own, but only what he sees the Father doing; for whatever the Father does, the Son does likewise. 20 The Father loves the Son and shows him all that he himself is doing; and he will show him greater works than these, so that you will be astonished.

21 Indeed, just as the Father raises the dead and gives them life, so also the Son gives life to whomever he wishes. 22 The Father judges no one but has given all judgement to the Son, 23 so that all may honour the Son just as they honour the Father. Anyone who does not honour the Son does not honour the Father who sent him.

24 Very truly, I tell you, anyone who hears my word and believes him who sent me has eternal life, and does not come under judgment, but has passed from death to life.

25 "Very truly, I tell you, the hour is coming, and is now here, when the dead will hear the voice of the Son of God, and those who hear will live. 26 For just as the Father has life in himself, so he has granted the Son also to have life in himself; 27 and he has given him authority to execute judgement, because he is the Son of Man.

28 Do not be astonished at this; for the hour is coming when all who are in their graves will hear his voice 29 and will come out— those who have done good, to the resurrection of life, and those who have done evil, to the resurrection of condemnation.

30 "I can do nothing on my own. As I hear, I judge; and my judgement is just, because I seek to do not my own will but the will of him who sent me. 31 "If I testify about myself, my testimony is not true. 32 There is another who testifies on my behalf, and I know that his testimony to me is true.

33 You sent messengers to John, and he testified to the truth. 34 Not that I accept such human testimony, but I say these things so that you may be saved. 35 He was a burning and shining lamp, and you were willing to rejoice for a while in his light.

36 But I have a testimony greater than John's. The works that the Father has given me to complete, the very works that I am doing, testify on my behalf that the Father has sent me. 37 And the Father who sent me has himself testified on my behalf. You have never heard his voice or seen his form, 38 and you do not have his word abiding in you, because you do not believe him whom he has sent.

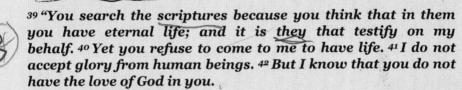

39 "You search the scriptures because you think that in them you have eternal life; and it is they that testify on my behalf. 40 Yet you refuse to come to me to have life. 41 I do not accept glory from human beings. 42 But I know that you do not have the love of God in you.

43 I have come in my Father's name, and you do not accept me; if another comes in his own name, you will accept him. 44 How can you believe when you accept glory from one another and do not seek the glory that comes from the one who alone is God?

45 Do not think that I will accuse you before the Father; your accuser is Moses, on whom you have set your hope. 46 If you believed Moses, you would believe me, for he wrote about me. 47 But if you do not believe what he wrote, how will you believe what I say?"

Luke 3 John the baptist.

voice crying in the desert!

Psalm 2:7 ?

13. Logos. Fulfilment. Spirit. Eternal Life

To an extent, this is the final aspect of the Nature of the Logos that John wants to reveal, before going back to supply us with more detail and nuance. In these first five chapters:

- He introduced the Logos as the Manifestation of God. (God the Father, as Jesus now teaches us to call Him.)
- Then we saw the Logos as the Fulfilment of Moses and the Old Testament.
- Jesus then declared himself the Source of the Spirit, the source of Living Water; Living Bread.
- And now, he is the Giver of eternal life, from the Father, to those who trust in the Son.

John will return to all of these themes in increasing richness of understanding as the gospel proceeds, but this discourse of Jesus comes now, to sum up the meaning of life, and his part in it. Jesus clarifies the purpose of the Logos – as 'the Son of Man' – which is to give eternal life, from the Loving Father, to those who choose to be on his side.

"Do not be astonished." I repeat to you Jesus's words, because doubtless many at this point will feel that credibility has been stretched unjustifiably far.

In response, I might plead that if God does not exist, nothing makes sense, but that if He does, then, for all its outrageous elaborateness, the Logos story does hang together.

You might then retort that being (just about) logically coherent is one thing, but being the only possible consequence of a divinely inspired Big Bang – that is another story.

Jesus was well aware that his listeners might be thinking, (like some of you??), that he was off his trolley. He therefore added infinite weight to his passionate plea with two inescapable points:

Firstly, he is not just a good person, he is THE good person – so why would he lie?

Secondly, if you still do not want to believe him, he pointed out (as we have already seen) that he has witnesses: the Spirit; Moses, and "the Father himself". The Spirit because his followers had seen its power in the Signs; Moses because the entire Jewish culture and faith centred on him, and it seemed now that he pre-figured Jesus; and the Father, because He had sent His Word to abide in his disciples, and they felt it in their hearts.

Tough, impenetrable, mind-blowing, barely credible. But what else could make sense of the Baptist's words about Jesus; the three Signs; the overwhelmingly powerful discourse that came from this Nazarene carpenter; and the sense that this all seemed to be making, deep within them, of a religion which might have previously seemed just a set of tough rules.

Pause for reflection: At the same time as claiming to be the fulfilment of Moses, Jesus was turning the Mosaic religion on its head. What he saw in the religious leaders was vanity, self-righteousness, intolerance and self-deception.

Please do not mistake for Christianity any shameful inadequacies or wearisome hypocrisies of organised religion.

14. Chapter 6   Bread. Real yeast. Real food

[1] *After this Jesus went to the other side of the Sea of Galilee, also called the Sea of Tiberias.* [2] *A large crowd kept following him, because they saw the signs that he was doing for the sick.* [3] *Jesus went up the mountain and sat down there with his disciples.*

[4] *Now the Passover, the festival of the Jews, was near.*

[5] *When he looked up and saw a large crowd coming toward him, Jesus said to Philip, "Where are we to buy bread for these people to eat?"* [6] *He said this to test him, for he himself knew what he was going to do.* [7] *Philip answered him, "Six months' wages would not buy enough bread for each of them to get a little."* [8] *One of his disciples, Andrew, Simon Peter's brother, said to him,* [9] *"There is a boy here who has five barley loaves and two fish. But what are they among so many people?"*

[10] *Jesus said, "Make the people sit down." Now there was a great deal of grass in the place; so they sat down, about five thousand in all.* [11] *Then Jesus took the loaves, and when he had given thanks, he distributed them to those who were seated; so also the fish, as much as they wanted.*

[12] *When they were satisfied, he told his disciples, "Gather up the fragments left over, so that nothing may be lost."* [13] *So they gathered them up, and from the fragments of the five barley loaves, left by those who had eaten, they filled twelve baskets.*

[14] *When the people saw the sign that he had done, they began to say, "This is indeed the prophet who is to come into the world."* [15] *When Jesus realized that they were about to come and take him by force to make him king, he withdrew again to the mountain by himself.*

[16] *When evening came, his disciples went down to the sea,* [17] *got into a boat, and started across the sea to Capernaum. It was now dark, and Jesus had not yet come to them.* [18] *The sea became rough because a strong wind was blowing.*

19 When they had rowed about three or four miles, they saw Jesus walking on the sea and coming near the boat, and they were terrified. 20 But he said to them, "It is I; do not be afraid." 21 Then they wanted to take him into the boat, and immediately the boat reached the land toward which they were going.

22 The next day the crowd that had stayed on the other side of the sea saw that there had been only one boat there. They also saw that Jesus had not got into the boat with his disciples, but that his disciples had gone away alone. 23 Then some boats from Tiberias came near the place where they had eaten the bread after the Lord had given thanks. 24 So when the crowd saw that neither Jesus nor his disciples were there, they themselves got into the boats and went to Capernaum looking for Jesus.

25 When they found him on the other side of the sea, they said to him, "Rabbi, when did you come here?" 26 Jesus answered them, "Very truly, I tell you, you are looking for me, not because you saw signs, but because you ate your fill of the loaves. 27 Do not work for the food that perishes, but for the food that endures for eternal life, which the Son of Man will give you. For it is on him that God the Father has set his seal."

28 Then they said to him, "What must we do to perform the works of God?" 29 Jesus answered them, "This is the work of God, that you believe in him whom he has sent." 30 So they said to him, "What sign are you going to give us then, so that we may see it and believe you? What work are you performing? 31 Our ancestors ate the manna in the wilderness; as it is written, 'He gave them bread from heaven to eat.'"

32 Then Jesus said to them, "Very truly, I tell you, it was not Moses who gave you the bread from heaven, but it is my Father who gives you the true bread from heaven. 33 For the bread of God is that which comes down from heaven and gives life to the world." 34 They said to him, "Sir, give us this bread always."

35 Jesus said to them, "I am the bread of life. Whoever comes to me will never be hungry, and whoever believes in me will never

be thirsty. 36 But I said to you that you have seen me and yet do not believe.

37 Everything that the Father gives me will come to me, and anyone who comes to me I will never drive away; 38 for I have come down from heaven, not to do my own will, but the will of him who sent me. 39 And this is the will of him who sent me, that I should lose nothing of all that he has given me, but raise it up on the last day. 40 This is indeed the will of my Father, that all who see the Son and believe in him may have eternal life; and I will raise them up on the last day."

41 Then the Jews began to complain about him because he said, "I am the bread that came down from heaven." 42 They were saying, "Is not this Jesus, the son of Joseph, whose father and mother we know? How can he now say, 'I have come down from heaven'?"

43 Jesus answered them, "Do not complain among yourselves. 44 No one can come to me unless drawn by the Father who sent me; and I will raise that person up on the last day. 45 It is written in the prophets, 'And they shall all be taught by God.' Everyone who has heard and learned from the Father comes to me. 46 Not that anyone has seen the Father except the one who is from God; he has seen the Father.

47 Very truly, I tell you, whoever believes has eternal life. 48 I am the bread of life. 49 Your ancestors ate the manna in the wilderness, and they died. 50 This is the bread that comes down from heaven, so that one may eat of it and not die. 51 I am the living bread that came down from heaven. Whoever eats of this bread will live forever; and the bread that I will give for the life of the world is my flesh."

52 The Jews then disputed among themselves, saying, "How can this man give us his flesh to eat?" 53 So Jesus said to them, "Very truly, I tell you, unless you eat the flesh of the Son of Man and drink his blood, you have no life in you. 54 Those who eat my flesh and drink my blood have eternal life, and I will raise them up on the last day; 55 for my flesh is true food and my blood is

true drink. ⁵⁶ *Those who eat my flesh and drink my blood abide in me, and I in them.* ⁵⁷ *Just as the living Father sent me, and I live because of the Father, so whoever eats me will live because of me.*

⁵⁸ *This is the bread that came down from heaven, not like that which your ancestors ate, and they died. But the one who eats this bread will live forever."*

⁵⁹ *He said these things while he was teaching in the synagogue at Capernaum.*

⁶⁰ *When many of his disciples heard it, they said, "This teaching is difficult; who can accept it?"*

⁶¹ *But Jesus, being aware that his disciples were complaining about it, said to them, "Does this offend you?* ⁶² *Then what if you were to see the Son of Man ascending to where he was before?* ⁶³ *It is the spirit that gives life; the flesh is useless. The words that I have spoken to you are spirit and life.*

14. Bread. Real yeast. Real food

This familiar passage is the only event, between the Baptism of Jesus, and his triumphal entry into Jerusalem, which is recorded in all four gospels. For John, it was a seminal moment: a miracle which struck a profound chord within him. A wonder that he had to think about for five decades or more before writing down. Bread. 'Real Food'. So many people. Twelve baskets. A miraculous day of adoration. Then, the next day, rejection.

This, the fourth Sign, was clearly linked to Jesus's puzzling mystical reference to himself as food – the Bread of Life. First hints had come at the Samaritan well. Now, just in the way that at Cana he miraculously produced a prodigious flow of wine; in this pleasant green space he was showing himself to be the source of a similar superabundance of bread. Jesus is building up what at first appears to be a metaphor relating to the New Covenant, of the Logos as the true life within us, our rich food and drink.

Given, however, that Jesus knew that young John would be deeply influenced by this profoundly significant Sign, and that he would later be inspired to record the details in his gospel, what else of significance was Jesus trying to convey?

Four things occur to me.

Firstly, immediately that the people saw the extraordinariness of the miracle of the loaves and fishes, they felt a natural exuberance, and wanted to express their newfound passion in an earthly rather than spiritual way. They wanted to make Jesus their King.

Presumably with something of a weary sigh, Jesus pushed off to the mountains and left them – telling them off roundly when he next sees them. Did they not understand that the Messiah, God's anointed one, did not need their help? That he did not come to save their stomachs, but rather their souls?

In between the two days of the event, he walks on water, (the fifth Sign), and calms the storm – a mind-blowing demonstration of his supernatural capabilities. This was surely incontrovertible testimony that anything Jesus might say was to be believed? And yet they could not think beyond an inspiring fish-sandwich picnic.

Secondly, 'the Passover was approaching', where people ate unleavened bread – flat bread made without yeast. This 'matzo' could be bread of any of the five grains, including barley, but needed to be made without yeast. This was to commemorate the flight of the Israelites from Egypt in a rush. They left immediately after the first Passover, the night when the Angel of Death killed the Egyptian first-borns, but spared those Israelites whose homes had been sprinkled with the blood of a sacrificial lamb. After a night of terror, Moses rushed them off into the wilderness, and there was no time to make leavened bread before they left.

Maybe, then, the boy was on his way to the Passover feast at Jerusalem, and his bread was 'matzo'. Maybe Jesus wanted to be saying that, in the same way that yeast transforms bread, so the Spirit transforms people: those eating unleavened bread with faith. Certainly, there is a commonality between wine and bread in that they both need yeast to nurture them into what they are supposed to become.

Thirdly, why twelve baskets of left-overs? The main point seems to be the super-abundance of the miracle, mirroring the bountifulness of the Bread of Life. However, is it a coincidence that Moses led twelve tribes through the desert? That Jesus had even chosen twelve apostles to reflect the twelve tribes?

This leads to the fourth and most profound point. When giving God's Law to the Israelites, Moses had said that "The Lord your God will raise up for you a prophet like me from among you"[1]. Jesus has already declared himself to be the fulfilment of Moses in many ways, (eg that, like Moses, he will set his people free; that, like Moses, he will give them springs of living water; that, like the serpent-staff of Moses, believers will look on the cross of Jesus to be saved; etc).

He was not a new Moses, however, but a fulfilment of Moses — the new Ark of the New Covenant. Now, just as Moses asked God to feed the Israelites with manna in the desert, so Jesus asks the Father to provide Living Bread. Jesus points out, here and elsewhere, that nothing of his claims are new: in their own scriptures they will find the references that the Prophet was to be raised up from within their people; that God would be their Father; that they would be 'taught by God' — and if his words seemed too extraordinary to believe, well then believe the Signs.

But they were not happy. Then comes the crunch. Instead of trying to assuage and persuade them, to draw them in more gently, to soothe the wound that was developing, he wades in with his most outrageous statement yet: Water; Wine; Bread — they were not just metaphors for spiritual refreshment and food brought by the Logos. No. They just pointed towards the REAL Truth, that it was Jesus himself — his flesh and blood — which needed to be physically devoured.

Even to our modern ears, this sounds crazy. If Jesus had meant these words to be an even more profound metaphor, he did not say so at the time. Perhaps this was to allow people to make a choice: For some, Jesus had touched their very soul with his presence, his words, and his Signs. Even these faithful few, however, were left dumbfounded by this 'flesh and blood' speech. Dumfounded, but on his side.

By contrast, for the lukewarm, their superficial faith had been tested — and had been found wanting.

Later in John's gospel, the profound significance of the Bread and Wine develops more and more weight, leading to the institution of the Bread and Wine of 'Communion', ('Eucharist'), at the Last Supper. More of this later, and of what Jesus might have meant on that crucial day by the lake. But for the moment, we can say this:

Jesus wanted people to leave that massive patch of crumb-spattered grass realising that, yes of course, the Messiah would be the fulfilment of Moses, the Prophet, the one who brings a new Law, new Water, new Healing, new Manna, new Passover Lamb, new Ark ... a new Covenant.

Instead, they were just grateful for the grub, and now they were looking for a King to see off the Romans.

He wanted those who knew that he walked on water to realise that if someone with such supernatural power said something even outrageous, it was nevertheless true.

Instead, they abandoned him, the loving miracle-worker who yesterday had fed them.

Pause for reflection: The feeding of the five thousand is as authentic an historical event as Julius Caesar's invasion of Britain.

Jesus thought that Bread was so fundamentally important, as to lose most of his followers over.

What about me? How important is that Bread in my life?

Reference: 1. Deut 18:15

15. Time to choose, when the going gets tough

⁶⁴ But among you there are some who do not believe." For Jesus knew from the first who were the ones that did not believe, and who was the one that would betray him. ⁶⁵ And he said, "For this reason I have told you that no one can come to me unless it is granted by the Father."

⁶⁶ Because of this many of his disciples turned back and no longer went about with him. ⁶⁷ So Jesus asked the twelve, "Do you also wish to go away?" ⁶⁸ Simon Peter answered him, "Lord, to whom can we go? You have the words of eternal life. ⁶⁹ We have come to believe and know that you are the Holy One of God."

⁷⁰ Jesus answered them, "Did I not choose you, the twelve? Yet one of you is a devil." ⁷¹ He was speaking of Judas son of Simon Iscariot, for he, though one of the twelve, was going to betray him.

15. Time to choose, when the going gets tough

The last reflection needed several pages of close-packed metaphysics to express why the 'Flesh and Blood' discourse was of such fundamental importance to Jesus ... so important that it was worth losing so many followers over.

Well aware that in those intense pages I might ironically have also lost many readers, I will keep this reflection short.

Jesus said that no-one can come to him unless it is first granted by the Father. This cannot mean that we are predestined to be either Christian or non-Christian. Rather, it must mean that the pre-requisite for choosing Jesus, is to have the capacity to choose. The Father might choose us, but we also have to choose Him.

Only those able to consider what is right and what is wrong – those with a 'soul' – can truly be held to account for the choices they make. And Jesus is saying that there is no more important choice than this: whose team are you on – Jesus, or the Opposition?

If, like the Pharisees and Judas, you are with the Opposition, then their hallmarks were vanity, self-deception, and intolerance.

Jesus has not yet expanded on the characteristics, benefits, and persecutions of being his follower, except to say that at the heart, it is about faith. About feeling, deep inside, a child-like trust in this mystical, powerful, extraordinary person; a deep longing and a love that goes beyond worldly instincts ... and holding on to that, even when not understanding it.

Jesus offered no 'stay-in-the-dressing-room' option, for those who were not sure which side to play for.

Pause for reflection: Whose side am I on? Jesus, representing the Supernatural; or Judas, representing the World? If I am on the side of Love, then, no matter how weak a player I am, God is my Captain. May I become the player He wants me to be.

16. Chapter 7: Hated for telling the Truth

¹ *After this Jesus went about in Galilee. He did not wish to go about in Judea because the Jews were looking for an opportunity to kill him.* ² *Now the Jewish festival of Booths was near.* ³ *So his brothers* said to him, "Leave here and go to Judea so that your disciples also may see the works you are doing;* ⁴ *for no one who wants to be widely known acts in secret. If you do these things, show yourself to the world."* ⁵ *(For not even his brothers believed in him.)*

⁶ *Jesus said to them, "My time has not yet come, but your time is always here.* ⁷ *The world cannot hate you, but it hates me because I testify against it that its works are evil.* ⁸ *Go to the festival yourselves. I am not going to this festival, for my time has not yet fully come."* ⁹ *After saying this, he remained in Galilee.*

¹⁰ *But after his brothers had gone to the festival, then he also went, not publicly but as it were in secret.* ¹¹ *The Jews were looking for him at the festival and saying, "Where is he?"* ¹² *And there was considerable complaining about him among the crowds. While some were saying, "He is a good man," others were saying, "No, he is deceiving the crowd."* ¹³ *Yet no one would speak openly about him for fear of the Jews.*

¹⁴ *About the middle of the festival Jesus went up into the temple and began to teach.* ¹⁵ *The Jews were astonished at it, saying, "How does this man have such learning, when he has never been taught?"* ¹⁶ *Then Jesus answered them, "My teaching is not mine but his who sent me.* ¹⁷ *Anyone who resolves to do the will of God will know whether the teaching is from God or whether I am speaking on my own.* ¹⁸ *Those who speak on their own seek their own glory; but the one who seeks the glory of him who sent him is true, and there is nothing false in him.*

¹⁹ *"Did not Moses give you the law? Yet none of you keeps the law. Why are you looking for an opportunity to kill me?"* ²⁰ *The crowd answered, "You have a demon! Who is trying to kill you?"* ²¹ *Jesus answered them, "I performed one work, and all*

of you are astonished. ²²Moses gave you circumcision (it is, of course, not from Moses, but from the patriarchs), and you circumcise a man on the sabbath. ²³If a man receives circumcision on the sabbath in order that the law of Moses may not be broken, are you angry with me because I healed a man's whole body on the sabbath?

²⁴Do not judge by appearances, but judge with right judgment."

(By the way, just to explain about Jesus's 'brothers': In the type of setting in which Jesus would have been raised in Nazareth, nuclear families were not the norm. Instead, men worked together on 'men's work' (or war), and women worked in a sorority, sharing child-care between them. Children growing up in such rustic communities made little distinction between 'brother' and 'cousin'. Indeed, this situation still pertains in many communities today, where people still greet each other as 'Brother /Sister /Mother /Father', irrespective of genetic relationship.

On whether Mary had other children after Jesus, I will not venture an opinion. However, the point is that it is not necessarily implied by the use of the term 'brothers' in this text.)

16. Hated for telling the Truth

The Festival of Tabernacles or 'Booths' or 'Shelters' took place over a week, when people camped out in temporary shelters. It was initiated by Moses, as a reminder of the tents in the desert that the fleeing Israelites had lived in. However, it was a major celebration with music and dancing – a sort of harvest festival – and must have felt a bit like a Hebrew Glastonbury.

Part of the ritual of the week was to visit the temple in pilgrimage, to celebrate the harvest having been gathered – recognising that, like manna from heaven, the harvest comes from God. In a daily climax of the feast, water, (which had been carried from the sacred Pool of Siloam outside Bethlehem), was ceremonially sprinkled over the altar, whilst the worshippers danced and sang with exuberant joy, remembering the Scripture[1] which said, "With joy you will draw water from the wells of salvation."

Moses; manna; water of salvation – you are one step ahead of me, I expect – yes, this should have been yet another situation in which the Messiah would explain why he was the fulfilment. However, his initial instinct was not even to go to the festival. We are not told why he changed his mind, but he arrived all guns blazing at the Jewish hierarchy.

Bear in mind that he knew that they had plans to kill him for having cured someone on the Sabbath. Imagine the frustration he must have felt. Have you ever tried to help a situation, then subsequently been not just maltreated, but blamed? Well, multiply that by infinity – the Logos been targeted for death for wanting to help humanity – and that about sums up Jesus's exasperation with the Sanhedrin. He had taught directly from God; he had demonstrated how he fulfilled the Scriptures; and he had backed this up with Signs as his witness. And he always told the truth. Yet they did not believe.

How could they not see that the very thing which had excited them to murderous thoughts – his healing someone on the Sabbath – was itself a celebration of the gift of the Sabbath *from his Father, via Moses? Indeed, it was yet another fulfilment of his role as the Prophet promised by Moses himself.*

And if they doubted his word, how could they not believe the miracle – that they witnessed with their own eyes!!!

Pause for reflection: Preconception. How harsh a judge it can be! I wonder how much of my response to people around me, is driven by prejudices I do not even realise that I have?

Even when the truth is there before me, if I could but see it ...

Reference: 1. Isaiah 12:3

17. "Let anyone who is thirsty come to me!"

25 Now some of the people of Jerusalem were saying, "Is not this the man whom they are trying to kill? 26 And here he is, speaking openly, but they say nothing to him! Can it be that the authorities really know that this is the Messiah? 27 Yet we know where this man is from; but when the Messiah comes, no one will know where he is from." 28 Then Jesus cried out as he was teaching in the temple, "You know me, and you know where I am from. I have not come on my own. But the one who sent me is true, and you do not know him. 29 I know him, because I am from him, and he sent me."

30 Then they tried to arrest him, but no one laid hands on him, because his hour had not yet come. 31 Yet many in the crowd believed in him and were saying, "When the Messiah comes, will he do more signs than this man has done?" 32 The Pharisees heard the crowd muttering such things about him, and the chief priests and Pharisees sent temple police to arrest him.

33 Jesus then said, "I will be with you a little while longer, and then I am going to him who sent me. 34 You will search for me, but you will not find me; and where I am, you cannot come." 35 The Jews said to one another, "Where does this man intend to go that we will not find him? Does he intend to go to the Dispersion among the Greeks and teach the Greeks? 36 What does he mean by saying, 'You will search for me and you will not find me' and 'Where I am, you cannot come'?

37 On the last day of the festival, the great day, while Jesus was standing there, he cried out, "Let anyone who is thirsty come to me, 38 and let the one who believes in me drink. As the scripture has said, 'Out of the believer's heart shall flow rivers of living water.'" 39 Now he said this about the Spirit, which believers in him were to receive; for as yet there was no Spirit, because Jesus was not yet glorified.

40 When they heard these words, some in the crowd said, "This is really the prophet." 41 Others said, "This is the Messiah." But some asked, "Surely the Messiah does not come from Galilee,

does he? 42 Has not the scripture said that the Messiah is descended from David and comes from Bethlehem, the village where David lived?" 43 So there was a division in the crowd because of him. 44 Some of them wanted to arrest him, but no one laid hands on him.

45 Then the temple police went back to the chief priests and Pharisees, who asked them, "Why did you not arrest him?" 46 The police answered, "Never has anyone spoken like this!" 47 Then the Pharisees replied, "Surely you have not been deceived too, have you? 48 Has any one of the authorities or of the Pharisees believed in him? 49 But this crowd, which does not know the law—they are accursed."

50 Nicodemus, who had gone to Jesus before, and who was one of them, asked, 51 "Our law does not judge people without first giving them a hearing to find out what they are doing, does it?" 52 They replied, "Surely you are not also from Galilee, are you? Search and you will see that no prophet is to arise from Galilee." 53 Then each of them went home.

17. "Let anyone who is thirsty come to me!"

Finally, on the last day of the festival, the dam-gates burst open, and Jesus declares his significance to this festival – the relationship of the Logos to the Festival of Shelters. Bear in mind that each day there had been a frenzy of exhilarating dance and music in the Temple, at the out-pouring of Siloam water on the altar. Holy water on the holy place.

In the desert, God had given life-giving water to the people of the Old Covenant, as part of His Promise of Salvation.

In the New Covenant, in the very place and the very ceremony which represented this water of salvation to the Israelites, the Logos declares that, under the New Covenant, he, Jesus, is the source of this water. No more going to the sacred pool at Siloam, but instead go straight to Jesus.

Of profound importance was what Jesus said next. In this new arrangement, it would not involve, (as in the desert), a passive reception of some water that needed replenishment each day. Instead, the Water of Life would well up within the person of faith, and they themselves would become a source of Living Water to others. Suddenly, believers would have a role to play in themselves carrying the Spirit within them, and in being used by the Spirit to refresh the lives of others.

Even more startling was the idea that the key to being saved would not be, as in the past, those who kept the Law: the righteous. Now, the key would be faith. Instead of water being poured on the altar, now Salvation and the Spirit would be poured out on those who believed. Jesus set no other condition. His one request: faith. In saying this, he turned the Pharasaical approach utterly on its head – and they did not like it.

Before leaving the Festival, there are two more thoughts that occurs to me. Firstly, Jesus chose not to justify himself by pointing out that he was indeed David's descendant born in David's town. In fact, his modus operandi was never to try to justify himself – and why should he? When the English Queen opens Parliament, for instance, she does not carry evidence of her bona fides in her handbag. She is who she is. And Jesus is who he is. It is up to me, not him, to find out what that means for me.

Secondly, Jesus said that from now on, instead of Water being poured onto the altar, it would be poured into our hearts. Does this mean that, in the New Covenant, believers would represent the altar of the Temple?

In Biblical times, the altar was the place upon which sacrifice to God was made – the life and blood of an animal offered to God ... as well as being the place where water was poured – to signify life-renewal rather than life-taking.

A place of death – then life. Born again? Blood then Water. Sacrificial Lamb then Spirit.

If I now represent that altar, what can that mean for my life?

Pause for reflection: Faith and sacrifice. If I meet these demands of me, then I will be a source of the Spirit. The actual Spirit of God.

That is an awesome thought.

As this is all going on in my heart, I presume that I will be told what sacrifices I should make ...?

18. Chapter 8 Forgiveness

¹ Jesus went to the Mount of Olives. ² Early in the morning he came again to the temple. All the people came to him and he sat down and began to teach them.

³ The scribes and the Pharisees brought a woman who had been caught in adultery; and making her stand before all of them, ⁴ they said to him, "Teacher, this woman was caught in the very act of committing adultery.

⁵ Now in the law Moses commanded us to stone such women. Now what do you say?" ⁶ They said this to test him, so that they might have some charge to bring against him. Jesus bent down and wrote with his finger on the ground.

⁷ When they kept on questioning him, he straightened up and said to them, "Let anyone among you who is without sin be the first to throw a stone at her." ⁸ And once again he bent down and wrote on the ground.

⁹ When they heard it, they went away, one by one, beginning with the elders; and Jesus was left alone with the woman standing before him. ¹⁰ Jesus straightened up and said to her, "Woman, where are they? Has no one condemned you?" ¹¹ She said, "No one, sir."

And Jesus said, "Neither do I condemn you. Go your way, and from now on do not sin again."

18. Forgiveness

In the first seven chapters of John's gospel, Jesus's actions, Signs and words have been designed to illustrate who Jesus is: the Logos; the fulfilment of Moses; the Son of Man sent from the Father; the Prophet; the bringer of the New Covenant.

Now Jesus begins to move from establishing his credentials to putting out his message. "OK – I showed by the Signs that I am from God. I told you about living water, wine, bread. Now I am telling you more of what God the Father is like ..."

And what is God like? Here is challenge: Jesus gave us just one prayer to talk to the Father, and it had in it only one instruction. What was that instruction? I'll give you a minute to think.

The answer: '...as we forgive those that sin/trespass against us'. We had one prerequisite for being on his side: faith. Now we have one activity – one key sacrifice – that shows we are playing his game: forgiveness. Faith and forgiveness – the hallmarks of Team God.

In the case of this adulterous woman, the forgiveness was for an archetypal human weakness. I was reminded of the power of our natural urges recently, when we were walking in the Cotswolds. The lambs now seemed halfway to being adults – sort of adolescent sheep. They no longer skipped and frisked, but moodily shadowed their mums, their expressions seeming to say, "O Mum, do I HAVE to? It's SOOO unfair!" The ewe replies, "What happened to you Larry? You used to be SUCH a frisky lamb!" Meanwhile, the rams were not even allowed in the same field.

We too have behaviours and desires which have their roots in our animal nature. But we also have another nature. We have a spirit, born of God, and destined to live with God in Eternity.

Our natural body will die, but our job here is to preserve the health of the spiritual one. When Paul talks to the Romans[1] about not 'living according to the flesh', he meant that we should not allow our nature – whether aggressive, lustful, irritable, or any natural potentially negative urge – to be the final controller of our destiny. Therein lies peace.

However, we mainly do not manage this, and judged by the Law of Moses, most of us fall short. God needed a new plan. The answer was a new type of salvation, and a new Passover Lamb – Jesus.

Jesus 'went to hell', and back, to pay for all our sins. (More of this later.) From then on, righteousness was not earned, but was a gift from God for those who believed.

The new Law was not a thick book of rules, but instead was something written on our hearts, that could be summed up in one word – forgiveness. We have been forgiven. We are asked humbly to forgive. Humbly, because it is often our vanity which holds us back.

Pause for reflection: As we struggle to put aside our nature, the key to unlocking the power of the Spirit is forgiveness.

However much of a sacrifice it might be, why not, right now, forgive someone for something you have been brooding about

... and see whether it sets you free?

Reference: Romans 8:5

19. The Light of the world

12 Again Jesus spoke to them, saying, "I am the light of the world. Whoever follows me will never walk in darkness but will have the light of life."

13 Then the Pharisees said to him, "You are testifying on your own behalf; your testimony is not valid."

14 Jesus answered, "Even if I testify on my own behalf, my testimony is valid because I know where I have come from and where I am going, but you do not know where I come from or where I am going.

15 You judge by human standards; I judge no one. 16 Yet even if I do judge, my judgment is valid; for it is not I alone who judge, but I and the Father who sent me.

17 In your law it is written that the testimony of two witnesses is valid. 18 I testify on my own behalf, and the Father who sent me testifies on my behalf."

19 Then they said to him, "Where is your Father?"

Jesus answered, "You know neither me nor my Father. If you knew me, you would know my Father also."

20 He spoke these words while he was teaching in the treasury of the temple, but no one arrested him, because his hour had not yet come.

19. The Light of the world

Here, then, is another description of God's nature – Light.

John typically uses metaphors rather than parables to describe the nature of God. Jesus has talked of his being Water and Bread, and now describes himself as 'Light'. Water, bread, light – the essentials of life, without which, we cannot live. And the most primordial of these is light. This metaphor is so fundamental, that John puts it in the very first paragraph of his gospel: 'What has come into being in him was life, and the life was the light of all people. The light shines in the darkness, and the darkness did not overcome it'.

This idea of the Lord as light is a recurrent one through Jewish Scripture – especially in the prediction of the coming Messiah by Isaiah[1]: 'The Lord will be your everlasting light'.

When light shines, it has a number of effects: It gives life, for example by photosynthesis. It gives meaning to life, without which everything is black and featureless. But it also shows up what is happening. The thief with the loot in his hand, climbing over the wall, picked out by the security light. In this sense, light not only gives life, and gives meaning, but also it judges. It judges not because it makes a judgement, but because it shows things as they are.

The followers of Jesus – especially John himself – had felt that light inside themselves, at Jesus's words, and at his Signs. They understood that this Light, this feeling within themselves, was itself a witness to the authenticity of Jesus as being from God.

By contrast, the Pharisees, in their darkness, just saw an annoying would-be prophet stirring up the people with his nonsense.

This was particularly ironic, given where and when this discourse was happening. Although the translation says 'in the Temple treasury', this conversation was taking place in the 'Court of the Women', where the collection boxes were for people donating money. In this exact same place, precisely at the Feast of Tabernacles, four huge (25 metre-high) candelabras were lit all night at the height of this precise feast, to commemorate God as the pillar of fiery light leading the Israelites through the desert at night[2].

As not even this poignancy was enough to illuminate most of the Pharisees, Jesus once more asserted the inescapable point that if he were speaking the truth, then what he said was valid.

It is strange, however, the way he initially puts this. He says that he should be believed because 'he knows where he has come from'. Not 'because of where he comes from', because he <u>knows</u> it. What can that mean, that <u>knowing</u> where he has come from justifies him?

The short answer is that I do not know. I do believe that John was there when Jesus said it, and that John picked up on every word that Jesus said. He was later prompted by the Spirit to remember each part of the Jesus story in vivid detail, and to make sense of it in a profoundly meaningful way.

Pause for reflection: Jesus calls himself the light, and says that he knows where he has come from. He is claiming not just to be the light-bulb, but the conduit of electricity, coming from its very source.

In the Old Covenant, God was both the source and the light.

In the New Covenant, maybe, He is the electricity, and we are his LEDs.

References: 1. Isaiah 60 – esp v19   2. Exodus 13:21

20. God the Father

21 Again he said to them, "I am going away, and you will search for me, but you will die in your sin. Where I am going, you cannot come." 22 Then the Jews said, "Is he going to kill himself? Is that what he means by saying, 'Where I am going, you cannot come'?" 23 He said to them, "You are from below, I am from above; you are of this world, I am not of this world. 24 I told you that you would die in your sins, for you will die in your sins unless you believe that I am he."

25 They said to him, "Who are you?" Jesus said to them, "Why do I speak to you at all? 26 I have much to say about you and much to condemn; but the one who sent me is true, and I declare to the world what I have heard from him." 27 They did not understand that he was speaking to them about the Father.

28 So Jesus said, "When you have lifted up the Son of Man, then you will realize that I am he, and that I do nothing on my own, but I speak these things as the Father instructed me. 29 And the one who sent me is with me; he has not left me alone, for I always do what is pleasing to him." 30 As he was saying these things, many believed in him.

31 Then Jesus said to the Jews who had believed in him, "If you continue in my word, you are truly my disciples; 32 and you will know the truth, and the truth will make you free." 33 They answered him, "We are descendants of Abraham and have never been slaves to anyone. What do you mean by saying, 'You will be made free'?"

34 Jesus answered them, "Very truly, I tell you, everyone who commits sin is a slave to sin. 35 The slave does not have a permanent place in the household; the son has a place there forever. 36 So if the Son makes you free, you will be free indeed. 37 I know that you are descendants of Abraham; yet you look for an opportunity to kill me, because there is no place in you for my word.

20. God the Father

When Jesus began to talk in the Temple about his Father, those who were trying to decide what level of respect to bestow upon him would have initially assumed that he was talking about his genetic father.

Despite the miraculous signs and extraordinary words that came from Jesus, most of the Pharisees automatically saw everything from the perspective of this world. They would have liked to know the name of Jesus's Nazarene father, to see if it was an important enough name for them to take seriously.

In fact, the human ancestry of Jesus was uniquely complex. Two genealogies are given in the synoptics – one in Luke, and the other in Matthew. The former is regarded by many as the genealogy of Mary, and the latter, the genealogy of Joseph, the adopted father of Jesus. Whereas both of them trace their ancestry to David, Mary's line was via David's son Nathan, and Joseph's was via David's son Solomon. Being son of Mary by the virgin birth, Jesus was the rightful heir to her lineage, and being the son of Joseph by adoption, he was the rightful heir to Joseph's.

Joseph and Solomon's line was the one through which David's kingship had flowed until the Kingdom was destroyed by the Babylonians. However, the very last King in that line had been told that no descendant of his would take up the throne of Judah. If the Messiah were truly to be in the lineage of David, he would therefore have had to be from one of David's other sons – such as Nathan, Mary's ancestor.

Certainly, the authenticity of Jesus as a Jew came from Mary – Judaism is unique in that Jewishness comes from one's mother, not one's father.

One way or another, then, it was actually possible that Jesus was the true heir to the worldly throne of Judah.

Had the Pharisees known all these facts about Jesus's heritage, they would have then delved into details of Jesus's birth in Bethlehem, hotfooted it back to their libraries, and pored over old scrolls to establish with what degree of earthly esteem they might endow him.

But: "Why do I speak to you at all?!", says Jesus in his frustration at their blindness. The whole point of the Messiah – how could they not know this – was to establish for mankind a spiritual relationship with God, in which <u>God Himself</u> is our Father. Father to us all! Just as Hosea prophesied[1]! Don't you know this? "Why do I speak to you at all?!"

In this continuation of his Court of the Women pronouncement, Jesus gets as close to what the Pharisees would have regarded as blasphemy, as at any point in his dealings with them so far.

For those who believed in him, however, he introduces two new elements – truth and freedom.

The Pharisees wrangle over the words of Jesus, finding them incompatible with their rigid and hypocritical framework of rules.

The followers of Jesus, by contrast, find that they feel in their hearts that words of the Logos are not just correct, but are indeed the essence of Truth. And through trust in Jesus, they feel free.

Pause for reflection: Joseph was the adopted father of Jesus, because Joseph chose to give his legitimacy to his adopted son. Jesus tells us that we have become adopted children of God Himself – again, an unearned birth-right by the choice of the adopted Father.

In fact, God is not just 'Father', Jesus says, but, like Joseph, He is 'Abba' – Dad.

The only condition – to believe that it is true.

Reference: Hosea 1:10

21. I AM

38 I declare what I have seen in the Father's presence; as for you, you should do what you have heard from the Father." 39 They answered him, "Abraham is our father."

Jesus said to them, "If you were Abraham's children, you would be doing what Abraham did, 40 but now you are trying to kill me, a man who has told you the truth that I heard from God. This is not what Abraham did. 41 You are indeed doing what your father does."

They said to him, "We are not illegitimate children; we have one father, God himself."

42 Jesus said to them, "If God were your Father, you would love me, for I came from God and now I am here. I did not come on my own, but he sent me.

43 Why do you not understand what I say? It is because you cannot accept my word. 44 You are from your father the devil, and you choose to do your father's desires. He was a murderer from the beginning and does not stand in the truth, because there is no truth in him. When he lies, he speaks according to his own nature, for he is a liar and the father of lies. 45 But because I tell the truth, you do not believe me.

46 Which of you convicts me of sin? If I tell the truth, why do you not believe me? 47 Whoever is from God hears the words of God. The reason you do not hear them is that you are not from God."

48 The Jews answered him, "Are we not right in saying that you are a Samaritan and have a demon?"

49 Jesus answered, "I do not have a demon; but I honour my Father, and you dishonour me. 50 Yet I do not seek my own glory; there is one who seeks it and he is the judge. 51 Very truly, I tell you, whoever keeps my word will never see death."

52 The Jews said to him, "Now we know that you have a demon. Abraham died, and so did the prophets; yet you say, 'Whoever keeps my word will never taste death.' 53 Are you greater than our father Abraham, who died? The prophets also died. Who do you claim to be?"

54 Jesus answered, "If I glorify myself, my glory is nothing. It is my Father who glorifies me, he of whom you say, 'He is our God,' 55 though you do not know him. But I know him; if I would say that I do not know him, I would be a liar like you. But I do know him and I keep his word.

56 Your ancestor Abraham rejoiced that he would see my day; he saw it and was glad."

57 Then the Jews said to him, "You are not yet fifty years old, and have you seen Abraham?"

58 Jesus said to them, "Very truly, I tell you, before Abraham was, I am."

59 So they picked up stones to throw at him, but Jesus hid himself and went out of the temple.

21. I AM

In 'The Lion, the Witch and the Wardrobe', the good little Lucy goes through the wardrobe to Narnia, and is followed by her naughty brother Edmund. Later, back in our world, Edmund pretends to Peter & Susan that Lucy made it all up.

Certainly, that would be much more believable than Lucy's magic world. Lucy has a rough time until someone points out that Lucy never lies, and Edmund often does. Then they began to see that, for all the wildness of the claim, Lucy indeed sounded like she was telling the truth ...

In the continuation of this Temple narrative, Jesus also claims to be telling the truth, making liars of those who deny him. Very annoying for those Pharisees to whom he was talking, but not yet blasphemy. Until then, his claims were just illusory metaphors, such as 'I am the light of the world'. But then: "My Father – God – glorifies me. I know him. Before Abraham was, I AM". Oh boy, now this Jesus has overstepped the mark!

Other than praise-names, the oldest name for God that we know of is simply 'El' – 'The One' – because the Maker of the Universe is not going to have a given name. ('I am Jim – Creator of All!' It doesn't work, does it?) From El we get Eli and Allah as names that we give God. But what does God call himself to humans?

We discover this in the story of Moses and the burning bush, when Moses is given his mission[1]. God calls himself 'I AM WHO I AM'. In ancient Hebrew, this is the four letters JHWH, sometimes pronounced Jehovah or Yahweh.

Jesus has upped the stakes infinitely in this statement. He is claiming at once to be the Son of God; in God's presence; ... and to <u>be</u> God: 'I AM'.

Wow. Jesus is saying unequivocally that he is the embodiment of the always-present Word of God. The Logos. Picking up stones to throw at him meant that they intended to kill him by stoning for this brazen blasphemy.

By contrast, listening to this proclamation must have sent shivers down the spine of 'the disciple Jesus loved' – John.

When he came to write his gospel, he builds up the tension from 'I am the bread of life'; through 'I am the light of the world'; to 'I AM'.

John carries on later to quote Jesus, using the 'I am' phrase, for three more descriptions of his identity: the gate; the good shepherd; and the true vine.

Then, in his final discourse, Jesus converts these I AM metaphors into what perhaps is the most important and mind-blowing claim that anyone has ever made: "I am the Way; the Truth; the Resurrection; and the Life". Here in the Temple, Jesus gives us a preview of this staggeringly profundity, saying "Whoever keeps my word will never see death".

Suddenly, to the young John listening to this, an upsurge of revelation must have erupted within him: Of course. If death were the end, then the whole elaborate mission of the Logos, planned since the beginning of time, would be, for the vast majority of people, a disappointing non-event. No. The meaning of our existence is to choose eternal life with God. Life through Jesus; Logos made Son of Man.

How fundamentally important and comforting, then, are these words of his: "If I am telling you the truth, why do you not believe me? The Truth will set you free ... from slavery to sin."

Pause for reflection: When our lives are burdened with normality; when everyday-ness numbs our spirituality; when we live in a culture of quick-thrill worldliness; Jesus's promises can sometimes seem just an impractical and unbelievable dream.

But be comforted, because he does not lie. It is actually true.

Reference: Exodus 3:13.

2 Cor 1 ? Mission through suffering

Suffering not a punishment — a reason?

22. Chapter 9 Blindingly obvious *in mission*

¹ As he walked along, he saw a man blind from birth. ² His disciples asked him, "Rabbi, who sinned, this man or his parents, that he was born blind?"

³ Jesus answered, "Neither this man nor his parents sinned; he was born blind so that God's works might be revealed in him.

⁴ We must work the works of him who sent me while it is day; night is coming when no one can work. ⁵ As long as I am in the world, I am the light of the world."

anointing?

⁶ When he had said this, he spat on the ground and made mud with the saliva and spread the mud on the man's eyes, ⁷ saying to him, "Go, wash in the pool of Siloam" (which means Sent). Then he went and washed and came back able to see.

⁸ The neighbours and those who had seen him before as a beggar began to ask, "Is this not the man who used to sit and beg?" ⁹ Some were saying, "It is he." Others were saying, "No, but it is someone like him." He kept saying, "I am the man."

¹⁰ But they kept asking him, "Then how were your eyes opened?" ¹¹ He answered, "The man called Jesus made mud, spread it on my eyes, and said to me, 'Go to Siloam and wash.' Then I went and washed and received my sight."

¹² They said to him, "Where is he?" He said, "I do not know."

¹³ They brought to the Pharisees the man who had formerly been blind. ¹⁴ Now it was a sabbath day when Jesus made the mud and opened his eyes. ¹⁵ Then the Pharisees also began to ask him how he had received his sight. He said to them, "He put mud on my eyes. Then I washed, and now I see."

¹⁶ Some of the Pharisees said, "This man is not from God, for he does not observe the sabbath." But others said, "How can a man who is a sinner perform such signs?" And they were divided.

¹⁷ So they said again to the blind man, "What do you say about him? It was your eyes he opened." He said, "He is a prophet."

¹⁸ The Jews did not believe that he had been blind and had received his sight until they called the parents of the man who

had received his sight ¹⁹ and asked them, "Is this your son, who you say was born blind? How then does he now see?"

²⁰ His parents answered, "We know that this is our son, and that he was born blind; ²¹ but we do not know how it is that now he sees, nor do we know who opened his eyes. Ask him; he is of age. He will speak for himself." ²² His parents said this because they were afraid of the Jews; for the Jews had already agreed that anyone who confessed Jesus to be the Messiah would be put out of the synagogue. ²³ Therefore his parents said, "He is of age; ask him."

22. Blindingly obvious

Given that John's gospel builds up, each chapter on the previous one, what do you think will happen next?

Jesus has gone to the feast of Light and Water, and has claimed to actually <u>be</u> Light and Water – and Life – to those who believe. As the water from Siloam was poured out on the altar, he cried out for people to come to him, all who were thirsty.

He went on to claim to be the Messiah – having backed up his claim with the five Signs and the Spirit of God. They who had set themselves up as judges of Israel did not believe his testimony, so, what next?

Well, in a trial, the judge gets to hear a summing up before finally deciding which side to believe – so Jesus now delivers two more spectacularly poignant and symbolic Signs to sum up his position.

The first is this healing of the blind man on the Sabbath – so packed with meaning, that surely they must have got the point?

Just to recap: until this moment, the delivery of the Israelites from the Egyptians had been celebrated in the Temple, at the Feast of Tabernacles, with light and water. This was to remind the Jews of God's fiery pillar that led Moses and their ancestors across the wilderness to the Promised Land; and the water-from-the-rock that gave them life. In the Feast, sacred[1] water is carried from the Pool of Siloam to sprinkle on the altar of God's Presence.

With five Signs and the Spirit to testify on his behalf, Jesus now proclaims that he is the Messiah, and that this Logos-Son of Man is the new source of Light, Water and Life. In rich symbolism, he shows that he is the fulfilment of Moses and the Old Covenant. He is the Lord of the New Covenant. But his opponents seem blind to his message.

He therefore symbolically finds a blind man, and sends him to the very pool of Siloam, where he is cured of his blindness by the Lord.

Furthermore, he is cured specifically on the Sabbath, to signify that the Son of Man is indeed Lord of the New System – where we are born again in the Spirit; where the Law is written on our hearts; where we ourselves are the Temple; where it is faith that justifies, not Judaic 'righteousness'.

They of course will have read Isaiah: "Then the eyes of the blind will be opened[2]". Surely the power and significance of this Sign will not be lost on them?

Oops. Yes it is. Instead of believing him, they want to kill him.

There is one further message from this passage that occurs to me. Why did Jesus not actually go to the Pool of Siloam? Surely God could have organised for the blind man to be there? Instead, he sent him – to the Pool whose name, 'Siloam', means 'sent'.

Could it be that this is also a directive also for us? We have established that faith is a pre-requisite of being redeemed by Jesus. We have seen that forgiveness is the characteristic we should then show. But neither of those two things moves us out of our comfy chair.

Maybe we also have to recognise that our spiritual sight is not perfect, that we do not see things quite as they are, and that we also need to be <u>sent</u> – to find the Water of Life?

Pause for reflection: Is there something I am being stubbornly blind about?

Is there somewhere that I should be physically going?

Something I should be actually doing?

Reference: 1. Isaiah 8:6   2. Isaiah 35:5

23. Selective blindness

24 So for the second time they called the man who had been blind, and they said to him, "Give glory to God! We know that this man is a sinner." 25 He answered, "I do not know whether he is a sinner. One thing I do know, that though I was blind, now I see." 26 They said to him, "What did he do to you? How did he open your eyes?" 27 He answered them, "I have told you already, and you would not listen. Why do you want to hear it again? Do you also want to become his disciples?"

28 Then they reviled him, saying, "You are his disciple, but we are disciples of Moses. 29 We know that God has spoken to Moses, but as for this man, we do not know where he comes from." 30 The man answered, "Here is an astonishing thing! You do not know where he comes from, and yet he opened my eyes. 31 We know that God does not listen to sinners, but he does listen to one who worships him and obeys his will. 32 Never since the world began has it been heard that anyone opened the eyes of a person born blind. 33 If this man were not from God, he could do nothing." 34 They answered him, "You were born entirely in sins, and are you trying to teach us?" And they drove him out.

35 Jesus heard that they had driven him out, and when he found him, he said, "Do you believe in the Son of Man?" 36 He answered, "And who is he, sir? Tell me, so that I may believe in him." 37 Jesus said to him, "You have seen him, and the one speaking with you is he." 38 He said, "Lord, I believe." And he worshiped him.

39 Jesus said, "I came into this world for judgement so that those who do not see may see, and those who do see may become blind." *opportunity to sin?*

40 Some of the Pharisees near him heard this and said to him, "Surely we are not blind, are we?" 41 Jesus said to them, "If you were blind, you would not have sin. But now that you say, 'We see,' your sin remains.

Self righteousness

Self righteousness

Spec's - relationship with Jesus?

focussed!

23. Selective blindness

My favourite TV detective series is the Sherlock Holmes version based in New York. It is beautifully made, with at its heart Sherlock's unique selling point – that he notices things that others miss. Time after time, he averts miscarriage of justice by seeing what others might not have noticed. It is not his eyes that are better than theirs, but rather his mind, which does not allow prejudice nor preconception to cloud his judgement.

The Pharisees could have done with a Sherlock when interviewing the man born blind: "What thinkest thou, Sherlock?"

> *"Let me gather the facts: He truly was blind before. He truly now can see. This must have been a miracle. The miracle-performer must then be a prophet. We know that if this were THE Prophet, opening the eyes of the blind would be something we might expect to see.*

> *Furthermore, he claims to be the 'I AM'. He has witnessed this claim with five other Signs. In his presence, we feel his Spirit. Brothers, until we have any better evidence, we have to regard this Jesus as the Messiah. Even if that means re-examining our understanding of the Sabbath. Elementary, my dear Pharisees!"*

Certainly, that was the position taken by the man born blind. The man could not only now see, but also he could see the hypocrisy of the Pharisees.

Is what Jesus meant, then, when he said that he would make the blind see – not only physically, but metaphorically? That they would be Sherlock-like in their ability to discern the truth about others? I am not sure that such sight would be a great gift. Plenty of opportunity for forgiveness, but a life dominated by a sense of injustice? Certainly, the New York Sherlock was a sad and lonely man.

There are two other ways, however, in which Jesus might make me see more clearly.

I might see better the truth about myself, and my inadequacies. If so, then the humility might make me a better and happier person.

Much more importantly, however, I might see the truth about Jesus. I might then, like the man in the story, believe in him. I might, then, like the man in the story, stand up for Jesus. Thereafter, I would not only have this life turned around, but also have the unearned gift of life that conquers death.

It seems like good news, then, that Jesus ".... came into the world .... so that those who do not see may see."

But what of the rest of the sentence: "I came ... for judgement ... so that those who do see may become blind"? Is that not a bit harsh?

He later clarifies that when he says "that those who see may become blind", he means 'those who <u>claim</u> that they can see, (but cannot)'. And we have already noted that the most important 'sight' is the ability recognise, in Jesus, and in his words, Signs and Spirit, that he is the Messiah. From 'those who claim that they can see', does Jesus then take away this ability to see him as he is?

No. Remember that this is all part of the discourse in which Jesus claimed to be the Light of the World. Light does not take anything away from anyone. It simply shows them as they are. The Light comes into the world to judge – but not by making a judgement, but rather by simply being there. By revelation – of truth, and of hypocrisy.

Pause for reflection: This, the sixth Sign, was, as we have seen, a sort of summing up of the story so far.

We are at this point supposed to be close to making our choice as to whose side we are on: God; Love; Logos; Light; Water; Bread; Sight; Life. Or ... or what? What else makes sense?

Faith — personal act of will. (doing)

24. Chapter 10 The Good Shepherd

[1] "Very truly, I tell you, anyone who does not enter the sheepfold by the gate but climbs in by another way is a thief and a bandit. [2] The one who enters by the gate is the shepherd of the sheep. [3] The gatekeeper opens the gate for him, and the sheep hear his voice. He calls his own sheep by name and leads them out.

[4] When he has brought out all his own, he goes ahead of them, and the sheep follow him because they know his voice. [5] They will not follow a stranger, but they will run from him because they do not know the voice of strangers."

[6] Jesus used this figure of speech with them, but they did not understand what he was saying to them.

[7] So again Jesus said to them, "Very truly, I tell you, I am the gate for the sheep. [8] All who came before me are thieves and bandits; but the sheep did not listen to them. [9] I am the gate. Whoever enters by me will be saved, and will come in and go out and find pasture. [10] The thief comes only to steal and kill and destroy. I came that they may have life, and have it abundantly.

[11] "I am the good shepherd. The good shepherd lays down his life for the sheep. [12] The hired hand, who is not the shepherd and does not own the sheep, sees the wolf coming and leaves the sheep and runs away — and the wolf snatches them and scatters them. [13] The hired hand runs away because a hired hand does not care for the sheep.

[14] I am the good shepherd. I know my own and my own know me, [15] just as the Father knows me and I know the Father. And I lay down my life for the sheep.

[16] I have other sheep that do not belong to this fold. I must bring them also, and they will listen to my voice. So there will be one flock, one shepherd.

¹⁷ For this reason the Father loves me, because I lay down my life in order to take it up again. ¹⁸ No one takes it from me, but I lay it down of my own accord. I have power to lay it down, and I have power to take it up again.

I have received this command from my Father."

¹⁹ Again the Jews were divided because of these words.

²⁰ Many of them were saying, "He has a demon and is out of his mind. Why listen to him?"

²¹ Others were saying, "These are not the words of one who has a demon. Can a demon open the eyes of the blind?"

24. The Good Shepherd

Jesus had established his credentials, and had talked of himself metaphorically as Light; Bread/Food/Blood/Wine/Drink; and Water. Do you notice, however, that all those descriptions of the 'I AM' are not sentient? They are things – albeit things which add up to Life. aware of life

It is only now, finally, having made his position exactly clear on being the Messiah, the Logos, the I AM, the Fulfilment of Moses, that he begins to unpack who this Messiah is. He switches his metaphor from being various vital aspects of Life, to being a person – the Good Shepherd.

For those with eyes to see it, this was of course a deeply symbolic comparison. His listeners would have been very familiar with the Psalms, which are attributed to King David, forefather of the Messiah.

In his youth, David was himself a good shepherd, and it was therefore natural for him to think of his Lord as 'my Shepherd', in Psalms[1] still popular after 3,000 years.

Even Abraham, father of all, was a 'Hebrew', meaning sort of wanderer, whose tribe's very existence depended on following their sheep through various pastures. From 'pasture' we get the word 'pastoral' which these days implies 'looking after'.

In using this time-honoured comparison, then, Jesus is telling us that he has an active part to play in our protection and day-to-day care. To this he adds that to be eligible for this care, you need to come via him – the gate of the sheepfold.

However, he then describes an even more active role in our salvation, which will involve giving up his life for his sheep. Whereas the caring, protective Good Shepherd was an easy metaphor for his listeners to assimilate, a shepherd who died for his sheep was not.

Indeed, it was usually the other way around: the sheep dying to preserve the shepherd. This might have been simply that a sheep needed to die to feed the shepherd.

However, in Abraham's day, sacrificing one of the sheep to appease the gods was a common pagan practice, and Abraham himself was asked to sacrifice a sheep to God as part of the pact between them[2].

Many generations later, it was a lamb, innocent and precious, whose blood was spilt by Moses and the Israelites to protect them from the Angel of Death in the first Passover[3].

Subsequently, John the Baptist refers to Jesus as 'the Lamb of God, who takes away the sins of the world'[4]. In this imagery, he was building on the prophecy of Isaiah[5], who at times portrays the Messiah as: "... oppressed and afflicted, yet he did not open his mouth; he was led like a lamb to the slaughter ..."

A Shepherd, then ... but also a Lamb. A shepherd can become a great Patriarch or King – like Abraham and David. But a lamb?

Perhaps John the evangelist, listening to this, was beginning to get the idea that this Messiah was not going to be the sort of King that everyone had been expecting ...

Pause for reflection: Do you, like Jesus's listeners, also find yourself uncomfortably unsure that this makes any sense? Uncomfortably unsure that this entirely kill-able man might be the bringer of eternal life to all who believe?

Surely he who describes his role has helping people to see, is not asking us for blind belief? ...

Cue the Spirit ...

References: 1. Psalms 23; 77; 79; 80; 95; 100   2. Genesis 22:2-13
3. Exodus 12: 1-14   4. John 1:29 &36   5. Isaiah 53:7

25. Selective deafness

²²At that time the festival of the Dedication took place in Jerusalem. It was winter, ²³and Jesus was walking in the temple, in the portico of Solomon. ²⁴So the Jews gathered around him and said to him, "How long will you keep us in suspense? If you are the Messiah, tell us plainly." ²⁵Jesus answered, "I have told you, and you do not believe. The works that I do in my Father's name testify to me; ²⁶but you do not believe, because you do not belong to my sheep.

²⁷My sheep hear my voice. I know them, and they follow me. ²⁸I give them eternal life, and they will never perish. No one will snatch them out of my hand. ²⁹What my Father has given me is greater than all else, and no one can snatch it out of the Father's hand. ³⁰The Father and I are one."

³¹The Jews took up stones again to stone him. ³²Jesus replied, "I have shown you many good works from the Father. For which of these are you going to stone me?" ³³The Jews answered, "It is not for a good work that we are going to stone you, but for blasphemy, because you, though only a human being, are making yourself God." ³⁴Jesus answered, "Is it not written in your law, 'I said, you are gods'? ³⁵If those to whom the word of God came were called 'gods' — and the scripture cannot be annulled — ³⁶can you say that the one whom the Father has sanctified and sent into the world is blaspheming because I said, 'I am God's Son'?

³⁷If I am not doing the works of my Father, then do not believe me. ³⁸But if I do them, even though you do not believe me, believe the works, so that you may know and understand that the Father is in me and I am in the Father." ³⁹Then they tried to arrest him again, but he escaped from their hands.

⁴⁰He went away again across the Jordan to the place where John had been baptizing earlier, and he remained there. ⁴¹Many came to him, and they were saying, "John performed no sign, but everything that John said about this man was true." ⁴²And many believed in him there.

25. Selective deafness

In preceding chapters, in all sorts of ways, Jesus laid claim to his rightful title, surrounding his words with deep symbolism and his actions with supernatural power. He persistently referred to God as his Father.

Finally, he claimed to be the 'I am who AM'. This was staggeringly bold. Even today, some devout Jews regard it as sinful just to say the word 'JHWH' /I AM about God. But for Jesus, 2000 years ago, to have said it about himself, was astounding.

Despite all this, we now hear some of his listeners asking him to speak plainly! "I've already told you!!!!", says Jesus. "And (please excuse my paraphrase) in case you are in any doubt at all, here it is in a nutshell: I am the One sent by God. He is my Father. I am one with Him. I have come to claim those who hear my voice and believe it. To them, my Father will give eternal life – in exchange for my life. Is that clear enough?!!"

"Yes!" said some.

"You are off your trolley!" said others.

It would take John a lifetime of study, thought, inspiration and revelation to understand how Jesus's actions and words had indeed spoken plainly.

Indeed, more than plainly: how Jesus had answered questions never even put to him, by his immensely rich poignancy and symbolism.

So perhaps it is not unreasonable that some of those listening to this last discourse were still confused. It is true enough they <u>should</u> have just believed him – they had seen the miracles; and they must have felt the Spirit. Nevertheless, some were still hovering on the edge of commitment.

"OK," says the Son of Man. "Last chance! One more Sign. And this will be a humdinger!" (Again, my words, not the Lord's!)

Pause for reflection: Here is the sequence that Jesus asks us to sign up to, in return for forgiveness of sins, and subsequent eternal life. We are asked, (with the help of the internal rechargeable battery of faith), to believe that:

- *That God exists,*
- *That He made the world for the purpose of love.*
- *That this needed us to be separated from Him in this life,*
- *and to suffer both adversity and temptation.*
- *That, before the end of this life, we had to make a choice – for good, or for evil.*
- *That, having chosen good, we needed redemption, which itself called for a Messiah – the Logos, the Word of the Father, made flesh.*
- *That Jesus is that Logos.*
- *That his life and death were the fulfilment of the Old Covenant, and the creation of the New, where God Himself is Our Father.*

Put like that, it takes a monumental leap of faith to accept in its entirety ...

until you try to come up with an alternative explanation of: the origin of the universe; the existence of love and evil; the miracles of Jesus and his followers; the belief in One Overarching God in just about any civilisation that has ever existed;

and the feeling, within us, when we love, when we forgive, when we believe, that it might, actually, all be true ...

26. Chapter 11 Heading for trouble

1 Now a certain man was ill, Lazarus of Bethany, the village of Mary and her sister Martha. 2 Mary was the one who anointed the Lord with perfume and wiped his feet with her hair; her brother Lazarus was ill. 3 So the sisters sent a message to Jesus, "Lord, he whom you love is ill."

4 But when Jesus heard it, he said, "This illness does not lead to death; rather it is for God's glory, so that the Son of God may be glorified through it."

5 Accordingly, though Jesus loved Martha and her sister and Lazarus, 6 after having heard that Lazarus was ill, he stayed two days longer in the place where he was.

7 Then after this he said to the disciples, "Let us go to Judea again." 8 The disciples said to him, "Rabbi, the Jews were just now trying to stone you, and are you going there again?"

9 Jesus answered, "Are there not twelve hours of daylight? Those who walk during the day do not stumble, because they see the light of this world. 10 But those who walk at night stumble, because the light is not in them."

11 After saying this, he told them, "Our friend Lazarus has fallen asleep, but I am going there to awaken him." 12 The disciples said to him, "Lord, if he has fallen asleep, he will be all right." 13 Jesus, however, had been speaking about his death, but they thought that he was referring merely to sleep.

14 Then Jesus told them plainly, "Lazarus is dead. 15 For your sake I am glad I was not there, so that you may believe. But let us go to him." 16 Thomas, who was called the Twin, said to his fellow disciples, "Let us also go, that we may die with him."

26. Heading for trouble

These few verses are just setting the scene for the majestic moment about to come, where Jesus will perform the definitive Sign, to witness utterly unequivocally, that what he has said was true. The Seventh Sign. (Seven was a significant word in John's world – implying completeness or perfection.)

We are not told where Jesus had gone to, except that it was outside Judaea. His disciples must have regarded it as something of a relief, but Jesus must have known what was soon to come, and I imagine that he would have been profoundly troubled in spirit during those days.

I expect that John picked up on this, and that a shadow had begun to spread a dark wing over the inner circle of Jesus. A far cry from the heady days of wine, loaves and fishes.

Given that John has an eye and an ear for the deep mysticism of Jesus's discourses, the one conversation he chooses to report from this sombre time, is this seeming non-sequitur:

Q: "Are you going there again?"
A: "Are there not twelve hours of daylight?"

Should not the answer have been: "I must go, because there is something important I have to do." Or, "I must go and face up to a final confrontation." But instead Jesus makes a point about the light of the world – presumably himself – and not stumbling when he, the Light, is around.

There are two implications here.

Firstly, that there will be a time when this Light is not around, and that will be a dark time indeed.

Secondly, is he implying that even his own followers will be stumbling when he himself is not with them? Judas, hearing those words, might have felt a chilling fear. For the others, maybe it was just a warning?

For John, it was perhaps a call to be by Jesus's side?

Pause for reflection. With the benefit of hindsight, knowing that Jesus was going back to Jerusalem to be crucified; and that all his followers (except John) would be scattered, what do you now make of this response of Jesus:

> *The disciples said to him, "Rabbi, the Jews were just now trying to stone you, and are you going there again?"*
>
> *9 Jesus answered, "Are there not twelve hours of daylight? Those who walk during the day do not stumble, because they see the light of this world. 10 But those who walk at night stumble, because the light is not in them."*

Note that he says "the Light is not in them", as opposed to around them.

There is evil in this world, and there are people who do not have the light within them.

As we will see when we get to Jesus quoting Psalm 22, Jesus was going to meet this evil head on.

27. The Resurrection and the Life

17 When Jesus arrived, he found that Lazarus had already been in the tomb four days. 18 Now Bethany was near Jerusalem, some two miles away, 19 and many of the Jews had come to Martha and Mary to console them about their brother. 20 When Martha heard that Jesus was coming, she went and met him, while Mary stayed at home.

21 Martha said to Jesus, "Lord, if you had been here, my brother would not have died. 22 But even now I know that God will give you whatever you ask of him." 23 Jesus said to her, "Your brother will rise again." 24 Martha said to him, "I know that he will rise again in the resurrection on the last day."

25 Jesus said to her, "I am the resurrection and the life. Those who believe in me, even though they die, will live, 26 and everyone who lives and believes in me will never die. Do you believe this?" 27 She said to him, "Yes, Lord, I believe that you are the Messiah, the Son of God, the one coming into the world."

28 When she had said this, she went back and called her sister Mary, and told her privately, "The Teacher is here and is calling for you." 29 And when she heard it, she got up quickly and went to him.

30 Now Jesus had not yet come to the village, but was still at the place where Martha had met him. 31 The Jews who were with her in the house, consoling her, saw Mary get up quickly and go out. They followed her because they thought that she was going to the tomb to weep there.

32 When Mary came where Jesus was and saw him, she knelt at his feet and said to him, "Lord, if you had been here, my brother would not have died." 33 When Jesus saw her weeping, and the Jews who came with her also weeping, he was greatly disturbed in spirit and deeply moved. 34 He said, "Where have you laid him?" They said to him, "Lord, come and see." 35 Jesus began to weep.

36 *So the Jews said, "See how he loved him!"* 37 *But some of them said, "Could not he who opened the eyes of the blind man have kept this man from dying?"*

38 *Then Jesus, again greatly disturbed, came to the tomb. It was a cave, and a stone was lying against it.* 39 *Jesus said, "Take away the stone." Martha, the sister of the dead man, said to him, "Lord, already there is a stench because he has been dead four days."* 40 *Jesus said to her, "Did I not tell you that if you believed, you would see the glory of God?"* 41 *So they took away the stone.*

And Jesus looked upward and said, "Father, I thank you for having heard me. 42 *I knew that you always hear me, but I have said this for the sake of the crowd standing here, so that they may believe that you sent me."*

43 *When he had said this, he cried with a loud voice, "Lazarus, come out!"* 44 *The dead man came out, his hands and feet bound with strips of cloth, and his face wrapped in a cloth. Jesus said to them, "Unbind him, and let him go."*

45 *Many of the Jews therefore, who had come with Mary and had seen what Jesus did, believed in him.* 46 *But some of them went to the Pharisees and told them what he had done.* 47 *So the chief priests and the Pharisees called a meeting of the council, and said, "What are we to do? This man is performing many signs.* 48 *If we let him go on like this, everyone will believe in him, and the Romans will come and destroy both our holy place and our nation."*

49 *But one of them, Caiaphas, who was high priest that year, said to them, "You know nothing at all!* 50 *You do not understand that it is better for you to have one man die for the people than to have the whole nation destroyed."* 51 *He did not say this on his own, but being high priest that year he prophesied that Jesus was about to die for the nation,* 52 *and not for the nation only, but to gather into one the dispersed children of God.*

53 *So from that day on they planned to put him to death.* 54 *Jesus therefore no longer walked about openly among the Jews, but went from there to a town called Ephraim in the region near the wilderness; and he remained there with the disciples.*

55 *Now the Passover of the Jews was near, and many went up from the country to Jerusalem before the Passover to purify themselves.* 56 *They were looking for Jesus and were asking one another as they stood in the temple, "What do you think? Surely he will not come to the festival, will he?"*

57 *Now the chief priests and the Pharisees had given orders that anyone who knew where Jesus was should let them know, so that they might arrest him.*

27. The Resurrection and the Life

Another I AM statement: I am the Resurrection and the Life.

The Seventh Sign: An actual resurrection.

What more witness could Jesus possibly have given?
What more light could he possibly have shone?
But the light needs to be in us, not just around us.

"One man must die for the people", dark Caiaphas said

... and he was right ...

Pause for reflection: Jesus wraps up the first part of his ministry with a rising from the dead. This sums up everything in one act, at the same time as giving incontrovertible testimony to the authenticity of Jesus: "I truly am the Resurrection and the Life. I AM!"

In the final part of John's story of Jesus also wraps up with a resurrection – that of Jesus himself.

The Power of the Father eternally flowing through His Logos.

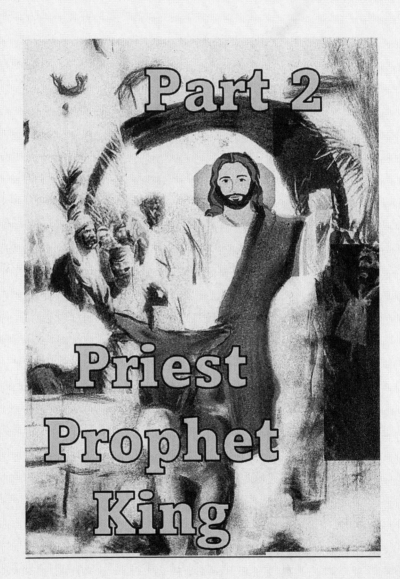

Part 2

Priest
Prophet
King

28. Chapter 12 The anointing

¹ *Six days before the Passover Jesus came to Bethany, the home of Lazarus, whom he had raised from the dead.* ² *There they gave a dinner for him.*

Martha served, and Lazarus was one of those at the table with him. ³ *Mary took a pound of costly perfume made of pure nard, anointed Jesus' feet, and wiped them with her hair. The house was filled with the fragrance of the perfume.*

⁴ *But Judas Iscariot, one of his disciples (the one who was about to betray him), said,* ⁵ *"Why was this perfume not sold for three hundred denarii and the money given to the poor?"* ⁶ *(He said this not because he cared about the poor, but because he was a thief; he kept the common purse and used to steal what was put into it.)*

⁷ *Jesus said, "Leave her alone. She bought it so that she might keep it for the day of my burial.* ⁸ *You always have the poor with you, but you do not always have me."*

28. The anointing

I once worked as Medical Superintendent of a mission hospital in Africa. With time, I began to understand that the diseases had their roots in the community, and so I began to develop our community outreach clinics.

It then became apparent that poverty underpinned so much of the poor health, and I became deeply involved in community development. The next step would have been to try to influence the political systems that fostered this inequality.

Then, one day, an old grandma brought in the small baby she had been left to look after whilst the mother had returned to back-breaking work on a farm. The only water available to them was polluted river water, and the baby arrived at the point of death from diarrhoea. Despite my efforts for the next hour, the baby died. As I handed the baby back to its grandmother, tears ran down her cheeks and mine. Our eyes met, and, across the enormous culture divide, something immensely profound passed between us.

From that moment, I realised that, much as the big picture needed dealing with – poverty; inequality; injustice – the thing that counts most of all, the thing that unleashes the most powerful repercussions on the world, is the love that I am showing right now to the person in front of me. It is a profound truth which can only be experienced. It is not susceptible to logical argument, or even, as in this case, practicality.

Martha had chosen to anoint Jesus, and to do it with as much humility and love as she could muster – not daring to touch above his feet; using her hair to wipe off the oil.

Silly? – possibly.
Embarrassing? – definitely.
Impractical? – unequivocally.
But loving? Profoundly.

In Biblical times, anointing was a ceremony where the pouring of oil represented a request for the pouring of blessing from heaven on the person, as they entered a new situation. On becoming a King, a prophet, a priest – even a guest – the anointing bestowed on the person not just love and fidelity, but legitimacy. Anointing was a way of inviting God to manage the transition from Prince to King; from stranger to guest; to take what was, and to make it what it should be.

It was therefore natural that this culture of anointing was extended to the anointing of the dead, calling down the blessing of God on them, asking that they be reborn in heaven.

Martha made the food; Judas tut-tutted; the guests were stunned into silence ... and Mary anointed the Saviour of the World.

Love. The thing that counts.

Pause for reflection: Which of the people present do we mainly identify with, if the truth were told?

Judas, with an angry sense of political injustice?

Martha, who maybe felt a little hard done-by as she slaved in the kitchen?

Those around who might have been deeply embarrassed at this unconventional display of emotion and humiliation?

... or Mary, who was driven by an immense love, which dared to declare itself?

... or Jesus, whose love was so great, that he was making ready to die for sinful humanity?

29. Triumphal entry and everlasting peace

⁹ When the great crowd of the Jews learned that he was there, they came not only because of Jesus but also to see Lazarus, whom he had raised from the dead. ¹⁰ So the chief priests planned to put Lazarus to death as well, ¹¹ since it was on account of him that many of the Jews were deserting and were believing in Jesus.

¹² The next day the great crowd that had come to the festival heard that Jesus was coming to Jerusalem. ¹³ So they took branches of palm trees and went out to meet him, shouting, "Hosanna! Blessed is the one who comes in the name of the Lord — the King of Israel!"

¹⁴ Jesus found a young donkey and sat on it; as it is written: ¹⁵ "Do not be afraid, daughter of Zion. Look, your king is coming, sitting on a donkey's colt!"

¹⁶ His disciples did not understand these things at first; but when Jesus was glorified, then they remembered that these things had been written of him and had been done to him.

¹⁷ So the crowd that had been with him when he called Lazarus out of the tomb and raised him from the dead continued to testify. ¹⁸ It was also because they heard that he had performed this sign that the crowd went to meet him.

¹⁹ The Pharisees then said to one another, "You see, you can do nothing. Look, the world has gone after him!"

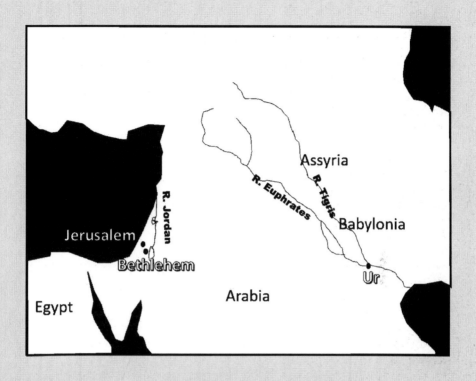

29. Triumphal entry and everlasting peace

Jerusalem had been a holy place since records began. When God spoke to Abraham nearly two thousand years before Jesus, he directed him to Jerusalem, to what would be the heart of the Promised Land.

When he got there, fresh from a successful battle, Melchizedek, King of Jerusalem, prophet, and 'priest of God Most High', brought out bread and wine to Abraham, and blessed him[1]. The city was called 'Salem' in those days – a name related to the greeting 'Shalom' – 'Peace'.

In Abraham's religion, the One God was 'El' or 'Eli', but 'Peace' (Salem) might well have been one of His ancient titles, which was then perhaps borrowed by the Canaanite predecessors of Melchizedek, to name their holy city. Anyway, Abraham and Melchizedek clearly both belonged to the same religion of adoration of Eli, the One God.

How that came about is a matter of conjecture. The first ever recorded organised religion in the first ever civilisation, arose between 5000 and 4000 BC in Sumer, between the Tigris and Euphrates.

Two millennia downstream, the last vestige of Sumerian culture flourished for a while in Ur. Ur was the birthplace of Abraham a century or two later. Ur is almost directly East of Bethlehem, so when, two thousand years later, Jesus was born, and Kings came from the East, did they come from Ur? Did they emulate Abraham's own journey? Indeed, did the Magi, Abraham and Melchizedek all belong to the same religion – the very first religion ever?

A thousand years after Abraham's triumphal entry into Melchizedek's Jerusalem, King David was getting old, and there was rebellion in the air. He therefore had his son Solomon anointed as King, put him on a donkey, and, with loud music and praises, King Solomon made a triumphal entry into Jerusalem[2]. Coming on a donkey as opposed to a warhorse, signifies coming in peace.

The king came in peace to the ancient 'City of Peace'.

In the beleaguered centuries that followed, the prophets of Israel every so often took time off from reprimands to remind that one day, from David's line, the Messiah would bring everlasting peace to the city of peace[3]: "Rejoice greatly, Daughter Zion! Shout, Daughter Jerusalem! See, your king comes to you, righteous and victorious, lowly and riding on a donkey, on a colt, the foal of a donkey ... He will proclaim peace to the nations. His rule will extend ... to the ends of the earth.

As for you, because of the blood of my covenant with you, I will free your prisoners from the waterless pit ... The LORD their God will save his people ... as a shepherd saves his flock."

Fast forward another thousand years from David, and in a spectacularly beautiful fulfilment, Jesus, Messiah, Son of David, Priest, Prophet and recently-anointed King, makes a triumphal entry into Jerusalem!

The crowd cried out David's own words in praise[4]! What a moment! No wonder Jesus told the scoffers that if he silenced the cheering crowd, the very stones themselves would cry out for joy!

Pause for reflection: It was a long wait from Solomon to Jesus. But when he finally arrived, the blessing was infinitely more than anyone had imagined: not just a spell of peace until we die, but actual, everlasting, peace, for all who are on the side of the true King.

References: 1. Genesis 14:18-20   2. 1 Kings 1:32-48   3. Zechariah 9:9-11 & 16   4. Psalm 118

30. New life

[20] *Now among those who went up to worship at the festival were some Greeks.* [21] *They came to Philip, who was from Bethsaida in Galilee, and said to him, "Sir, we wish to see Jesus."* [22] *Philip went and told Andrew; then Andrew and Philip went and told Jesus.*

[23] *Jesus answered them, "The hour has come for the Son of Man to be glorified.*

[24] *Very truly, I tell you, unless a grain of wheat falls into the earth and dies, it remains just a single grain; but if it dies, it bears much fruit.*

[25] *Those who love their life lose it, and those who hate their life in this world will keep it for eternal life.*

[26] *Whoever serves me must follow me, and where I am, there will my servant be also.*

Whoever serves me, the Father will honour.

30. New life

On the face of it, it is a straightforward metaphor: we have to, in some way, 'die', in order to subsequently bear fruit. And it must be a metaphor, not an instruction to be taken literally, as it would be difficult to see how we might bear fruit if we were dead.

'To die', then, might mean 'to submit', in the same way that a seed has no say whatever in its own destiny, but submits itself to the hand of the thrower, to the wind on which it was thrown, and to the soil on which it lands. So it is that we, perhaps are called to submit ourselves to God, the one who sews, trusting in His Hand to sew us well?

Or, more poignantly, perhaps 'to die' might mean 'to serve' – a word mentioned twice in this short passage? Jesus knows himself to be the fulfilment of Isaiah's Messianic prophecies, and understands infinitely more deeply than any of us could, that part of the Messiah's destiny is to be the 'Suffering Servant[1]':

> "... He was despised and rejected by mankind, a man of suffering, and familiar with pain
>
> ... Surely he took up our pain and bore our suffering ... he was pierced for our transgressions, he was crushed for our iniquities ... and by his wounds we are healed.
>
> We all, like sheep, have gone astray ... each of us has turned to our own way; and the LORD has laid on him the iniquity of us all.
>
> ... he was led like a lamb to the slaughter ... After he has suffered, he will see the light of life and be satisfied; by his knowledge my righteous servant will justify many, and he will bear their iniquities."

However, we have already seen how in John's gospel, the author picks up on the significant nuances and subtleties of Jesus's actions and words.

Looking beyond the obvious, then, it suddenly strikes me as odd that this anguished speech of Jesus comes, not at an intimate meeting of his closest Jewish friends, but after having been approached by some Greeks. Greeks, by definition, could not have been close friends. In those days, however, Greeks such as those asking to see Jesus, would have been sophisticated and enlightened gentiles, with a culture rooted in the golden age of philosophy. It may even be that the word 'Greek' here would signify to the people of that era, 'enlightened gentile'.

With this in mind, is Jesus hinting that his suffering will not just be for Jews, but for all? That the 'fruit' he will bear will be for all those who believe, Jew and gentile alike?

Seen from that perspective, the seed metaphor takes on a different significance: perhaps the seed is the Old Covenant, which contains the life and essence of the New Covenant, but which has to fulfil its purpose and then disappear, before the New Covenant can bear fruit?

One more point: A seed does not die. It changes. It morphs. The Old Covenant would not die, but it would be fulfilled. In using the word 'die', despite subsequently being very much alive and bearing much fruit, Jesus was therefore pointing at a new and spectacular impermanence to death itself.

Jesus was indeed going to die ... but then be resurrected. The Logos, the Messiah, the King, the Suffering Servant ... the Resurrection and the Life.

Pause for reflection: Am I holding on to something old, which must be renewed?

Something which must 'die', only to be reborn in a much more fruitful form?

Reference: Isaiah 58

31. Light, Judgement and Salvation

27 *"Now my soul is troubled. And what should I say — 'Father, save me from this hour'? No, it is for this reason that I have come to this hour.* 28 *Father, glorify your name." Then a voice came from heaven, "I have glorified it, and I will glorify it again."*

29 *The crowd standing there heard it and said that it was thunder. Others said, "An angel has spoken to him."* 30 *Jesus answered, "This voice has come for your sake, not for mine.*

31 *Now is the judgment of this world; now the ruler of this world will be driven out.* 32 *And I, when I am lifted up from the earth, will draw all people to myself."* 33 *He said this to indicate the kind of death he was to die.*

34 *The crowd answered him, "We have heard from the law that the Messiah remains forever. How can you say that the Son of Man must be lifted up? Who is this Son of Man?"*

35 *Jesus said to them, "The light is with you for a little longer. Walk while you have the light, so that the darkness may not overtake you. If you walk in the darkness, you do not know where you are going.* 36 *While you have the light, believe in the light, so that you may become children of light."*

After Jesus had said this, he departed and hid from them. 37 *Although he had performed so many signs in their presence, they did not believe in him.*

38 *This was to fulfil the word spoken by the prophet Isaiah: "Lord, who has believed our message, and to whom has the arm of the Lord been revealed?"* 39 *And so they could not believe, because Isaiah also said,* 40 *"He has blinded their eyes and hardened their heart, so that they might not look with their eyes, and understand with their heart and turn — and I would heal them."* 41 *Isaiah said this because he saw his glory and spoke about him.*

42 *Nevertheless many, even of the authorities, believed in him. But because of the Pharisees they did not confess it, for fear that they would be put out of the synagogue;* 43 *for they loved human glory more than the glory that comes from God.*

44 *Then Jesus cried aloud:* "Whoever believes in me believes not in me but in him who sent me. 45 And whoever sees me sees him who sent me. 46 I have come as light into the world, so that everyone who believes in me should not remain in the darkness.

47 I do not judge anyone who hears my words and does not keep them, for I came not to judge the world, but to save the world.

48 The one who rejects me and does not receive my word has a judge; on the last day the word that I have spoken will serve as judge, 49 for I have not spoken on my own, but the Father who sent me has himself given me a commandment about what to say and what to speak.

50 And I know that his commandment is eternal life. What I speak, therefore, I speak just as the Father has told me."

31. Light, Judgement and Salvation

"Now my soul is troubled." <u>Now</u>. Now that I have said to the scoffers everything I had to say; now that I have showed the Signs; now that they have felt and ignored the Spirit; now that they have seen the true fulfilment of everything they have been brought up to believe in – and rejected it. Now.

From now on, Jesus would reveal some profound mysteries to his chosen, but to the unbelievers, he has said all he wants to say. Notice that he does not even answer their questions in this passage – he just sums up his message.

At the heart of that message is Light.

When the amazing Simon and Garfunkel broke up, (yes, I am that old), we heard little of poor Art Garfunkel on the international stage thereafter. It was clear who the genius was. But that did not make Garfunkel wrong, or a bad musician. It is just that he was not 50% of the partnership.

I imagine that Jesus's listeners on that day, especially the learned, were trying to work out to what degree Jesus was the genius, and to what degree their own interpretation was correct. "We are right about this ... he is right about that ..." In other words, perhaps the less convinced, listening to Jesus, thought that maybe both the Chief Priest and Jesus had a point, and that the truth was somewhere in between.

However, instead of talking of two components, each contributing something, that together make harmony, Jesus made it clear that he was instead talking about two opposites. Himself and the unbelievers. Light and Dark.

Jesus was not trying to argue the percentage that he was contributing to the debate. He was not saying, "Well, you have a point there, but even so ..." He was saying, "I am the Light of the world. I AM." Light or Dark – your choice, but there is no third way.

If the Light was not in them, at least until then it had been around them. Jesus was warning them that when he was lifted to heaven, they would then realise what true 100% darkness was. There was nothing about evil that could make harmony with good. Nothing about wrongness that could make harmony with rightness. They would be judged according to which side they picked.

We have already seen how Jesus makes us think deeply by sometimes claiming to be our judge, and sometimes claiming not to be.

Here, however, he makes it clearer: he is the vehicle through which judgement arrives, but he, as a person, will not be judging in the way that the Jews of the day would have been familiar with. He is the Word. The Light. And when light shines, it cannot help but judge, because it shows things as they are.

Jesus's own summary of his ministry to the sceptics, then, is this: "I am from the Father. I am Light. The Light will save you. I have proven this to you, by my words, Signs and Spirit. But you have chosen darkness".

From this point, Jesus withdraws completely from public life, until the time of his arrest. But to his disciples, he still has so much more to say and do ...

Pause for reflection: The corollary of this is that Salvation is for those with Light in them. Those who, when shown up by the Light to be what they truly are, are willing to accept the embarrassing truth. This has two implications.

Firstly, humility. Am I willing to let go of my foolish vanities and conceits?

Secondly, tolerance. Am I willing to accept that both myself and others, are not yet perfect?

32. Chapter 13 The Servant King

1 Now before the festival of the Passover, Jesus knew that his hour had come to depart from this world and go to the Father. Having loved his own who were in the world, he loved them to the end. 2 The devil had already put it into the heart of Judas son of Simon Iscariot to betray him.

And during supper 3 Jesus, knowing that the Father had given all things into his hands, and that he had come from God and was going to God, 4 got up from the table, took off his outer robe, and tied a towel around himself. 5 Then he poured water into a basin and began to wash the disciples' feet and to wipe them with the towel that was tied around him.

6 He came to Simon Peter, who said to him, "Lord, are you going to wash my feet?" 7 Jesus answered, "You do not know now what I am doing, but later you will understand." 8 Peter said to him, "You will never wash my feet."

Jesus answered, "Unless I wash you, you have no share with me." 9 Simon Peter said to him, "Lord, not my feet only but also my hands and my head!" 10 Jesus said to him, "One who has bathed does not need to wash, except for the feet, but is entirely clean.

And you are clean, though not all of you." 11 For he knew who was to betray him; for this reason he said, "Not all of you are clean."

12 After he had washed their feet, had put on his robe, and had returned to the table, he said to them, "Do you know what I have done to you?

13 You call me Teacher and Lord—and you are right, for that is what I am. 14 So if I, your Lord and Teacher, have washed your feet, you also ought to wash one another's feet. 15 For I have set you an example, that you also should do as I have done to you.

¹⁶ Very truly, I tell you, servants are not greater than their master, nor are messengers greater than the one who sent them.

¹⁷ If you know these things, you are blessed if you do them. ¹⁸ I am not speaking of all of you; I know whom I have chosen. But it is to fulfil the scripture, 'The one who ate my bread has lifted his heel against me.' ¹⁹ I tell you this now, before it occurs, so that when it does occur, you may believe that I am he.

²⁰ Very truly, I tell you, whoever receives one whom I send receives me; and whoever receives me receives him who sent me."

encompassing all the commandments

humble

32. The Servant King

The public ministry of Jesus is over. John now gives us five chapters of what happened at the Last Supper, the words and actions of which must have been etched deeply on his heart.

The more symbolic and transcendental parts of these precious moments can be better understood when seen as the Messiah establishing on earth his Church of the New Covenant. Not his Roman Church, nor his Anglican Church, nor his Baptist Church, nor his religious tradition, but his Church – the collection of people, starting with these intimate friends, who will be an interface through which the Spirit might come into the world in day-to-day life.

Until this point, the Logos, The Word made flesh, had spent three years showing that he was the Messiah, the Anointed One[1,2,3]. The Son of Man, the Everlasting King[4,5]. The Resurrection and the Life[6]. Son of David and Redeemer of Israel[7]. The One who will deliver His people[8]. Son of the Father[9,10]. The Child of Bethlehem taking David's throne[11].

Now, at the Last Supper, a new side of the Logos would be revealed to them. The Lamb of God[12]; the Suffering Servant[13,14].

In particular, Isaiah had already prophesied that the Messiah would come twice: once to die in ignominy to save us, and then again in glory, as a benevolent King for ever. Now, at this exact moment, the disciples found themselves precisely between these two manifestations of God.

What was only going to dawn on them very, very slowly, was that, from now on, our entire human existence prior to death would be between these two aspects of the Messiah – between the Son of Man who had asked us to believe in him, and Everlasting King who would lift us to everlasting life.

How would we – his believers, his friends, his 'Church' – spend that time? Jesus began with an example. Service. The sort of service normally performed by a slave. Not, however, with a slave's downturned and perhaps wounded eyes, but with eyes of deep love.

More than that, however, Jesus said that this service was a cleansing. A cleansing of the feet knowing full well that they would be dirty again very soon.

If we were to follow that example, then we were to be the means by which those in need of cleansing found the Spirit of Jesus at work through the incessant love of his followers.

Pause for reflection: The direction of the action is top down. Jesus shows his love for his disciples not because he is trying to please the Father, but because he loves them.

He washes their feet purely for the sake of love. What have I done today to follow that example, purely for the sake of love?

References: 1. 2 Samuel 1:14   2. Psalm 105:15   3. Isaiah 45:1   4. Daniel 9:25   5. Daniel 7:13-14   6. Ezekiel 37:9-14   7. Isaiah 11:1-10 & 32:1 & 33:17 & 42:1-9 & 52:9-10 & 61:1-2   8. Joel 2:28-32   9. 1 Chronicles 17:10-14   10. Zechariah 6:12-13   11. Micah 5:2-4   12. Isaiah Isaiah 53:3-12   13. Isaiah 42:1-9   14. Psalms 21, 22, 68, 69

33. Treachery is a choice

²¹ After saying this Jesus was troubled in spirit, and declared, "Very truly, I tell you, one of you will betray me." ²² The disciples looked at one another, uncertain of whom he was speaking.

²³ One of his disciples — the one whom Jesus loved — was reclining next to him; ²⁴ Simon Peter therefore motioned to him to ask Jesus of whom he was speaking. ²⁵ So while reclining next to Jesus, he asked him, "Lord, who is it?"

²⁶ Jesus answered, "It is the one to whom I give this piece of bread when I have dipped it in the dish." So, when he had dipped the piece of bread, he gave it to Judas son of Simon Iscariot.

²⁷ After he received the piece of bread, Satan entered into him. Jesus said to him, "Do quickly what you are going to do." ²⁸ Now no one at the table knew why he said this to him. ²⁹ Some thought that, because Judas had the common purse, Jesus was telling him, "Buy what we need for the festival"; or, that he should give something to the poor. ³⁰ So, after receiving the piece of bread, he immediately went out. And it was night.

33. Treachery is a choice

The Suffering Servant was predicted by Isaiah 700 years before, but these prophecies made no sense to the Pharisees at the time of Jesus.

Nor did they strike a chord with Judas, to whom the idea of giving oneself over to mockers and spitters was utterly at odds with his concept of the Messiah. Jesus, the Anointed One, was innocent and spotless, and yet was to be sacrificed? What a pointless anti-climax, Judas must have thought.

We have seen during the public ministry of Jesus how it was particularly important to him to be seen as the fulfilment of Moses – the new Ark / Temple; the new Manna; the Spring of Water; the Redeemer of Israel; the Healer; the New Covenant.

What could be more poignant, then, than to be the fulfilment also of the Passover initiated by Moses?

Yet even though Judas had been party to killing the innocent and spotless sacrificial Passover lamb every year of his adult life; and even though he probably knew much of Isaiah by heart; and even though he had lived three years with Jesus – and knew that John the Baptist had called him the Lamb of God ... he failed to see the connection.

The cross marked a seminal moment in the journey of Jesus: a choice he made to be true to himself and his destiny, even when it meant scorn and terror.

On this side of that decision he left behind public opinion, treachery, and death.

On the far side he found glory.

For Judas, the cross was a mistake.

For the Lamb of God, the cross, (and what was to follow the next day), were the means whereby the Suffering Servant would become the Resurrection and the Life.

For us, the decision to be true to ourselves and our destiny, whatever others might think, is a cross we take up daily, on our journey to the glorious Kingdom.

Pause for reflection: Lord, Lamb of God, you have shown me the Way.

May I brush off daily the dust of this world, and ever more truly rejoice and be glad in you ... and follow where you lead.

34. It's all about Love

31 When he had gone out, Jesus said, "Now the Son of Man has been glorified, and God has been glorified in him. 32 If God has been glorified in him, God will also glorify him in Himself and will glorify him at once.

33 Little children, I am with you only a little longer. You will look for me; and as I said to the Jews so now I say to you, 'Where I am going, you cannot come.'

34 I give you a new commandment, that you love one another. Just as I have loved you, you also should love one another.

35 By this everyone will know that you are my disciples, if you have love for one another."

34. It's all about Love

There is so much theology packed into these five short verses!

The first three are imbued with typically deep mysticism. John tells us that Jesus says, "Now ... God <u>has been</u> glorified". Hang on! <u>Has been</u> glorified? Isn't that yet to come? What can 'has been' mean?

I am afraid that I do not know. I recognise, however, that like any confusing part of the gospel, there must be deep significance to it – an 'Aha! moment' to come – or else why did the Spirit inspire John to remember these words as spoken in the past tense?

I can only offer this: 'Now' in this context can only mean 'Now that Judas has gone' – the immediately preceding event. Maybe Jesus 'has been glorified' by the decision – his own free choice – to allow Judas to betray him to the awfulness to come?

Presumably "He will glorify him in Himself, and glorify him at once" then refers to the Resurrection to come in just a couple of days.

But I suspect that there might be more to it than that ...

The next statement is yet another mystery – "where I am going, you cannot come". This presumably refers to the unfathomable clause in the Apostle's creed: 'he descended into hell' – of which more in the next reflection.

The final pair of verses are, in their own way, equally puzzling: 'A new Commandment'. The implication is that in three years on the road, he never before gave this commandment to love one another, but instead saved it for here, with his intimate believers, when establishing his Church.

It is true that John has not mentioned it before, and that in the synoptic gospels, Jesus talked in parables to describe the Kingdom of Heaven. However, we know from Mark's gospel[1], that Jesus had already reiterated the commandments of Moses[2] when asked what the greatest commandment was. This *included 'love the foreigner', which Jesus rendered as 'love your neighbour as yourself'. Matthew also has Jesus telling us to love our enemies[3].*

In John's way of telling the story, by contrast, Jesus in his public ministry had told any who might listen, that it was <u>Light</u> that needed to be within them. He had explained that the hallmark of that light was forgiveness.

Only in the intimacy of the upper room, had he then given an example of the behaviour to be practised by people of the Light – the service of foot-washing.

Now, he was giving that behaviour a more general name: Love. By this they will know that you are of my 'Church'; that you have the Light within you – that you love one another.

It was a new commandment, not because he had not mentioned love before, but rather because he was emphasising, in his New Covenant, his Church, that love rather than righteousness, was the overarching characteristic.

C.S. Lewis describes four types of love:
- *'Eros' – the romantic love between partners;*
- *'Storge' – the familiar love between parent and child;*
- *'Philia' – the strong-bond love between best friends; and*
- *'Agape' – the unconditional Love which flows through and beyond the other three, and touches even the most unlovable.*

Here's the rub: It is this limitlessness of this 'agape' love which Jesus was now beginning to reveal to his Church.

Pause for reflection: Who do I know who is unlovable? What might 'agape love' mean for that relationship?

References: 1. Mark 12:31   2. Deuteronomy 6:5 & 10:19   3. Matthew 5:44

35. To hell and back

36 Simon Peter said to him, "Lord, where are you going?"

Jesus answered, "Where I am going, you cannot follow me now; but you will follow afterward."

37 Peter said to him, "Lord, why can I not follow you now? I will lay down my life for you."

38 Jesus answered, "Will you lay down your life for me? Very truly, I tell you, before the cock crows, you will have denied me three times.

35. To hell and back

One of the times when I need to remind myself to show agape love, instead of brimming with indignation, is when I hear yet another sermon portraying the terrifyingly horrific death of Jesus on the cross as being the price paid for the sin of all humanity.

It is true that words cannot describe the horror of that day.

However, Jesus had had a relatively peaceful life, right up to his meal on Maundy Thursday. Just twenty-four hours later he was dead – the same type of crucifixion death subsequently suffered by thousands of his followers, many of them after prolonged torture.

How could a single day – of admittedly desperately horrendous and unjust human suffering – atone for every sin of billions of humans? It could not. The cross was not a destination. It was a gateway to hell. Jesus knew this, and soon enough, in utter agony, he would be nailed to a cross and quoting Psalm 22: 'My God, my God, why have you forsaken me?"

But if Jesus was the Word of God, how could God forsake him?

If Jesus is the 'I AM' subsumed into the infinity of God, how could he also 'go to hell', which, by definition, is the place where God is not? Hell – the utter horror of complete absence of Light, and complete presence of evil?

I think that the answer lies in the consideration of the different natures of Jesus when the Logos became Son of Man.

Firstly, as Son of Man, Jesus was a human being – body and blood.

Secondly, the 'soul' or 'Spirit' of Jesus was a separate entity from the Father. As was clear from so many of the discourses of Jesus, you cannot ask things of the Father; receive things from the Father; obey the Father; spend time in prayer with the Father, or say that "the Father is greater than I", if you ARE the Father.

Thirdly, Jesus was the Logos – the Manifestation of God, in which mysterious sense he was indeed one with the Father.

The body of Jesus was about to die; the blood about to be spilt. Thereafter, the Logos was to go to the Father, to become One I AM.

In between, however, for the duration of the Passover Sabbath, the Soul of Jesus was to go into the presence of all sin, and to call all who might love him, to Forgiveness, Redemption and Resurrection.

What that might actually mean, the human mind cannot imagine. That, however, was the infinite payment of all debt, next to which, the crucifixion was a walk in the park: The Manifestation of God, who had been in the presence of God from the beginning of time, chose to go where God was not, to seek out souls for Salvation.

It was the overwhelming foreboding of this infinitely terrifying journey, perhaps, that caused him to point out to Peter the weakness of even so faithful a friend.

Pause for reflection: St. Faustina, a Polish nun, gave us a prayer called 'the chaplet of Divine mercy.'

The core of the prayer is: "Eternal Father, I offer you the Body, Blood, Soul and Divinity of Our Lord Jesus Christ, in atonement for our sins, and those of the whole world. For the sake of His sorrowful Passion, have mercy on us and on the whole world."

I could say it a million times, and, like Peter, still not fully get it.

36. Chapter 14 The Way, the Truth and the Life

¹ "Do not let your hearts be troubled. Believe in God, believe also in me. ² In my Father's house there are many dwelling places. If it were not so, would I have told you that I go to prepare a place for you?

³ And if I go and prepare a place for you, I will come again and will take you to myself, so that where I am, there you may be also. ⁴ And you know the way to the place where I am going."

⁵ Thomas said to him, "Lord, we do not know where you are going. How can we know the way?"

⁶ Jesus said to him, "I am the way, and the truth, and the life. No one comes to the Father except through me. ⁷ If you know me, you will know my Father also. From now on you do know him and have seen him."

⁸ Philip said to him, "Lord, show us the Father, and we will be satisfied."

⁹ Jesus said to him, "Have I been with you all this time, Philip, and you still do not know me? Whoever has seen me has seen the Father. How can you say, 'Show us the Father'? ¹⁰ Do you not believe that I am in the Father and the Father is in me? The words that I say to you I do not speak on my own; but the Father who dwells in me does his works.

¹¹ Believe me that I am in the Father and the Father is in me; but if you do not, then believe me because of the works themselves.

¹² Very truly, I tell you, the one who believes in me will also do the works that I do and, in fact, will do greater works than these, because I am going to the Father. ¹³ I will do whatever you ask in my name, so that the Father may be glorified in the Son.

¹⁴ If in my name you ask me for anything, I will do it.

36. The Way, the Truth and the Life

His disciples have called him 'Son of God', 'Messiah', 'Son of David', 'King', and presumably many other titles.

Jesus himself, however, now reveals which title might best suit the purposes of his Church – the Way, the Truth and the Life. Jesus is the Way *to eternal life in the Father, through faith and love ... and yet mysteriously he is* in *the Father.*

That is our creed in a nutshell.

Given that no human explanation will ever get remotely close to unpacking this relationship between Jesus and the Father, it is quite incredible how much schism it has caused in the Church that Jesus established.

In the Arian schism, for instance, the debate centred on whether Jesus had eternally existed. In 325, when the Roman Empire was suddenly in favour of Christianity, the elders of the church came from all points of the compass to Nicene, to come up with an irrefutable declaration of belief. Every word and punctuation of the 'Nicene Creed' was designed to expunge all potential heresy, and to give a permanently explicit declaration of the faith ... um, except that there are now a dozen extant versions – not to mention all of the other older ones .

Picking extracts from various versions, the Nicene Creed now says that Jesus is "His only son ... eternally begotten of the Father ... begotten not made ... one in substance with the Father...". I'm not sure it was worth having the schism over, if literal interpretation is what is being demanded. How can anything be 'eternally begotten'? 'Begotten' implies a beginning. How can you be someone's son and yet be 'one in substance? You cannot be both. Literal interpretation of words does not cut the mustard.

At the Last Supper, Jesus was telling us all we needed to know of a supreme Truth, that could not actually make sense except by his metaphor: the Way, the Truth and the Life.

What does that mean for other religions, then? Jesus did not say that he was 'one of' the ways. He is THE Way. The Father is in him, and when we have seen Jesus, we have seen the Father. There is only one Father God.

I will not venture into these troubled waters, except to say that 'What is impossible for mortals is possible for God¹'.

Then – glory be!!! – having told us that he goes to God to prepare a place in heaven for those who believe, Jesus then goes on to promise that petitionary payer actually works! Believe in him, ask in his name, and we will receive! What extraordinarily extravagant promises!

Perhaps, like Philip, many people of the day would not have been quite ready to hear these stunning words. However, Jesus was making it quite clear that they were true:

> *Firstly, he had shown how the Jewish/Israeli story, based on adoration of the One God, was true, by his fulfilling of the prophets.*

> *He had then augmented this by showing, in the Signs, that the supernatural truly exists, and that it flowed through him at his word.*

> *He had then made sense of the loving nature of God.*

> *During all of this, they had felt the power of his Spirit.*

> *Now, the decisive point: "I am the Truth". If someone does not lie, then what they say is truth.*

Pause for reflection: Jesus promises that prayers in his name will be answered. Yet sometimes, I do not immediately receive what I had been expecting. Who has got it wrong, then? Jesus? ... Or my understanding of what I was asking for? ...

References: 1. Matthew 19:26   Mark 10:27   Luke 18:27

37. The Advocate, the Revelation – and Peace

15 "If you love me, you will keep my commandments. 16 And I will ask the Father, and he will give you another Advocate, to be with you forever. 17 This is the Spirit of truth, whom the world cannot receive, because it neither sees him nor knows him. You know him, because he abides with you, and he will be in you.

18 "I will not leave you orphaned; I am coming to you. 19 In a little while the world will no longer see me, but you will see me; because I live, you also will live. 20 On that day you will know that I am in my Father, and you in me, and I in you.

21 They who have my commandments and keep them are those who love me; and those who love me will be loved by my Father, and I will love them and reveal myself to them."

22 Judas (not Iscariot) said to him, "Lord, how is it that you will reveal yourself to us, and not to the world?"

23 Jesus answered him, "Those who love me will keep my word, and my Father will love them, and we will come to them and make our home with them. 24 Whoever does not love me does not keep my words; and the word that you hear is not mine, but is from the Father who sent me.

25 "I have said these things to you while I am still with you. 26 But the Advocate, the Holy Spirit, whom the Father will send in my name, will teach you everything, and remind you of all that I have said to you.

27 Peace I leave with you; my peace I give to you.

I do not give to you as the world gives.

Do not let your hearts be troubled, and do not let them be afraid.

28 You heard me say to you, 'I am going away, and I am coming to you.' If you loved me, you would rejoice that I am going to the Father, because the Father is greater than I.

29 And now I have told you this before it occurs, so that when it does occur, you may believe.

30 I will no longer talk much with you, for the ruler of this world is coming. He has no power over me; 31 but I do as the Father has commanded me, so that the world may know that I love the Father.

Rise, let us be on our way.

37. The Advocate, the Revelation – and Peace

Having explained that he was the Way to the Father – that faith in Jesus, and love, would lead to forgiveness – Jesus now strides straight on into the mystery of the Holy Spirit and the Holy Trinity.

Phew – tough theology for the nascent Church.

However, given that this very same Spirit was with John when he wrote this gospel, it is worth looking closely at the clues Jesus has given us:

'Advocate.
Spirit of Truth.
Abides in you – but not in the world.
Will teach you everything.
Will remind you of what I said.'

These phrases are perhaps better understood in the context of listeners who, all their lives, had regarded God as living in the Temple in Jerusalem. When prayers needed answering; or where sacrifices were made for love of God; or where one sought the true meaning of life; or where one delved deeply into the learning of the scriptures; or where legal cases needed resolving by God's justice; the Temple in Jerusalem was where it happened in the past[1].

But once Jesus had sent the Spirit, then the new Temple was the heart of the believer. That would be where prayers were answered; where love was made manifest; where truth might be revealed; where spiritual learning occurred; where forgiveness replaced harsh justice.

Furthermore, this was not to be a facility only available at times of pilgrimage, but rather something actually resident within.

Prayer. Love. Truth. Understanding. Forgiveness. All within.
Peace! The Peace of God, which passes all understanding, would guard our hearts and our minds in (the love of) Christ

Jesus[2]. Jesus seems to be saying that the Holy Spirit will be the bringer of these blessings.

Quite how that happens on a metaphysical level, to me is less important than that it does.

I know that explanations matter, (as these reflections testify!), and indeed St Paul spent much of his time making sense of Christianity to his readers and listeners. It seems helpful to point out, for instance, that faith, love and forgiveness are at the heart of the meaning of life.

However, it is useful to remember that when we come to those things infinitely beyond our comprehension, only metaphors suffice. (A millennium ago, the entire Christian Church on earth was torn in two by failure to agree on the 'filioque clause' in the Nicene creed. This clause, and its Latin suffix arrangement, suggested that the Spirit 'proceeded from the Son' as well as the Father. Why such angst over literal interpretation!!? It has to be a metaphor, because how does an infinite being 'proceed'?)

So, for me, what Jesus actually said, recorded by John under prompting of the Spirit, is enough: clear enough; mysterious enough. The Spirit of God dwells in those who love Him, who believe in Jesus, and who show it by their faith, love and forgiveness.

The Spirit of God lives within those who accept the invitation.

Pause for reflection: Why not, right now, invite that same Spirit to make you feel that peace of Jesus, soothing any inner hurt, answering any deep-seated need.

Reference: 1. Psalm 122   2. Philippians 4:7

38. Chapter 15 Love and the Vinegrower

[1] "I am the true vine, and my Father is the vinegrower. [2] He removes every branch in me that bears no fruit. Every branch that bears fruit he prunes to make it bear more fruit. [3] You have already been cleansed by the word that I have spoken to you.

[4] Abide in me as I abide in you. Just as the branch cannot bear fruit by itself unless it abides in the vine, neither can you unless you abide in me.

[5] I am the vine, you are the branches. Those who abide in me and I in them bear much fruit, because apart from me you can do nothing. [6] Whoever does not abide in me is thrown away like a branch and withers; such branches are gathered, thrown into the fire, and burned.

[7] If you abide in me, and my words abide in you, ask for whatever you wish, and it will be done for you. [8] My Father is glorified by this, that you bear much fruit and become my disciples.

[9] As the Father has loved me, so I have loved you; abide in my love. [10] If you keep my commandments, you will abide in my love, just as I have kept my Father's commandments and abide in his love. [11] I have said these things to you so that my joy may be in you, and that your joy may be complete.

[12] "This is my commandment, that you love one another as I have loved you. [13] No one has greater love than this, to lay down one's life for one's friends. [14] You are my friends if you do what I command you. [15] I do not call you servants any longer, because the servant does not know what the master is doing; but I have called you friends, because I have made known to you everything that I have heard from my Father.

[16] You did not choose me but I chose you. And I appointed you to go and bear fruit, fruit that will last, so that the Father will give you whatever you ask him in my name. [17] I am giving you these commands so that you may love one another.

38. Love and the Vine-grower

Having made it clear that it is the flow of love which characterises the relationship between ourselves and the Trinity, Jesus now gives us the analogy of a vine, where the flow of sap produces the fruit. In the same way, the flow of love in us will produce the spiritual fruits hoped of us in our presence here on Earth.

(A vine, whose image was represented both on coinage and on the Temple, was an ancient and poignant symbol for Israel.)

Along with 'fruit that lasts' comes the promise of prayer answered – as well as some painful pruning. (I presume that you cannot pray to avoid the pruning shears?) The pruning, we should remember, would not be of any flourishing parts of ourselves – those which have found good light, and have thrived – but instead the parts needing pruning are those parts of ourselves where energy is being drawn into darker places, where no fruit might be borne.

Amidst all this, the life-giving element of our spiritual plant is the sap: Jesus – the Way.

In a similar metaphor in Luke's gospel², Jesus describes himself not as the Way through which we need to come, nor the vine to which we need to be attached, but instead as the 'narrow door'. The narrowness, it seems to me, is not because only the righteous who never sin can enter, but instead it is narrow because we cannot take our baggage with us.

Our dark, useless baggage. Our dark useless branches. Uselessness needs, as in the vine story, to be pruned.

As we get nearer to the end of Jesus's final discourse to his disciples, he is using simple imagery to sum up the message. It is as if he is saying, after all the deep theological symbolism, "Look, don't worry if you don't get all that! Just stick with me. There will be a rough ride in places; but huge blessings – and then an eternity of love."

Pause for reflection: Pruning our darker areas.

Oh, so hard. Vanity. Deceit. Lust. Bitchiness. Wasting blessings. Greed. Forgetting God. So many sins.

What do you need to prune?

Here is a poem that might help:

> *I realise from time to time a poignant truth –*
> *and what a crime*
> *that fantasy and vanity should foster such profanity*
> *As I should ever lose my hold on Love and Solace...*
>
> *....Yet the cold and sordid world*
> *of discontent and bitterness,*
> *is ever bent on capturing my lazy will*
> *with thrills and promises,*
> *until I once again am lured into the sticky web.*
>
> *And there anew I helplessly awake,*
> *and cry for glory that has passed me by.*
>
> *Yet glory is the very thing surrounding my awakening –*
> *Evaporating guilt like mist before the sun.*
> *The warm insistence of the sense of hope surprises me.*
> *And sense denies the Past its power.*
> *For Truth, revealed, has won the day, and I am healed.*

Reference: 1 Psalm 80:8-19 2. Luke 13:23-30

39. The hate of the world

18 "If the world hates you, be aware that it hated me before it hated you. 19 If you belonged to the world, the world would love you as its own. Because you do not belong to the world, but I have chosen you out of the world—therefore the world hates you.

20 Remember the word that I said to you, 'Servants are not greater than their master.' If they persecuted me, they will persecute you; if they kept my word, they will keep yours also. 21 But they will do all these things to you on account of my name, because they do not know him who sent me.

22 If I had not come and spoken to them, they would not have sin; but now they have no excuse for their sin. 23 Whoever hates me hates my Father also. 24 If I had not done among them the works that no one else did, they would not have sin. But now they have seen and hated both me and my Father. 25 It was to fulfil the word that is written in their law, 'They hated me without a cause.'

26 "When the Advocate comes, whom I will send to you from the Father, the Spirit of truth who comes from the Father, he will testify on my behalf. 27 You also are to testify because you have been with me from the beginning.

Chapter 16   March 23 3. 23

1 "I have said these things to you to keep you from stumbling. 2 They will put you out of the synagogues. Indeed, an hour is coming when those who kill you will think that by doing so they are offering worship to God. 3 And they will do this because they have not known the Father or me.

4 But I have said these things to you so that when their hour comes you may remember that I told you about them. "I did not say these things to you from the beginning, because I was with you.

39. The hate of the world

Having assured us that we will not be abandoned, Jesus is inviting us to choose sides. These verses create a strong 'us and them' feel, that needs some deeper scrutiny:

It might be worth placing another piece of John's writing alongside this passage, to get a clearer feel for what he is saying.

John begins his first letter[1] giving us what appears to be a paradox: "... I am writing these things to you so that you may not sin. But if anyone does sin, we have an advocate with the Father, Jesus Christ ... the propitiation for ... the sins of the whole world. And by this we know that we have come to know him, if we keep his commandments. Whoever says "I know him" but does not keep his commandments is a liar, and the truth is not in him ..."

On the surface, this is a 'Catch 22': Those on Jesus's side will have their sins forgiven ... but if you sin, you can't be on his side.

Delving deeper, the only explanation is that 'sinning', and 'not keeping his commandments', are not precisely the same! That seems almost crazy until you then ask yourself what commandments Jesus actually did give in John's gospel. As we have seen time and again, the principles, (the 'sap of the vine'), were faith and love[2], from which come forgiveness.

Even in the synoptic gospels, Jesus does not pulpit-bash about the weaknesses and follies of the humble and the honest. Almost as an afterthought he might say, "Go away and sin no more."

Even in one of the most direct sermons he gives, the 'Sermon on the Mount'[3], he concentrates not so much on sin, but rather on the qualities that will free us from the misery of sin. Qualities that will give us spiritual health – 'salt' he called it.

A light for others to see, and to light our own way. Jesus recognised that when we sin through weakness, when we 'walk in the dark', it is we ourselves who are the poorer in so many ways.

Not 'keeping his commandments', in this context, was in an altogether different league from 'the flesh is weak'. To a modern ear, it might be expressed as 'being on his team'. In other words, accepting Jesus with faith; embracing life with love; asking his help; and humbly acknowledging our own weakness by giving and asking for forgiveness.

In short, 'sinning' is not the same as 'embracing a life of sin'.

Instead, those on his team will embrace Jesus, and ask that a life of sin be washed away, and a life of love be born. Therein they might find true joy. Joy in this life, and everlasting joy in the next ... so what's the catch?

Well, there are two. Firstly, deferred gratification rather than self-indulgence is sometimes hard – even painful – to do.

Secondly, as Jesus tells us in this chapter, part of the deal is persecutions.

Blessings untold, in this life and the next, but also persecutions. I cannot just walk into the 'Jesus United' team, and expect to play in the firsts for the rest of my life, without some effort and commitment on my part. And 'commitment' means seeing it through, even when the tough times come, in the certain knowledge that blessings will follow in this life and the next.

Pause for reflection: Jesus promised persecution as well as blessing.

He promised it to me, and he promised it to those that are persecuting me.

Spirit, give me love to see it through.

References: 1. 1 John 2:1-6   2 1 John 3:23   3. Matthew 5:1-16

40. The Spirit of Truth

5 But now I am going to him who sent me; yet none of you asks me, 'Where are you going?' 6 But because I have said these things to you, sorrow has filled your hearts.

7 Nevertheless I tell you the truth: it is to your advantage that I go away, for if I do not go away, the Advocate will not come to you; but if I go, I will send him to you.

8 And when he comes, he will prove the world wrong about sin and righteousness and judgment: 9 about sin, because they do not believe in me; 10 about righteousness, because I am going to the Father and you will see me no longer; 11 about judgment, because the ruler of this world has been condemned.

12 "I still have many things to say to you, but you cannot bear them now. 13 When the Spirit of truth comes, he will guide you into all the truth; for he will not speak on his own, but will speak whatever he hears, and he will declare to you the things that are to come.

14 He will glorify me, because he will take what is mine and declare it to you.

15 All that the Father has is mine. For this reason, I said that he will take what is mine and declare it to you.

40. The Spirit of Truth

At first sight, there is not much more to say about these references to the Spirit, the Advocate.

We have already seen that the reward for being on Jesus's side is that we will have the Spirit dwelling in our heart; that we will believe not because of logical arguments, but because of what we feel within; that we will ask for blessings and receive them; and that, when times of persecution come, we have a Comforter right there for us.

Typically, however, (being prompted by that same Spirit to remember!), John then muddies the water for us by the mysterious way in which this future manifestation of the Spirit was expressed by Jesus:

> "He will prove the world wrong about sin ... because they do not believe in me,
>
> He will prove the world wrong about ... righteousness because I am going to the Father, and
>
> He will prove the world wrong about ... judgement, because the ruler of this world has been condemned."

Phew, again! A strange sequence of reasoning. With all tough bits of John's gospel, however, packed within are gems of truth; and so it is here.

These words are perhaps better understood when we remember that Jesus was using this last discourse to establish his Church. His people. His team. The Spirit had not yet descended at Pentecost, but if Pentecost was the birth of the Church, then the last discourse of Jesus was its conception.

Furthermore, it is not subsequent events themselves that will be doing the 'proving', (meaning somewhere between 'convincing' and 'convicting'), but the Spirit of God Himself.

Given this setting, the Spirit would show people that they were wrong about sin, because the relentlessly harsh, punitive attitude to human frailty in Old Testament Judaism left a hollow fear in the heart of normal people.

By contrast, his Church would proclaim a loving and forgiving God ... where the only unforgiveable sin was against the Holy Spirit[1]: rejection of Jesus; rejection of love; rejection of forgiveness.

This same Spirit would reveal to our hearts that 'righteousness' was not the blind, intolerant dogmatism of Caiaphas the High Priest, but was instead faith and love. Both sides accepted that the origin and font of 'righteousness' was the God of Abraham. But – as his resurrection would prove – it was Jesus who was made one with the Father, not his opponents.

To Jewish eyes in Jesus's day, the stand-off about to take place between Jesus and the Sanhedrin had a different flavour to a modern court. There was no case for the prosecution based on a detailed police investigation.

Instead, two sides each called witnesses to convince, and then a judgement – or conviction – was made.

In this case, however, Jesus would call no human witnesses. He had already given his Signs as witnesses. Now, the Advocate would reveal to his Church that the two parties in this dispute were Jesus and 'Satan' – representing rejection of Love.

When Jesus 'descended into hell' and then 'rose to the Father', it was Satan, not Jesus, who in truth was utterly condemned.

Pause for reflection: Spirit of Truth, please keep me on the right side.

Reference: 1. Matthew 12:30-32

41. The Father loves you and is listening

[16] "A little while, and you will no longer see me, and again a little while, and you will see me."

[17] Then some of his disciples said to one another, "What does he mean by saying to us, 'A little while, and you will no longer see me, and again a little while, and you will see me'; and 'Because I am going to the Father'?" [18] They said, "What does he mean by this 'a little while'? We do not know what he is talking about."

[19] Jesus knew that they wanted to ask him, so he said to them, "Are you discussing among yourselves what I meant when I said, 'A little while, and you will no longer see me, and again a little while, and you will see me'? [20] Very truly, I tell you, you will weep and mourn, but the world will rejoice; you will have pain, but your pain will turn into joy.

[21] When a woman is in labour, she has pain, because her hour has come. But when her child is born, she no longer remembers the anguish because of the joy of having brought a human being into the world.

[22] So you have pain now; but I will see you again, and your hearts will rejoice, and no one will take your joy from you. [23] On that day you will ask nothing of me.

Very truly, I tell you, if you ask anything of the Father in my name, he will give it to you. [24] Until now you have not asked for anything in my name. Ask and you will receive, so that your joy may be complete.

[25] "I have said these things to you in figures of speech. The hour is coming when I will no longer speak to you in figures, but will tell you plainly of the Father. [26] On that day you will ask in my name.

I do not say to you that I will ask the Father on your behalf; [27] for the Father himself loves you, because you have loved me and have believed that I came from God.

[28] *I came from the Father and have come into the world; again, I am leaving the world and am going to the Father."*

[29] *His disciples said, "Yes, now you are speaking plainly, not in any figure of speech!* [30] *Now we know that you know all things, and do not need to have anyone question you; by this we believe that you came from God."*

[31] *Jesus answered them, "Do you now believe?* [32] *The hour is coming, indeed it has come, when you will be scattered, each one to his home, and you will leave me alone.*

Yet I am not alone because the Father is with me. [33] *I have said this to you, so that in me you may have peace.*

In the world you face persecution.

But take courage; I have conquered the world!"

41. The Father loves you and is listening

"Your pain will turn to joy ... Ask anything of the Father in my name ... and you will receive, so that your joy may be complete."

Wow. What a promise!

And this promise was from the Way, the <u>Truth</u> and the Life. The Truth — one who is the very definition of honesty; one who simply cannot deceive. He will deliver. In his name, we are given access to the Father. We are promised pain; but then joy; and answers to prayers.

It is worth at this point reminding ourselves that the word Jesus uses for 'Father' is 'Abba' — Daddy. There was no Old Testament precedent for this. Some of the most devout Jews, even today, do not dare to proclaim his Name — JHWH: I AM. Jesus, by contrast, used the most familiar term available to him — 'Daddy'.

These words about Abba / Daddy are the very last words that Jesus will say to his <u>disciples as a group</u>. In the next part of the gospel, he himself will pray to the Father, and then he will be arrested.

Jesus uses these final words to his embryo Church to pass on to them the familiarity that he has always had with Abba. From now on, his Church, in his name, could call directly on the Father, to be delivered from pain into joy.

Three thoughts occur to me in relation to this.

Firstly, this Church which was being conceived at the Last Supper was not a denomination. It had no name; no traditions; no hierarchy; no Canon Law. It was the <u>Brotherhood / Sisterhood of those who accepted Jesus — and his commandment of love — as the Way to God.</u>

Secondly, after the initial persecutions, the ease with which this new Way swept through the world was unprecedented and extraordinary. Within a few centuries, from a handful of people in the upper room, most of the civilised West was Christian.

Finally, why did John not talk of the institution of the Eucharist?

The other three gospels had described the Last Supper events in almost identical words – words we still use today in Communion services – where Jesus describes the broken bread as his body, offered for us; and the wine as his blood, 'blood of the new and eternal Covenant, that will be shed for you and for many for the forgiveness of sins'.

This is especially noteworthy, given that John's gospel highlights bread and wine – in the first Sign at Cana; in the fourth Sign, where he feeds the 5,000; and then particularly in the follow-up, where Jesus loses many of his fans by telling them to 'eat his flesh and drink his blood'.

John's omission of the 'Communion' aspect of the Last Supper is the subject of PhD study rather than a paragraph, but it is worth mentioning one thing: John's was the last gospel written, maybe even a couple of decades after Mark and Luke. Certainly, he was a young man standing at the cross of Jesus, and an old man when he wrote his gospel.

I expect that by the time he wrote it, not only was the idea of the Eucharist firmly established amongst believers, but also had already differentiated into multiple traditions, each thinking that they were the ones who had got it right.

Plus ça change.

Pause for reflection: If Jesus walked into my 'Church' next Sunday, how much of what he expounded in his last discourse, would he find thriving in my town?

42. Chapter 17 | May they be one in Us

¹ After Jesus had spoken these words, he looked up to heaven and said, "Father, the hour has come; glorify your Son so that the Son may glorify you, ² since you have given him authority over all people, to give eternal life to all whom you have given him.

³ And this is eternal life, that they may know you, the only true God, and Jesus Christ whom you have sent. ⁴ I glorified you on earth by finishing the work that you gave me to do. ⁵ So now, Father, glorify me in your own presence with the glory that I had in your presence before the world existed.

⁶ "I have made your name known to those whom you gave me from the world. They were yours, and you gave them to me, and they have kept your word. ⁷ Now they know that everything you have given me is from you; ⁸ for the words that you gave to me I have given to them, and they have received them and know in truth that I came from you; and they have believed that you sent me.

⁹ I am asking on their behalf; I am not asking on behalf of the world, but on behalf of those whom you gave me, because they are yours. ¹⁰ All mine are yours, and yours are mine; and I have been glorified in them.

¹¹ And now I am no longer in the world, but they are in the world, and I am coming to you. Holy Father, protect them in your name that you have given me, so that they may be one, as we are one. ¹² While I was with them, I protected them in your name that you have given me. I guarded them, and not one of them was lost except the one destined to be lost, so that the scripture might be fulfilled.

¹³ But now I am coming to you, and I speak these things in the world so that they may have my joy made complete in themselves.

¹⁴ *I have given them your word, and the world has hated them because they do not belong to the world, just as I do not belong to the world.*

¹⁵ *I am not asking you to take them out of the world, but I ask you to protect them from the evil one.* ¹⁶ *They do not belong to the world, just as I do not belong to the world.* ¹⁷ *Sanctify them in the truth; your word is truth.* ¹⁸ *As you have sent me into the world, so I have sent them into the world.* ¹⁹ *And for their sakes I sanctify myself, so that they also may be sanctified in truth.*

²⁰ *"I ask not only on behalf of these, but also on behalf of those who will believe in me through their word,* ²¹ *that they may all be one. As you, Father, are in me and I am in you, may they also be in us, so that the world may believe that you have sent me.*

²² *The glory that you have given me I have given them, so that they may be one, as we are one,* ²³ *I in them and you in me, that they may become completely one, so that the world may know that you have sent me and have loved them even as you have loved me.*

²⁴ *Father, I desire that those also, whom you have given me, may be with me where I am, to see my glory, which you have given me because you loved me before the foundation of the world.*

²⁵ *"Righteous Father, the world does not know you, but I know you; and these know that you have sent me.* ²⁶ *I made your name known to them, and I will make it known, so that the love with which you have loved me may be in them, and I in them."*

42. May they be one in Us

A seminal moment – not just in this story, but in the history of the world. A gruelling three-year mission on the road is over. He has had an infinitely poignant Passover meal with his disciples, during which he sews the seed of his Church. Job nearly done.

Finally, before his Passion, he prays. He gives the listeners, and those billions since who have heard or read the words, his High-Priestly Prayer – a Prayer for all people, of all time, whose words were emblazoned on the young John's heart.

So what is the essence of this prayer? Given its awesomeness, it seems almost sacrilege to unpick it, but in order to understand it better, perhaps shining a spotlight in a few places might help:

Jesus said that he was going to the glory that he had with God before the world existed. Furthermore, God had given Jesus his own name – JHWH – I AM – which indeed Jesus had already used. As the Name implies, God had made Jesus one with Him in the I AM; sharing everything.

God had then sent this part of His AM – His Logos now seems a good way of describing it – to the ones He had chosen on earth. To these, Jesus had demonstrated that he was indeed the I AM; the Logos; the Messiah; the Christ; the fulfilment of Adam, Abraham and Moses.

And they believed ... and the world hated them. Their reward awaited however, because they, too, would become an eternal part of the same I AM. And that 'AM' is Love.

Here is the best bit: We too are invited: to believe; to love; to face persecution; and to be an eternal part of the I AM. Even me!!!!

Furthermore, we are not invited as a cacophony of conceited individuals, but as One Orchestra of Love.

There is indeed a power of evil in the world, and we need protection from it. But he who is the Way, the Truth and the Life will 'consecrate us in the Truth' that is, set us apart from evil, and equip us against it, so that we might stand for what is good.

In short, this prayer by the Logos, this conversation with Abba-Father, sums up not only his mission, but nothing less than the purpose of existence: the unique soul that is 'I' is invited to reject evil; and to unite in love, in the name of Jesus, in the eternal glory of the Father.

Pause for reflection: The irony is that the Ultimate High Priest is about to officiate at the Ultimate Passover – with himself as the Ultimate Sacrificial Lamb.

Indeed, not only was he the Passover Lamb, but also the Atonement: since the time of Moses, a sacrificial animal had been offered in atonement for sin[1,2]; and now that sacrifice was the Logos Himself.

Deeper still, he who is part of the I AM, who is about to fulfil these eternal roles, still felt the need to make a petitionary prayer – not for himself, but for us.

Perhaps then, we need to say more often, "Lamb of God, who takes away the sin of the world, have mercy on us."

References: 1. Exodus 30:10   2. Leviticus 8:14 – 9:22

43. Chapter 18 Where are your friends now?

¹ After Jesus had spoken these words, he went out with his disciples across the Kidron valley to a place where there was a garden, which he and his disciples entered.

² Now Judas, who betrayed him, also knew the place, because Jesus often met there with his disciples. ³ So Judas brought a detachment of soldiers together with police from the chief priests and the Pharisees, and they came there with lanterns and torches and weapons.

⁴ Then Jesus, knowing all that was to happen to him, came forward and asked them, "Whom are you looking for?"

⁵ They answered, "Jesus of Nazareth."

Jesus replied, "I am he." Judas, who betrayed him, was standing with them. ⁶ When Jesus said to them, "I am he," they stepped back and fell to the ground. ⁷

Again he asked them, "Whom are you looking for?"

And they said, "Jesus of Nazareth."

⁸ Jesus answered, "I told you that I am he. So if you are looking for me, let these men go." ⁹ This was to fulfil the word that he had spoken, "I did not lose a single one of those whom you gave me."

¹⁰ Then Simon Peter, who had a sword, drew it, struck the high priest's slave, and cut off his right ear. The slave's name was Malchus. ¹¹ Jesus said to Peter, "Put your sword back into its sheath. Am I not to drink the cup that the Father has given me?"

¹² So the soldiers, their officer, and the Jewish police arrested Jesus and bound him. ¹³ First they took him to Annas, who was the father-in-law of Caiaphas, the high priest that year. ¹⁴ Caiaphas was the one who had advised the Jews that it was better to have one person die for the people.

¹⁵ Simon Peter and another disciple followed Jesus. Since that disciple was known to the high priest, he went with Jesus into the courtyard of the high priest, ¹⁶ but Peter was standing outside at the gate. So the other disciple, who was known to the high priest, went out, spoke to the woman who guarded the gate, and brought Peter in. ¹⁷ The woman said to Peter, "You are not also one of this man's disciples, are you?" He said, "I am not."

¹⁸ Now the slaves and the police had made a charcoal fire because it was cold, and they were standing around it and warming themselves. Peter also was standing with them and warming himself.

(verses 19 – 24 are dealt with in the next section)

²⁵ Now Simon Peter was standing and warming himself. They asked him, "You are not also one of his disciples, are you?" He denied it and said, "I am not."

²⁶ One of the slaves of the high priest, a relative of the man whose ear Peter had cut off, asked, "Did I not see you in the garden with him?"

²⁷ Again Peter denied it, and at that moment the cock crowed.

43. Where are your friends now?

OK, you have said your morning prayers, and the day is in front of you. If you had to pick a single thing you must do to be a Christian, what would it be? If someone said, "Quick! I only have a second for you to make me a Christian before I get on this train, and never see you again!" What one thing?

Well, thinking of the Lord's Prayer, or about Jesus's answer to 'Which is the greatest commandment', we would probably find ourselves saying "to love, praise and glorify God".

In the House of the High Priest, however, Peter – the boss Christian of his day – was not doing much loving or praising or glorifying. He was busy lying to save his skin.

I do say my morning prayers, but for me also, when everyday life kicks in, it does not involve much psalm-singing. Instead, I somewhat selfishly weave my way through the interactions and tasks of the day. I do not, like Peter, wear a sword, but maybe I offend an ear or two, as I apply my vanity, my time, and my blessings to suit my own purposes.

Let me ask the question again, then: Having said in the morning that I love God, and having praised Him, how, as a Christian, do I show it during the rest of the day?

Perhaps you are going to say, "Love your neighbour". Well, yes. But how?

The answer is one that we have already come across. We have noted that there is only one instruction for us in the Lord's Prayer, to manifest our love, and this from the same person who told us about loving one's neighbour. We are instructed to forgive.

After his denying the Lord to save himself, I expect that Peter found himself thinking very deeply about what mattered. For three years, he had faithfully followed Jesus, and yet here he was, abandoning him. He thought he had assimilated all the *lessons that Jesus had taught – he was a proper Christian – and now he found himself wanting in what really mattered: faith.*

In his subsequent leadership of the Church, I'll wager that he was more-than-forgiving of sin, when humility and self-knowledge were grounded in a faithful and loving heart like his own.

By contrast, I expect that he damaged quite a few arrogant and deceitful ears with the sword of his tongue, in the face of pompous, self-righteous intolerance, of the kind that Annas and Caiaphas were showing.

Luke tells us that after Peter's third denial, the Lord turned and looked straight at Peter. Maybe one of the things that look was saying was, "I forgive you. Now, teach others what forgiveness means."

Pause for reflection: Peter did not earn his forgiveness. Forgiveness is a gift from God, to those with faith.

It is paid for by the blood of Jesus.

But faith is also His gift, which we have chosen to accept. God trusts us with the gifts of forgiveness and faith. The deal is done and dusted.

Now that we have received both, what will we do with them today?

Deny him?

44. The King, The Truth

¹⁹ Then the high priest questioned Jesus about his disciples and about his teaching.

²⁰ Jesus answered, "I have spoken openly to the world; I have always taught in synagogues and in the temple, where all the Jews come together. I have said nothing in secret. ²¹ Why do you ask me? Ask those who heard what I said to them; they know what I said."

²² When he had said this, one of the police standing nearby struck Jesus on the face, saying, "Is that how you answer the high priest?"

²³ Jesus answered, "If I have spoken wrongly, testify to the wrong. But if I have spoken rightly, why do you strike me?"

²⁴ Then Annas sent him bound to Caiaphas the high priest.

(verses 24 – 27 see above)

²⁸ Then they took Jesus from Caiaphas to Pilate's headquarters. It was early in the morning. They themselves did not enter the headquarters, so as to avoid ritual defilement and to be able to eat the Passover. ²⁹ So Pilate went out to them and said, "What accusation do you bring against this man?" ³⁰ They answered, "If this man were not a criminal, we would not have handed him over to you."

³¹ Pilate said to them, "Take him yourselves and judge him according to your law." The Jews replied, "We are not permitted to put anyone to death." ³² (This was to fulfil what Jesus had said when he indicated the kind of death he was to die.)

³³ Then Pilate entered the headquarters again, summoned Jesus, and asked him, "Are you the King of the Jews?" ³⁴ Jesus answered, "Do you ask this on your own, or did others tell you about me?"

35 Pilate replied, "I am not a Jew, am I? Your own nation and the chief priests have handed you over to me. What have you done?"

36 Jesus answered, "My kingdom is not from this world. If my kingdom were from this world, my followers would be fighting to keep me from being handed over to the Jews. But as it is, my kingdom is not from here." 37 Pilate asked him, "So you are a king?"

Jesus answered, "You say that I am a king. For this I was born, and for this I came into the world, to testify to the truth. Everyone who belongs to the truth listens to my voice."

38 Pilate asked him, "What is truth?"

After he had said this, he went out to the Jews again and told them, "I find no case against him. 39 But you have a custom that I release someone for you at the Passover. Do you want me to release for you the King of the Jews?"

40 They shouted in reply, "Not this man, but Barabbas!" Now Barabbas was a bandit.

44. The King, The Truth

Terra Village School decides to put on a rock concert, and at the last moment, the lead guitarist gets ill. Rock star Mark Knoffler hears about it and he and the band step in.

In Terra, the talk was all about the amazing day with Dire Straits. In Dire Straits, however, (yes, that was the most recent band I could think of that I knew the lead singer), the talk was all about the day at Terra. Terra's perspective was all about Mark. Mark's perspective was all about Terra.

Similarly, we say that Jesus is 'Son of God'.

But in heaven, they call him 'Son of Man'.

'Son of God' is a human take, and 'Son of Man' is a heavenly one.

John's gospel rather rushes the meeting of Jesus with Caiaphas, (and maybe even gets events in slightly the wrong order). We know from the synoptics, however, that when, after numerous unproven accusations, the High priest asks Jesus straight up, "Are you the Messiah", Jesus's answer seems at first sight a bit shifty: "So you say". However, what he is in fact saying is, "That is your human word for one aspect of me, rather than what I am called in the infinite reality of heaven".

Similarly, when Pilate asks Jesus, "Are you the King of the Jews?", Jesus finally says, "You say that I am a King." In other words, in our attempt to put a label on Jesus, we are of course limited to human concepts – like 'Messiah' and 'King' – that cannot in any way do justice to the infinite AM. Jesus was indeed a direct descendent of David. I like to think that he was in fact THE direct descendent, the legitimate ruler. Furthermore, he was the ultimate 'King of the Jews', as the long-awaited Messiah.

However, when Caiaphas and Pilate asked their emotionally-charged questions, they were trying to limit Jesus not just to a word, but to their own personal interpretation of that word. To Caiaphas, the 'Messiah' would have been a Moses-like figure to dissolve away the Roman invaders. To Pilate, 'King' would have been a Hannibal-like person, planning insurrection. Jesus was neither – although he was indeed Messiah and King.

Thereafter, with a world-weary sigh, and with perhaps more than a touch of sarcasm, Pilate asks Jesus, "What is Truth?". How different the world would have been if Jesus had said, "Me", and Pilate had believed him.

But this was a dark day – the darkest – and the Spirit that might have revealed the true majesty of Jesus was hidden from their eyes. Pilate had lost his taste for truth. Caiaphas had taken the God-inspired gift of Scripture, wrapped it up tightly in his own meaning, and buried it. What was left to them was a caricature of reality. A dead idea in a spiritually dead soul.

Pause for reflection: What a human failing, to redefine truth! To make our own caricature of events, of interactions, of cultures; and to bind ourselves so tightly to these misconceptions that we become impervious to the fullness of the Truth, even when it stands in front of us.

Lord, in my dealings with my fellow human beings, let me never be too certain that I am right.

45. Chapter 19 The death of a King

¹ Then Pilate took Jesus and had him flogged. ² And the soldiers wove a crown of thorns and put it on his head, and they dressed him in a purple robe. ³ They kept coming up to him, saying, "Hail, King of the Jews!" and striking him on the face. ⁴ Pilate went out again and said to them, "Look, I am bringing him out to you to let you know that I find no case against him."

⁵ So Jesus came out, wearing the crown of thorns and the purple robe. Pilate said to them, "Here is the man!" ⁶ When the chief priests and the police saw him, they shouted, "Crucify him! Crucify him!" Pilate said to them, "Take him yourselves and crucify him; I find no case against him." ⁷ The Jews answered him, "We have a law, and according to that law he ought to die because he has claimed to be the Son of God."

⁸ Now when Pilate heard this, he was more afraid than ever. ⁹ He entered his headquarters again and asked Jesus, "Where are you from?" But Jesus gave him no answer. ¹⁰ Pilate therefore said to him, "Do you refuse to speak to me? Do you not know that I have power to release you, and power to crucify you?"

¹¹ Jesus answered him, "You would have no power over me unless it had been given you from above; therefore the one who handed me over to you is guilty of a greater sin." ¹² From then on Pilate tried to release him, but the Jews cried out, "If you release this man, you are no friend of the emperor. Everyone who claims to be a king sets himself against the emperor."

¹³ When Pilate heard these words, he brought Jesus outside and sat on the judge's bench at a place called The Stone Pavement, or in Hebrew Gabbatha. ¹⁴ Now it was the day of Preparation for the Passover; and it was about noon. He said to the Jews, "Here is your King!" ¹⁵ They cried out, "Away with him! Away with him! Crucify him!"

Pilate asked them, "Shall I crucify your King?" The chief priests answered, "We have no king but the emperor." ¹⁶ Then he handed him over to them to be crucified.

17 So they took Jesus; and carrying the cross by himself, he went out to what is called The Place of the Skull, which in Hebrew is called Golgotha. 18 There they crucified him, and with him two others, one on either side, with Jesus between them. 19 Pilate also had an inscription written and put on the cross. It read, "Jesus of Nazareth, the King of the Jews." 20 Many of the Jews read this inscription, because the place where Jesus was crucified was near the city; and it was written in Hebrew, in Latin, and in Greek.

21 Then the chief priests of the Jews said to Pilate, "Do not write, 'The King of the Jews,' but, 'This man said, I am King of the Jews.'" 22 Pilate answered, "What I have written I have written."

23 When the soldiers had crucified Jesus, they took his clothes and divided them into four parts, one for each soldier. They also took his tunic; now the tunic was seamless, woven in one piece from the top. 24 So they said to one another, "Let us not tear it, but cast lots for it to see who will get it." This was to fulfil what the scripture says, "They divided my clothes among themselves, and for my clothing they cast lots." 25 And that is what the soldiers did.

Meanwhile, standing near the cross of Jesus were his mother, and his mother's sister, Mary the wife of Clopas, and Mary Magdalene. 26 When Jesus saw his mother and the disciple whom he loved standing beside her, he said to his mother, "Woman, here is your son." 27 Then he said to the disciple, "Here is your mother." And from that hour the disciple took her into his own home.

28 After this, when Jesus knew that all was now finished, he said (in order to fulfill the scripture), "I am thirsty." 29 A jar full of sour wine was standing there. So they put a sponge full of the wine on a branch of hyssop and held it to his mouth.

30 When Jesus had received the wine, he said, "It is finished." Then he bowed his head and gave up his spirit.

31 Since it was the day of Preparation, the Jews did not want the bodies left on the cross during the sabbath, especially because that sabbath was a day of great solemnity. So they asked Pilate to have the legs of the crucified men broken and the bodies removed. 32 Then the soldiers came and broke the legs of the first and of the other who had been crucified with him.

33 But when they came to Jesus and saw that he was already dead, they did not break his legs. 34 Instead, one of the soldiers pierced his side with a spear, and at once blood and water came out. 35 (He who saw this has testified so that you also may believe. His testimony is true, and he knows that he tells the truth.)

36 These things occurred so that the scripture might be fulfilled, "None of his bones shall be broken." 37 And again another passage of scripture says, "They will look on the one whom they have pierced."

45. The death of a King

If the Truth is fully in you, you are truly who you should be, and you cannot stop being who you are. (Indeed, it often strikes me, that to BE comes before to DO.) Here, on Golgotha, Jesus has been handed over to crucifixion, and from the moment of the handing over until the moment of resurrection, he will DO nothing – only BE.

And in the tableau of that deadly mountain, the young John, standing at the foot of the cross, sees even in the improbable detail of the events, evidence of who Jesus truly is: The Way – that led to the cross.

The Truth that he had testified to Pilate.

The High Priest – high priests wear a garment woven without a seam so that it cannot be torn.

The Lamb of God – the Passover lamb was sacrificed at that hour, and had to have no blemish, and no broken bones.

The King, with a crown, albeit of thorns, and with a notice of his Kingship in three languages that together symbolised the entirety of humanity.

The Saviour and fulfilment of the Psalms[1].

The Suffering Servant[2], lifted up on a cross[3], drinking the sour wine to signify the acceptance of his bitter destiny.

The prophetic Son of Man, soon to be glorified[4].

The Light of the world, as the world went dark when he died.

More symbolism was to come. John, to whom the water of life and the blood of redemption had been profoundly important symbols, then witnessed the blood and water pouring from the side of Jesus. John was so deeply moved that he felt that these elements themselves were proclaiming, for all with ears to hear, the legitimacy of Jesus. Indeed, in his later letter[5], he refers to water and blood as 'witnesses'. Water and blood at the birth; water and wine at Cana; water in Jacob's Well and in the pool of Siloam at the Festival of Shelters; wine and blood at the Last Supper; blood and water at the end – full circle.

John was not the only person at the foot of the cross, however. He was accompanied by Mary, mother of Jesus, probably by Mary Magdalene, and perhaps by one or two other women from his home in Galilee.

John reports not a single word of any conversation. I expect because there was none, in that most profound of tortures, where Mary surely felt a sword pierce her very soul[6].

Some traditions regard Mary as 'The Immaculate Conception' – in other words, the one so much in touch with God, that she is untouched by any taint of sin. Being soul-in-soul with the crucified Lord, as she stood at the foot of the cross, there was nothing she could say or do. Nothing any of them could say or do.

Only be.

Pause for reflection: Sometimes, I need to drop my baggage, stop frenetically doing, and think about who I am. And who Jesus is. I might imagine him upon the cross, where he still would have gone through with that terrifying destiny, even if it were only for me.

It is true that actions speak louder than words, and that showing that I love is better than proclaiming that I love.

However, before doing, I must be. In my heart should BE only love.

References: 1. eg Psalms 42, 61 & 69 2. Isaiah 53:1-12 3. Isaiah 52:13 4. Daniel 7:13-14 5. I John5:7-8 6. Luke 2:35

46. Small decisions, big results

38 After these things, Joseph of Arimathea, who was a disciple of Jesus, though a secret one because of his fear of the Jews, asked Pilate to let him take away the body of Jesus. Pilate gave him permission; so he came and removed his body.

39 Nicodemus, who had at first come to Jesus by night, also came, bringing a mixture of myrrh and aloes, weighing about a hundred pounds.

40 They took the body of Jesus and wrapped it with the spices in linen cloths, according to the burial custom of the Jews.

41 Now there was a garden in the place where he was crucified, and in the garden there was a new tomb in which no one had ever been laid. 42 And so, because it was the Jewish day of Preparation, and the tomb was nearby, they laid Jesus there.

46. Small decisions, big results

"Where are you going, Nicodemus?", said his wife, a few months before the crucifixion of Jesus. "I am just nipping down to the market to get a barrow-load of myrrh and aloes, to prepare my body for my funeral, so that we are not caught short on the day."

"OK", she replied, "While you are there, can you also get another loaf of bread?"

"Do you like it?" said Joseph to his brother, when they had gone down from Arimathea to Jerusalem for a pilgrimage. "Well", said the other, "it will make a fabulous tomb, and it is right here next to the holy City ... but I think you paid over the odds ..."

OK, maybe it did not happen like that, but the point is that the embalming spices must have already been bought before the day, surely? And even the tomb must have belonged to Joseph already – or to someone with whom he had influence, who himself had been prompted to buy the cave but never to use it.

Then, on this, the most epoch-defining day in history, the tomb and the spice and the linen cloths, hitherto run-of-the-mill, became nothing less than centre-stage in the resurrection of Jesus.

All the circumstances – seemingly trivial and unconnected – which had cooperated to have spices, tomb and linen available, now, in retrospect, were vital links in a vital chain of events. A chain of events which finishes with these assets providing the backdrop to the most overwhelming event ever.

Maybe, then, coincidence is not always coincidence.

Maybe the unlikely host of circumstances that led to me meeting my future wife were not unplanned in heaven.

Maybe the Spirit had a hand in the incident or picture or experience that caused me to change my mind about what I was about to do.

Maybe that annoying delay turned out to be a blessing.

Or that turbulent day of hassle diverted my life onto a better road.

Or that illness made me see things in a new light.

Of course, not all events in life turn out to have been for my long-term physical or mental well-being. Indeed, one day, one such thing will kill me. However, God is still there, even in the small things, and the 'Desiderata[1]' is spot-on when it says:

"Whether or not it is clear to you, no doubt the universe is unfolding as it should".

Pause for reflection: We do not get to choose all the incidents and experiences that make up our lives. (And that is often a good thing.)

But we do get to choose our response to them.

What if that car that just 'cut you up' was in fact rushing someone to hospital?

What if an unknown blessing is about to enrich you, as a direct result of, say, your laptop breaking; the traffic delaying you; that person being mean to you; that illness that laid you flat?

Many times, the blessings will be at best invisible and at worst absent. Sometimes, however, some precious times, you might find that through that tribulation, you are about to be caught up in an enrichment of your life.

Maybe, in retrospect, you shouldn't have been so grumpy about it??

Reference: 1. https://en.wikipedia.org/wiki/Desideratat

Part 4

Resurrection and the Life

47. Chapter 20 How could they not understand?

¹ *Early on the first day of the week, while it was still dark, Mary Magdalene came to the tomb and saw that the stone had been removed from the tomb.* ² *So she ran and went to Simon Peter and the other disciple, the one whom Jesus loved, and said to them, "They have taken the Lord out of the tomb, and we do not know where they have laid him."*

³ *Then Peter and the other disciple set out and went toward the tomb.* ⁴ *The two were running together, but the other disciple outran Peter and reached the tomb first.* ⁵ *He bent down to look in and saw the linen wrappings lying there, but he did not go in.*

⁶ *Then Simon Peter came, following him, and went into the tomb. He saw the linen wrappings lying there,* ⁷ *and the cloth that had been on Jesus' head, not lying with the linen wrappings but rolled up in a place by itself.*

⁸ *Then the other disciple, who reached the tomb first, also went in, and he saw and believed;* ⁹ *for as yet they did not understand the scripture, that he must rise from the dead.*

¹⁰ *Then the disciples returned to their homes.*

47. How could they not understand?

How long was Jesus in the tomb?

Answer: One day, with a bit on either side. That day was the Sabbath.

In those times, the Jewish day began at 6pm – the average time for night-fall. (As indeed still happens in modern times in some countries near the equator, where days and nights are both more or less twelve hours.)

Although there is debate as to the exact time scale used in John's gospel, the most likely inference is that Jesus was being put into the tomb just before night was falling on the first day of his Passion. With nightfall, the calendar moved on, and the new day began – the second day.

Furthermore, that second day which was beginning was not just any day, it was the Sabbath – the holy day to commemorate the perfect Creation of the world, before sin appeared. Not just any Sabbath, moreover, but Passover, to commemorate the salvation of God's people from the evil grasp of the Egyptians.

However, despite the ministry of Moses, God's people remained in the grasp of evil. Indeed, they would always do so until they could in some way be permanently redeemed.

Whether or not his name was Adam, there must, at some time in the last ten millennia, have been the first ever human with a soul; with the capacity to make moral choice; and he or she committed the first ever sin. Since then, humanity – as we must now call Homo sapiens since that moment – has had the capacity to love ... and to sin. For which there has to be a Reckoning.

Incomprehensibly, for the duration of that monumental Passover Sabbath, Jesus was somehow 'in hell'.

His purpose, in some infinitely unfathomable way, was once more to save God's people from sin and evil.

That was why he came.

That was the whole meaning of the Messiah.

That was what his 'I am' statements pointed to.

That was the culmination of his Signs, especially his resurrection of Lazarus.

That is the crowning moment of his fulfilment of the heritage of Moses.

Then, when that terrifying Sabbath was over, on the third day, he rose from the dead.

"I am the Way, the Truth and the Life", he had said.

How crazy, then, that after three years of listening and following and witnessing and giving their lives, his two top disciples still had not realised, until that moment, what it was all about.

Pause for reflection: Have you also got to this point in the story of the Messiah, without properly realising what he has done for us? For you?

"No greater love hath man than this, that he lay down his life for a friend."

What a way to lay it down!

What a friend!

48. Mary Magdalene meets the risen Lord

[11] But Mary stood weeping outside the tomb. As she wept, she bent over to look into the tomb; [12] and she saw two angels in white, sitting where the body of Jesus had been lying, one at the head and the other at the feet.

[13] They said to her, "Woman, why are you weeping?"

She said to them, "They have taken away my Lord, and I do not know where they have laid him."

[14] When she had said this, she turned around and saw Jesus standing there, but she did not know that it was Jesus.

[15] Jesus said to her, "Woman, why are you weeping? Whom are you looking for?" Supposing him to be the gardener, she said to him, "Sir, if you have carried him away, tell me where you have laid him, and I will take him away."

[16] Jesus said to her, "Mary!"

She turned and said to him in Hebrew, "Rabbouni!" (which means Teacher).

[17] Jesus said to her, "Do not hold on to me, because I have not yet ascended to the Father. But go to my brothers and say to them, 'I am ascending to my Father and your Father, to my God and your God.'"

[18] Mary Magdalene went and announced to the disciples, "I have seen the Lord"; and she told them that he had said these things to her.

48. Mary Magdalene meets the risen Lord

I have never seen a tall, intelligent, slim person who incidentally suffered from Down's syndrome. A Down's syndrome sufferer is defined in almost every way – to a casual acquaintance at least – by his or her condition and its physical manifestations.

Will such a person look the same after rising from the dead? I expect not. When, therefore, I profess in the Nicene Creed that I believe in the resurrection of the body, what, exactly, do I mean? I cannot mean that someone with Down's syndrome will still have it.

I am totally certain, indeed, that there will be no trace of inferiority – or even of past inferiority – in the life to come.

What, then, can resurrection of the body mean? Jesus had already told us that resurrection of the body will occur; that we will have our true identity, like Abraham, Isaac and Jacob[1]; but that we will not be betrothed to each other[1]. Indeed, what would the point be of having reproductive systems in heaven?

Of course, my spiritual identity is my soul, not my body, and I have had a chance to make choices about belief and love and forgiveness that might make my soul eligible for the redeeming Grace of our Saviour. I cannot earn that Grace, however.

And what of those souls with extreme mental incapacity which never gives them the opportunity to make such a choice?

Anyway, we are not talking of souls – it is 'resurrection of the body' that we profess. Indeed, at the time of the resurrection of Jesus, many people saw alive, the resurrected bodies of those who had risen with Jesus[2]. To which experience we might add that of Lazarus.

One potential answer to this conundrum would be if we had many lives, before finally achieving our heavenly goal in a body which represented all the lives. This is what the Hindus believe, and they have believed it for the best part of four millennia. Their ancient religion had its roots in the migration of the Sumerians – the first ever civilisation – from their land between the Tigris and Euphrates, to the Indus river. Interestingly, the star of their civilisation finally set in the city of Ur, a century or so before Abraham was born there. All I can say to all who believe in reincarnation, is that it is not my tradition.

What is quite certain however, is that Jesus rose in the body.

Furthermore, although he seemingly bore the scars of his crucifixion, Mary did not recognise him at first. Maybe she was looking down; maybe it was twilight; maybe she was crying.

However, on at least three more occasions[3], his followers had not immediately recognised him. Given that this is not what an author would write if making up the tale, it seems then that this is the truth: that we will rise from the dead, and will somehow be ourselves, and somehow not.

One more point to make from this passage: The first person to see the risen Lord was not Peter; nor 'the disciple Jesus loved'; nor any of the eleven apostles; nor even his own mother; but a woman he met on his travels. A woman who had stood at the foot of the cross.

A woman whose inconsolable tears throughout that appalling Passover, had shown the depth of her love for the Lord Jesus as a person.

Pause for reflection: I wonder who that Laurence will be, who, hopefully, will stand before the throne of the Lamb, cleansed by his Blood[4].

One thing is certain: he will be defined by his depth of love for God-made-Man.

References: 1. Mark 12:24-26 / Matthew 22:30   2. Matthew 27:53   3. Luke 24:13-35 Luke 24:36-43 John 21:4   4. Revelation 7:9-10

49. Peace, Breath and the Holy Spirit

[19] When it was evening on that day, the first day of the week, and the doors of the house where the disciples had met were locked for fear of the Jews, Jesus came and stood among them and said, "Peace be with you."

[20] After he said this, he showed them his hands and his side. Then the disciples rejoiced when they saw the Lord.

[21] Jesus said to them again, "Peace be with you. As the Father has sent me, so I send you." [22] When he had said this, he breathed on them and said to them, "Receive the Holy Spirit."

[23] If you forgive the sins of any, they are forgiven them; if you retain the sins of any, they are retained."

49. Peace, Breath and the Holy Spirit

Jesus gave them peace twice. The first was the Jewish greeting, 'Shalom', used throughout the world. The second was Jesus's own peace, which came from heaven.

And then he breathed on them.

He breathed on them?? Why?! He surely did not have to? As the Logos now risen from the dead and one with the Father, ("He and I are one" ... "Anything you ask"... etc), he had immediate access to the Power of God! He did not have to breathe to make things happen!

On the other hand, he did have to: At this, arguably the most significant moment in Christianity, he would not have wasted the gesture for a half-considered whim. Nor would John have been prompted to remember it, to pass on to two millennia of believers.

Nevertheless, why did he do it? For that matter, it suddenly occurs to me to ask, why did Moses have to hit the rock with his staff to get the water out? Or strike the sea for it to part? Or lift a serpent on a stick for people to be cured?

In fact, whilst we are on Moses, why was there even an Ark of the Covenant within which was kept the stone tablets given by God? Nobody read them. If you were even to touch them, you would die.

Taking the thought further – why did you have to dip in the Jordan to be baptised? Why did the blind person need to wash in the Pool of Siloam?

The explanation can only be that these physical accompaniments enhance, not the immensity of the manifestation of God, but rather our understanding of it.

Then it begins to make more sense. Breath is physical life; the Spirit is Spiritual Life. Breath moves; the Spirit moves. Breath is largely unseen; the Spirit is largely unseen. The breath of Jesus comes from Jesus. The Spirit of Jesus comes from Jesus.

In fact, as I start to make a list, I see that the breath symbolism could continue to add to my understanding literally every time I contemplate it.

By contrast, saying instead: 'The Spirit arrived' would have left much to be desired. Indeed, when I come to think of it, we are immersed in a unique world prodigiously rich in spiritual metaphor. God's creation not only looks after me physically, but gives me any number of pointers to its Creator: light; water; fire; vines, fruit and crops; lambs; wind ... and breath[1].

As I now re-read the passage, I can see that the breath is immediately linked to Power. Power from on High. And what Power did these bastions of early Christianity receive first? Hulk-like strength to fight the Romans? Spider-man agility to slip away from the Sanhedrin?

No.

It was the Power to Forgive.

Pause for reflection: It is all about forgiveness.

The Salvation coming from the Logos was God's forgiveness of our sins.

The first act of Jesus when meeting his Church was to empower them to pass forward that forgiveness.

Risen Lord, help me bask in your forgiveness of me, and help me pass it forward – with the same breath of peace that you gave the disciples.

Reference: 1. Ezekiel 37:9

50. Future belief

24 But Thomas (who was called the Twin), one of the twelve, was not with them when Jesus came. 25 So the other disciples told him, "We have seen the Lord."

But he said to them, "Unless I see the mark of the nails in his hands, and put my finger in the mark of the nails and my hand in his side, I will not believe."

26 A week later his disciples were again in the house, and Thomas was with them. Although the doors were shut, Jesus came and stood among them and said, "Peace be with you."

27 Then he said to Thomas, "Put your finger here and see my hands. Reach out your hand and put it in my side. Do not doubt but believe."

28 Thomas answered him, "My Lord and my God!"

29 Jesus said to him, "Have you believed because you have seen me? Blessed are those who have not seen and yet have come to believe."

30 Now Jesus did many other signs in the presence of his disciples, which are not written in this book.

31 But these are written so that you may come to believe that Jesus is the Messiah, the Son of God, and that through believing you may have life in his name.

50. Future belief

We are nearly at the end of these reflections. As with John's gospel itself, "these are written so that you may come to believe that Jesus is the Messiah, the Son of God, and that through believing you may have life in his name."

The Son of Man who invited his friend Thomas to explore his wounds was the same Son of Man prophesied by Daniel[1]:

"... there before me was one like a son of man, coming with the clouds of heaven. He approached the Ancient of Days and was led into his presence.

He was given authority, glory and sovereign power; all nations and peoples of every language worshiped him.

His dominion is an everlasting dominion that will not pass away, and his kingdom is one that will never be destroyed."

John, 'the disciple Jesus loved', had witnessed the entire ministry of Jesus, right up until the moment of his death. This same John, (we think), many years later, had a very similar vision to Daniel[2]:

"After this I looked, and there was a great multitude that no one could count, from every nation, from all tribes and peoples and languages, standing before the throne and before the Lamb, robed in white, with palm branches in their hands.

[10] They cried out in a loud voice, saying, "Salvation belongs to our God who is seated on the throne, and to the Lamb!"

OK, that is a great end to the story, but surely this is all too much to take in, far less to believe?

And yet, even before we factor in the historically attested Signs and ministry of Jesus, could you have come up with any better explanation of the meaning of life? Of what was before the beginning? Of what is beyond the end? Of how love and moral choice could possibly exist?

It's all about faith, and faith will be given to us, if we try not to wrap up our soul in the tight bindings of our preconceptions and our appetites.

Then, when we love, when we forgive, we will feel that Witness inside, that Spirit, affirming to us that, incredibly, God is real.

It is the truth.

He is the Truth, so why would we not believe?

Pause for reflection: I only have this life to get to know the Jesus whom I hope will recognise me; and the Father whom I hope to adore for eternity.

Reference: 1. Daniel 7:13-14   2. Revelation 7:9-10

51. Chapter 21: The Rock

After these things Jesus showed himself again to the disciples by the Sea of Tiberias; and he showed himself in this way. ² Gathered there together were Simon Peter, Thomas called the Twin, Nathanael of Cana in Galilee, the sons of Zebedee, and two others of his disciples. ³ Simon Peter said to them, 'I am going fishing.' They said to him, 'We will go with you.' They went out and got into the boat, but that night they caught nothing.

⁴ Just after daybreak, Jesus stood on the beach; but the disciples did not know that it was Jesus. ⁵ Jesus said to them, 'Children, you have no fish, have you?' They answered him, 'No.' ⁶ He said to them, 'Cast the net to the right side of the boat, and you will find some.' So they cast it, and now they were not able to haul it in because there were so many fish.

⁷ That disciple whom Jesus loved said to Peter, 'It is the Lord!' When Simon Peter heard that it was the Lord, he put on some clothes, for he was naked, and jumped into the lake. ⁸ But the other disciples came in the boat, dragging the net full of fish, for they were not far from the land, only about a hundred yards off.

⁹ When they had gone ashore, they saw a charcoal fire there, with fish on it, and bread. ¹⁰ Jesus said to them, 'Bring some of the fish that you have just caught.' ¹¹ So Simon Peter went aboard and hauled the net ashore, full of large fish, a hundred and fifty-three of them; and though there were so many, the net was not torn.

¹² Jesus said to them, 'Come and have breakfast.'

Now none of the disciples dared to ask him, 'Who are you?' because they knew it was the Lord.

¹³ Jesus came and took the bread and gave it to them, and did the same with the fish. ¹⁴ This was now the third time that Jesus appeared to the disciples after he was raised from the dead.

15 When they had finished breakfast, Jesus said to Simon Peter, 'Simon son of John, do you love me more than these?' He said to him, 'Yes, Lord; you know that I love you.'

Jesus said to him, 'Feed my lambs.'

16 A second time he said to him, 'Simon son of John, do you love me?' He said to him, 'Yes, Lord; you know that I love you.'

Jesus said to him, 'Tend my sheep.'

17 He said to him the third time, 'Simon son of John, do you love me?' Peter felt hurt because he said to him the third time, 'Do you love me?' And he said to him, 'Lord, you know everything; you know that I love you.'

Jesus said to him, 'Feed my sheep.

18 Very truly, I tell you, when you were younger, you used to fasten your own belt and to go wherever you wished. But when you grow old, you will stretch out your hands, and someone else will fasten a belt around you and take you where you do not wish to go.' 19 (He said this to indicate the kind of death by which he would glorify God.) After this he said to him, 'Follow me.'

20 Peter turned and saw the disciple whom Jesus loved following them; he was the one who had reclined next to Jesus at the supper and had said, 'Lord, who is it that is going to betray you?' 21 When Peter saw him, he said to Jesus, 'Lord, what about him?' 22 Jesus said to him, 'If it is my will that he remain until I come, what is that to you? Follow me!' 23 So the rumour spread in the community that this disciple would not die. Yet Jesus did not say to him that he would not die, but, 'If it is my will that he remain until I come, what is that to you?'

24 This is the disciple who is testifying to these things and has written them, and we know that his testimony is true. 25 But there are also many other things that Jesus did; if every one of them were written down, I suppose that the world itself could not contain the books that would be written.

51. The Rock

How do we know whether the gospels are historically accurate, or whether they are just stories and legends?

Of course, this is a matter to which a vast array of scholarly talent has applied itself, over nearly two millennia. The consensus is very much that, rather than being fables, the gospels are written as biographies, in the same way that, for instance, Plutarch wrote a biography of Julius Caesar a few decades after John's gospel.

However, I might intend to write a biography, but I might fabricate material to get my point across, or to sell more copies. There are therefore numerous methodologies and criteria for attesting the likelihood of historical accuracy – such as whether the author had authority and legitimacy; or whether multiple sources agree; or whether the event would have been unlikely for the author to invent, but happened anyway; etc. (An example of which we have already noted, that immediately after the resurrection, on four occasions, people did not immediately recognise Jesus.)

In John's gospel in particular, however, one recurrent note of authenticity keeps ringing through – the apparent eye-witness nature of the account.

In this vignette to finish John's gospel, we once more are treated to a description which clearly seems to have been seen through the very eyes of the writer. Casual details are incidentally added in: it was Peter's idea; seven of the eleven went fishing; Peter was naked; they caught nothing all night. (By the way, whether the number of fish being 153 was an inconsequential detail, or symbolic number, no-one seems certain!)

We are given this gentle everyday scene, then, as an authoritative account of the ratification of the appointment of the first ever leader of the Christian Church. The first Pope; President; Moderator; Patriarch; Archbishop; Primate.

Jesus refers to Peter as Simon Son of Jonas three times, to coincide with Peter's three denials.

Thereafter, he completes the ceremony not with applause, nor congratulation, nor with a ceremonial mitre ... but with a prophecy that this job will be an uphill task. (With something nasty waiting at the top.)

Peter's response – as we can see from, for example, the Acts of the Apostles – was to accept with joy and humility.

And maybe also with relief, that he had been forgiven, and that he would now get a chance to serve the Lord.

St. Peter the Rock had arrived.

Pause for reflection: A whole generation or two seems now to have to a large extent abandoned organised religion.

I understand: I also get fed up of ideological rigidity, stuffiness, unfriendliness and even hypocrisy in some of the churches I have attended.

But there is only one Christian Church, and of that One, if we choose, we are all members.

52. Epilogue

Either the Supernatural exists, or everything we do and experience is just Nature.

Either it is all true, or nothing spiritual means anything.

Either God exists, or else true love is hard to account for – indeed, the whole universe is hard to account for.

I believe that God does indeed exist, and that Love truly exists.

It makes sense to me, to say that these are at the heart of the purpose for our existence.

It is then a leap of faith to suggest that God's plan was mediated via the Logos, but if it is true, it is a story that makes more sense of our existence than any other I have come across.

However, Jesus had two witnesses to attest to this version of events – one was the supernatural Signs that he performed; the other was the Spirit of God which inexplicably came to people of faith, which both changed and empowered them.

Nevertheless, even without any witnesses, the existence and ministry of Jesus is as historically accurate as the existence and works of, say, Socrates, or Julius Caesar, or Darius the Great – indeed more, so, as the personal impact of Jesus was more profound than any of these.

This leaves us with this vastly important point, made by Jesus himself – a man whose quintessence was utter integrity: "If I am telling you the Truth, why don't you believe me?"

I expect and hope that this has left you with many questions ... but ultimately, there is one question which subsumes all the rest:

Whose team are you on?

Pause for reflection:

John's gospel asks us to believe that Jesus was – is – the Logos: the Messiah; the Bread of Life; the Light of the World; the Door / the Way; the Good Shepherd; the True Vine; the Resurrection; the Truth; and the Life.

We are told that we may regard God the Almighty as ... Abba – Daddy.

We are invited to pause in our lives, to put down our baggage, and to look upon the Lord, that we might learn love and forgiveness.

What 'things of Earth' do I need to put down, so that I can stand up straight, lift my head, and look in His Wonderful Face?

Maybe when you have time, check out: Turn your eyes upon Jesus: https://www.youtube.com/watch?v=fzDx_lgodGc

Dave 07927 691634

Printed in Great Britain
by Amazon

Staying Positive

THE STORY OF 'THE REAL'
PAUL BANKE

PAUL BANKE AND PAUL ZANON

First published by Pitch Publishing, 2019

Pitch Publishing
A2 Yeoman Gate
Yeoman Way
Worthing
Sussex
BN13 3QZ
www.pitchpublishing.co.uk
info@pitchpublishing.co.uk

ISBN 978 1 78531 540 4

Typesetting and origination by Pitch Publishing
Printed and bound in India by Replika Press Pvt. Ltd.

CONTENTS

'How did Paul survive after all he went through in life? It wasn't a miracle. It was destiny.'

Yolanda Miranda, Paul's mother

ACKNOWLEDGEMENTS

A BIG thank you to everyone who took the time to share some stories for my book. Special thanks to Jaime Cantu, Alfred Godinez, Ronnie Essett, Connie Lynn Brown, Steve Rosenzweig, Jeff Fenech, Mario Miranda, Karl Abrams, Paul Vaden, Freddie Roach, Mauricio Sulaimán, Pepe Sulaimán, Steve Banke, Tim Munz, Rebecca Munz, Yolanda Miranda, Michele Chong, Louie Valenzuela, Victor Valenzuela, Sherman Henson, Bob King, Ricky Romero, Carlos Palomino, Robert Shannon, Eddie Pagan, Ray Mancini, Roberto Garcia, Hector Lizarraga, Paula Munson, Mack Kurahara, Wayne McCullough, Ruben Castillo, Henry Tillman and Zack Padilla. Also, a big thank you to Luca Rosi for taking the time to go through and diligently edit and pull it up another level.

I'd like to add a note about John Maresca. John's originally from New Jersey, owned a gym out there, was training fighters, then sold that gym and came here to the West Coast in 2001. In 2015, he organized a fundraiser for the late Bobby Chacon and I was there, being my usual chatty, energetic self. John thought, 'This guy is nuts!', but in a fun way.

He then started managing fighters out here and we kept seeing each other at boxing events. Then he made the mistake of getting my number to talk about some business stuff and I started bombarding him with 35 phone calls at all hours of the day. When he spoke to my ghostwriter Paul Zanon, he told him, 'You get talking to him and get attached to him. He pisses you off, but somehow you miss him if you don't get a phone call from him every hour!'

We have a few standing jokes between us now. Once we were both at the West Coast Boxing Hall of Fame and John had Ronnie Essett, Carlos Palomino and me standing next to him. John said, 'Let's take a picture.' I said, 'I'll be right back,' but I had no intention of returning, just to wind John up. John started mumbling a load of bad words under his breath. 'That little son of a…' To this day, John won't let me get into pictures with him. I have to sneak my way in.

Here's another example of us in full flow. One day I decided he was going to be my manager. I wrote on a napkin that John was my manager and then signed it. Since that day, I've hired and fired him thousands of times, sometimes up to 20 times a day. I'll write on Facebook, 'My ex-manager,' just to piss him off. We have a Tom and Jerry relationship. We piss each other off, but we always remain good friends.

Fast forward to 2018. John had been trying to help me get my autobiography written for a few years. Without him, this book would never have happened. Going through my life helped me to reconnect with friends and family I may have drifted from, and pushed me to look at my boxing career from the first day I ever put on a pair of gloves up to this present day.

Thank you for everything, John.

INTRODUCTION

WHEN I received a message on social media from a certain John Maresca Ed.D, claiming, 'I have a story for you,' I was a little sceptical. I get approached several times a week by people with similar intentions, but the reality is a story needs to have some kind of jaw-dropping content to make it book-worthy and also for me to commit the better part of a year to complete it. After receiving a summary from John about a certain Paul Banke, it soon became evident that this was one hell of a story.

Shortly after the introduction from John, I received a video call from Paul. Within moments the energy and honesty from him was overflowing and we formed an instant friendship. I did, however, wonder why he was calling me at 11am (I'm based in the UK), which meant it was 3am on the West Coast. As it goes, 3am would be our calling slot.

One thing that quickly became evident on Paul's social media trail was how he calls people 'brother' or 'sister'. He's got an endearing way of drawing you into his positive slipstream of enthusiasm, and if you're ever having a bad day, he'll pick you up in a heartbeat. I also realiz1ed he's the undisputed king of Facebook and selfies. If you've ever crossed paths with him, you'll know exactly what I mean.

I hope you have as much pleasure walking in his shoes over the next 35 chapters as I have, reliving the highlights of his brilliant boxing career, but also the darker times, which sometimes catch you by surprise. Paul Banke is one of the richest men on the planet and I hope you'll understand why by the time you reach the final chapter.

Paul Zanon
March 2019

FOREWORD

YOU'VE got to respect and admire what Paul Banke achieved in the ring. It's hard enough for anybody to become world champion, but to beat one of the greatest world champions ever in that division in Daniel Zaragoza was something else. People sometimes don't understand the lighter weights, but Paul was a special fighter, he really was. When we used to cross paths at boxing functions in the 1990s, he was always very polite and complimentary, telling me he was a fan of my fights. The fact is, I was actually a fan of his.

Timing is everything as far as life and love goes. Same applied to Paul's time as a professional boxer. If he was fighting now on network television, he would have been a million-dollar fighter. Another Arturo Gatti. He was rough and tough, and brought the fight to the opponent, and that's what the fans loved about him. Paul understood that also. It's like he realized he had an obligation to the fans to give his best, be that all-out performer. A lot of fighters have the heart and want to do that, but not a lot of anything else. Paul could actually deliver. He had the tools. He was that guy.

Unfortunately, without major television coverage, he was known more as a local hero. Back then, if you didn't fight in New York, a lot of people didn't know about you. Paul stayed loyal to his fans, boxed in California and won the world title in California. The West Coast will always have love for him because of that.

And as a person? When I met Paul back in the 1990s, I didn't know his full story, but when I found out, it blew me away. Back then, having AIDS was a death penalty. That was it. You were dead. Nobody knew about the correct medication and many couldn't afford it. How did Paul manage to live on a daily basis not knowing how long he had left on this planet? I admire him. I gotta tell you – I can't imagine how, after getting that news, he could go ahead and try to live a full life. A life of love and happiness. How happy could you be knowing you're living with a death sentence?

When Magic Johnson was diagnosed with HIV, he gave major awareness to the virus. People back then heard about entertainers getting AIDS and were like, 'That's their lifestyle, they deserve it. It's going to happen.' But Magic helped to dispel myths about HIV and to educate. Paul was right after that, but he was not on the world scale of Magic.

What Paul did have was the ability to speak to and represent the majority of people who either had AIDS or were at risk of getting it. The guys who weren't celebrities. The guys who were sharing needles and having unsafe sex who would never make the front cover of a magazine. Paul could speak to the people on the streets and the homeboys in the barrios. He could speak to the people at the community centers, because he was one of them and could identify with them. He explained the lifestyle he was living and the ramifications of living that life. And here's the thing – he's never stopped since.

What he's done in terms of acceptance and helping others has been so profound and inspirational. I see him now going to the gym, training people, and he speaks with everyone, but always with a smile. In fact, he's always smiling, laughing and joking! His joy of living and his endearing personality is tremendous to see, it really is. I have a lot of love for Paul and am so very proud of him.

Ray 'Boom Boom' Mancini
WBA lightweight champion, 1982–84

DOWN IN THE DUMPSTERS

I WENT from being a broke kid in a poor area to earning $600,000 as a professional boxer, to then retiring as a broke drug addict.

When you're world champion, everyone wants to invite you to parties, show you off and give you things for nothing. I didn't get the exposure like fighters get these days, but I was well known enough to get hangers-on. Then when I stopped boxing, they disappeared, along with some so-called friends. My good friends were with me throughout the good and the bad times and are still close to me now, but the guys who hung out with you to get entry to a party, meet a celebrity or get a free boxing ticket were never to be seen again.

You blow money quick when you're out of control. I wish I had some of that money now because I would have bought some real estate or made some other investments. But back then, I couldn't think straight.

After retiring, I still needed to survive. The intention was to get work in Utah and stay there for a while, but instead I drove to Vegas and got a job in construction because I got bored of Utah after a couple of days. There I was, 29 years old, a former world champion, working as a laborer. It was a union job working on freeways. I was earning $16.07 an hour which, don't get me wrong, was good money back then. Unfortunately, I couldn't maintain a steady lifestyle and it soon started falling apart because of my drug use. I didn't work when I really needed to and started calling out sick at least once a week.

I actually stopped using drugs for a few months but then I became addicted to gambling. I wasn't gambling down the big Strip as that was for tourists. Instead I'd stay local and go to places like El Cortez or a Western hotel. I was making about $1,500 a month in construction and remember one night, I came back from a casino and wanted to make some breakfast. I opened the refrigerator and there was no fucking food. I'd blown all my money gambling. I switched one addiction for another. I was back to square one again.

No money, addicted and hungry. After about a month, I was no longer sober, had kicked the gambling habit, but was back on the drugs again.

Las Vegas was probably the worst place I could have picked in terms of dope. Any kind of drug I wanted was available to me, whenever I wanted it, and that's when I got even more messed up. Understandably, no boss would put up with that shit and I wasn't working for long. Shortly after, I was homeless and living out of my truck.

One night, it was either a Friday or Saturday, the fights were going on. I wasn't going to the boxing much back then and I drove up to a gas station behind one of the big hotels. I think it might have been The Mirage. I used to go there all the time to slam dope. I was so good at slamming that people would pay me to stick a needle in their arm because I was that fast and accurate. Not something to be proud of, I know.

I've pulled up and people are putting gas in their cars, but I didn't give a shit if they looked. Next thing, I saw from the corner of my eye Vinny Pazienza. I jumped out the car and said, 'Hey Vinny! What's up man!' He gave me a hug and said, 'What's up, Paul.' He had absolutely no idea what I was about to do. Hard to believe that 12 years before we were training together in Colorado to fight in the Olympics. What had happened to me?

Here I was now living off the streets. When I first ran out of money and became homeless, I was calling my brother Tim and he'd wire me money through UPS. If my truck broke down or anything like that, he was the first person I'd call and he'd come see me and help me out. He did that for months, until one day his wife said he needed to stop sending me money because the second I got it, I'd blow it, which was totally true.

Eventually, my family and friends stopped sending me money and I was eating out of dumpsters.

I'd been homeless in California for a couple of weeks, but I was staying at a shelter for about two months. This was the first time actually on the streets.

I'd see people who would recognize me and would be getting themselves coffee and say, 'Hey. You're Paul Banke! World champion!' Then they'd take a good look at me and say with that pity in their voice, 'How you doing, champ? You want anything to eat?' I'd always say, 'No. I'm good thanks.' I had too much pride to accept anything in public like that. They knew I was on the streets, but I didn't want to show that I was desperate, even though I was. The truth is, I was ready to pass out, I was so hungry.

One night, after not having eaten for three days, walking around high and starving, I decided to find some food. It was about 9pm, warm outside, and I saw this big dumpster full of trash, outside Burger King, just by the Stratosphere Hotel on Vegas Boulevard. The place is still there now.

Vegas is a 24/7 town, so there were people everywhere. I waited for about 45 minutes, but every time I tried to jump in people kept appearing and I'd back off. On my third attempt, I just jumped in. I didn't give a shit who was watching. I was rummaging around when I came across this bag, opened it up and there was a little cheeseburger with only one bite from it. One bite. Oh my gosh. I felt so lucky and became emotional. I'd reached new lows.

I was laying on my back in the trash eating this burger, real comfortable, and looked at the moon as the warm air blew gently in my face and I thought to myself, 'How the fuck did I end up like this?' This is what life had given me. This is how drugs turned my life upside down. You're in a fucking trash can eating a burger. I'd like to say that moment was a turning point, but far from it.

* * *

You'd see a lot of people down on their luck walking up and down Hollywood and Vegas with backpacks, but I never wore one because that was a sign of being homeless. They could probably tell I was anyway, but it was more of a pride thing.

I hated being homeless, but I soon started to get to grips with finding places that could help me to survive on the streets. I was attending AA [Alcoholics Anonymous] meetings, but more for the benefits that came with them, instead of genuinely trying to get clean. One place I used to visit a lot was on California Street, off Main Street, and was called The Turning Point. I think it had been there since the 1960s, but it doesn't exist any more now. It became a regular hangout for me.

At the time, I was living and sleeping out of my little 1989 Toyota truck, which kept breaking down. I'd bought it straight after a fight and it was one of the few things left which I'd been able to afford through boxing, so I became attached to it. Thankfully, at The Turning Point, I had my little spot where I'd park my truck, but I wasn't the only one there. A lot of people were living in their cars back then and I stayed in that lot for several weeks.

Turning Point had rooms and a 24-hour café over it. I attended the meetings all the time back then so I could get a roof over my head, somewhere to wash, free food and it was also a place where people would walk in looking for laborers. 'You need work?' Yeah, I needed work. It became a new home for me. Everybody knew me there and that social side of things was important. That feeling of belonging. Being lonely eats you up real fast.

There was also another house about two miles away from there. Here's how I found out about it. One day, some of the guys I was hanging out on the street with were off somewhere and I said, 'Where you going?' and they said, 'We're going to eat. Come with us in the morning.' I met them in the morning and we walked and walked and walked until we finally got to this house, which I think was connected to the church somehow. There were a lot of homeless people walking in and out of there. Anyway, we got in and the guy inside gave us oatmeal and a sandwich. The sandwich was like bread, a piece of baloney and maybe a piece of cheese. No mayo, no mustard and some oatmeal. I said to myself, 'This will work!' I was starving.

That first homeless stint in Vegas lasted about three weeks, maybe a month, then I went back home to live with my mom in her second-floor apartment on Venice Beach. When I arrived, she looked at me, looked at my arm and she saw my track marks. I'll never forget the way she looked at me and then said upset, 'Oh son. What have you done?' That was a horrible feeling.

Unfortunately, I couldn't kick the habit when I was at my mom's and ended up getting kicked out of the house because I was always high. This routine went on for a long time and I was in and out with my mom for years. I ended up living homeless on Venice Beach for a while, but it wasn't great. Some people were happy living in parks and on the beach, but I preferred to be in a shelter. At least I knew my clothes were safe and I had a little lockup to put my case in. Not to mention they fed you, allowed you to take a shower, shave and try and get your life back together again.

I also stayed with my brother Tim at his house a few times over a few months. He had a successful roofing business and was a damn good worker. I worked with him for a little while and, let me tell you, that was hard work. Like mom, though, Tim could tell I was out of control, but knew that he couldn't help me because I just couldn't stay off the drugs. I can't imagine how terrible a feeling that must have been for him and my loved ones back then, but it's a feeling I'd be able to sympathize with years later, when seeing some of my own family go through it.

The longest period I was homeless in one go was about four months, in Hollywood, and that was my next destination. I hated being homeless with a passion, but compared to Venice Beach and Vegas, Hollywood treated you better and you ate better. You have to remember that West Hollywood has money. It's just next door to Bel Air and Rodeo Drive. The rich people out there treated the homeless better.

One church in particular stood out when I was in Hollywood. It was called PATH – People Assist The Homeless. The place was like a jail because there were lots of crazy people in there screaming, shouting, wanting to fight and who smelt real bad. You'd go in, grab your spot and your bed. You had to be real quick to get that bed, though, because about 150 people were fighting over them. I used to go there for about three or four hours, listen to a church service, get fed, take a shower, which included soap and razors, then I'd leave. They were open seven days a week and I'd go there fairly often.

* * *

For many, like myself, their drug habit is what put them on the street. Others become drug addicts when they become homeless. They might start with drinking beer to take the edge off the day, then get addicted to that. When that buzz doesn't give the needed highs, they'll move on to something stronger.

While I was starving on the streets, I still needed to fuel my drug habit. I was selling dope, but it wasn't easy. The sad thing was I was aware of everything crumbling down around me, but couldn't stop. The addiction took over. You don't think when I was selling little bags of dope on the streets in Vegas, homeless, when my family didn't want me, my friends didn't want me, that I didn't want to stop and straighten myself out? Of course I wanted to. You'd think that all the discipline that got me a world championship belt could help me focus and get clean, but it couldn't. I just couldn't stop taking dope.

A lot of guys in prison won't want to admit that they've had to do a lot of shit to get those drugs. They're embarrassed to say it. Some people jack people up, but that wasn't me. I've probably only stolen a handful of times, but it's what I tried to steer clear of. When I was world champion, people be like, 'Hey Paul, we got some stuff. Let's go hang out.' I thought it was a privilege to have drugs for free, but that was the start of a very slippery slope. When my boxing career started to slide and the parties and pay checks were fewer and fewer, the drug habit called me more than ever and I didn't have the money or free access I had previously. When you're desperate, you would do anything you needed to do for that dope. I did everything I needed to do to get that dope, apart from kill somebody.

* * *

A hard part about living on the streets is loneliness. You talked to people, but it wasn't talking, it was short sentences exchanging a bit of information. No emotion. I didn't appreciate how lucky I'd been to be loved by another person up to that point. One bus trip in particular highlighted just how much that was the case.

Buses were a great way of killing time and cooling down. A lot of homeless people in Vegas did it back then. A few times, I'd get the bus in the middle of the night, which went from Hollywood all the way to Santa Monica. When you got there, they'd kick you off, but you'd jump back on the next one and it would take you all the way back to LA. It was a good 45-minute drive and you could get some comfortable sleep with air con, because it didn't drop below 110 degrees during the summer. Then you'd do the same again when you got to LA.

On this particular day, I jumped on this bus in Vegas and it was packed. After a few stops, this girl came on. I don't remember what she looked like. She could have been short, fat, tall, slim, black, white or Mexican, who knows, but what I do remember is that the bus was packed and she chose to sit next to me. Now remember, I was living on the streets, so I must have smelt real bad. I was embarrassed about what she must have been thinking as she came over.

As she sat down, her leg touched my leg. Oh my gosh. Another human touching me. That felt so fucking good. Wow. I don't mean in a sexual way at all, I mean that another human was willing to come that close to me, in the state I was in. That's pretty sad if you think about it. Everybody else was steering clear of me, but this lady didn't. She had no idea of what she did that day. It made me realize how lonely I was and that I needed people around me.

Those little things you take for granted every day, like saying hello and goodbye to people, get taken away when you're lonely and homeless. Nobody wants to even make eye contact with you, never mind say hello. It's the closest to being invisible you'll ever experience. I made over half a million dollars as a pro boxer, was all over the TV and press and here I was on a Greyhound bus with a paper bag in my hand, smelling terrible and nobody saw me.

Hygiene is a big thing when you're homeless. I used to see homeless people looking smelly and dirty and I didn't want to look like that, so I'd use any bathroom available. You name it, Burger King, Taco Bell, McDonald's, but when they see you a few times, they'd throw you out. About 90 per cent of all the restaurants in Vegas and LA had [and still do] a security code you needed to punch in at the door, to stop the homeless people getting in. But you'd speak to the other homeless people and they'd give you the codes.

I didn't make any friends on the streets. I made acquaintances who were my drug buddies and on the whole, I couldn't tell you their names or even what they looked like now. This wasn't a regular group of guys I'd see, it was a case of whoever and whenever I was in town. A drug addict has no need to get high with others, they can do it by themselves. Either way, I met some interesting guys from all backgrounds. I remember one guy coming up to me and saying, 'You're Paul Banke! I watched all of your fights.' This guy had two master's degrees, but he got strung out on crack cocaine and ended up on the streets. The dope don't care. It doesn't matter if you're poor, rich, black, white, Hispanic, dope will take you down.

Before I was homeless, I used to look at people on the street and just felt bad and sorry for them. Now I was one of them. There's any number of reasons why people end up homeless. Messed-up marriages, war veterans, you name it.

I'd met many vets who'd served in Vietnam, the Gulf War, Bosnia, Afghanistan, all the places imaginable. I used to have lunch with these guys sometimes and being a nosey person, I'd ask them how they ended up on the streets. It made me realize, 'Your story ain't that special compared to some of these guys.'

They'd done their tours of duty, maybe sustained an injury or came back with post-traumatic stress disorder. Basically, the war fucked them up and they didn't have the money or support to get through it. Many didn't want to face the reality, feel the hurt and the loneliness, so they'd drink and take drugs to take away that feeling. You self-medicate to make yourself feel numb. To me, that made sense. There's logic to it. Not saying it's good logic, but it's easy-to-follow logic.

It was the summer of 1995. I'd hit rock bottom. Nothing could be lower than this. Or so I thought.

CHAPTER 1

PAUL ANDRE BANKE

*'You've got to be born with a love of people
and a hatred for injustice if you want to be a
union organizer – and a lack of sense about
when to keep your mouth shut'*

Yolanda Miranda, *Los Angeles View*

C HICANO. Where I grew up. That's what they called Mexican-Americans. This Chicano was born at 4.30am on 1 March 1964 in Blythe, California, Riverside County.

I was delivered prematurely at seven months, weighing five pounds, and was only 13 inches in length. Being born premature didn't matter, though, because I was a healthy baby with a tremendous appetite. My mom never had me on a feeding schedule. Whenever I cried, she fed me and I went from five to eight pounds in six weeks.

Banke. It's not the name you associate with a Mexican-American, but there's a good explanation for that. It's not from Mexico or America! My great-grandfather on my dad's side was a sheep herder from San Sebastián, which is on the border of Spain and France in Europe, in the Basque country. He then came over to the United States and met my great-grandmother, and married her. The last name, Banke, is pronounced 'Baaan-kay' back in Europe, but 'Ban-key' over here. Either way, the Banke name isn't what raised me, my two brothers Steve and Tim and sister Rebecca. My dad left soon after I was born and I only saw him a handful of times right the way up to adulthood. The person who raised us was a lady by the name of Yolanda Miranda. Mom.

My mom's family also had a lot of history to it. She has Native American blood from Arizona and her grandparents from her mom's side were Yaqui. That means I have Basque, Mexican, Yaqui and US heritage. All of that crammed into me. That's a lot of cultures!

My mom came from a very poor migrant farmworker family in the United States. They had money but they were never financially free of poverty and that's something she didn't want us to experience when we became adults. Mom was one of 14. Seven girls and seven boys, and had more cousins than I could name. They didn't have what you'd call a fixed home because they followed the crops, something me and my brothers and sister would also grow up doing as kids. It was a way of life for us and still is for many.

At that time, mom and her brothers and sisters were child labor. Not because her parents wanted to but because it took all of them to get the work completed in the fields when crop-picking seasons were in. During the winter, the weather situation prevented them from working in the fields, so her papa and mama would rent a house and stay there until spring, at which time they could start working again. My mom always said, 'We were financially very poor, but traditionally, very rich in culture and language.' When they did work, they lived in camps that the owners of the farms and governments provided for migrant farm workers. Not the best, but they were sheltered and had wooden floors, with bathrooms outside and so forth.

Mom had a brother, Billy, who did amazing things campaigning with labor leader and civil rights activist Cesar Chavez who, alongside Dolores Huerta, co-founded the National Farm Workers Association. Unfortunately, Billy was murdered at the age of 22. This didn't stop mom's passion for the cause, though.

Chavez was a big name amongst Mexican-Americans. Back in the day, there were posters by Chavez that said, 'Cherish your heritage. The harvest is great.' Chavez and Billy built up a good friendship and between her brother's work alongside Chavez and him dying young, that inspired her to take everything to the next level in terms of continuing the work he was doing. She used to tell us, 'Cesar taught me the importance of having hopes and dreams. Without them, you can't overcome your fears and stand up for your rights on the job.' Wise words.

Due to being a product of those fields, her culture and the area she was raised in, mom became very passionate about the working conditions of her fellow migrants and became a union worker fighting hard for the rights of Mexicans and Mexican-Americans. She started off by helping to organize farm workers and then started working for the union. That was a calling for her. With her experience, in the coming years she started working with other unions also, including construction workers, registered nurses, pre-school teachers and newspaper workers.

She went on to write a number of articles for magazines and newspapers about the movement, and is still very passionate about it to this very day. Sometimes though, that passion has got her in trouble. Once, while leafleting on one of her rallies, some guy in a van intentionally hit her. When she realized she wasn't badly hurt, she picked herself up and chased the van down the street as everyone started cheering.

But back then, as a result of the campaigning, we were constantly on the move as a family. We were raised by her ways of dealing with life. Where she went, we went. We moved all over California, sometimes for very short periods of time, moving as far north as Santa Rosa in Sonoma County. One year in one place, three years in another, one year somewhere else.

Northern California was full of farm workers, which meant my mom was constantly involved in her union stuff. If she went to a picket line or a boycott, we went and when she had vacation time – well, let's just say it wasn't a traditional vacation. Then in the summertime we'd travel, because that's when the crops were out, which meant the union workers were out. We just tagged along.

My mom used to pick grapes in the San Joaquin Valley in Fresno, California when she was a kid and during our vacation time she'd take us to vineyards because she wanted to show us how hard it was to be a farm worker. Everything from how to use the land correctly to putting barbecues in the ground. She wanted to show that if we didn't go to school and learn, no matter how hard we worked in those fields, the pay was always going to be low. She wanted us to realize we had a chance to make a difference in our own lives by studying.

Her brother, who passed away, had showed the difference he had made with the movement and she also had a cousin who used to work with her in the farmer days, who decided to leave the fields and try to become something in the world of entertainment. He succeeded. His name is Luis Valdez. He's a famous playwright and founded El Teatro Campesino. He did a lot of plays about the culture of farm workers and his other brother, Daniel, was a songwriter, composer and actor who was musical director for *Zoot Suit* and *La Bamba*. They both became successful in Hollywood. The latest thing he's been a part of was playing the voice of Tío Berto in the film *Coco*.

Back to those vineyards. I remember picking grapes as a little kid and kept saying to my mom, 'When we gonna eat? Why we doing this? Why? Why?' You could complain as much as you wanted, but she was very strict about making

33

sure we went on vacation to those fields to work. Looking back, it certainly made us appreciate a lot about what we had and how much more we could get out of life if we tried.

However, we also realized that being preached to about working hard wasn't always practised by the preachers! One time, I remember picking grapes in the 1970s. I was about 11 years old. There was me, Steve, mom, my uncles and a few others. As me and Steve were picking grapes like crazy, we turned and saw the rest of them taking a long break, smoking weed. Then someone called, 'Lunch'. All the Mexicans just stopped in the fields and had their food. I remember being tired after working real hard and two of my two uncles were sitting on their asses, smoking weed and laughing. I looked at Steve thinking, 'They ain't doin' no work! That's bullshit!'

Despite being poor, I don't remember starving at any point and when you have an appetite like mine, trust me, that's something you wouldn't forget. However, I knew we were poor and living just above the broke line. I learned how to cook and wash my clothes when I was young, not because mom wasn't always there, but because that was the way she'd brought us up. I didn't cook anything fancy. Things like eggs or potatoes, basic food to survive.

We had a stable home, TV, clothes, went to school and did all the normal things a kid did. I became very proud of what we had and the houses we rented. My mom still laughs now when she remembers what I was like back then. If she had to work and we had to stay home after school, I was like a butler. I cleaned the kitchen and Steve did the washing. Then, when she would come from work and start dinner, I would be there right after her saying, 'Pick that up. Wipe that down.' I'd want the kitchen spotless.

Outside of the house, I loved making rock gardens, exploring and had a big fascination with animals. Birds, fishing, cats, dogs, you name it. But that exploring tendency did get me into trouble on a few occasions. The first episode I don't remember that well, but I was fascinated to try what the mice were being fed. It turns out rat poison ain't so good for you. When my brother found me covered in powder all around my mouth and down my front, my mom took me straight to hospital to get my stomach pumped. I was only three at the time.

By the age of five, I raised the bar. Me and my brother Steve were at a friend's house and there was an old barn that we used to play in, as you do when you're kids. To get back to our place from the barn, we had to climb a steel fence that was barbed at the top. There was a tree next to it and we used to climb the tree and the fence at the same time to get over. But on this occasion, I slipped and cut my arm real bad. The blood was literally flowing. Off we went to the emergency room again. I've still got the scar on my arm. That was the first serious injury I had and the first time I ended up having stiches, although it wouldn't be the last.

If there's one thing me and Steve were good at as kids, it was being resourceful. When mom was organizing for the union back in the day and you had a group of people together, there was always the opportunity for a little hustle to make some money. We used to buy watermelons, slice them up and start selling them to the people. Especially when it was hot, you couldn't sell those slices quick enough.

Food wasn't our only money-making idea, though. There was this carpet store and we used to go through the garbage, finding bits and pieces. Back then, a lot of the farmers didn't have a good standard of living and lived in real shabby places, so we took the offcuts of carpet and started selling them. Some of them were already cut and sometimes we'd cut them to the size they wanted, but either way, we made some cash. The only thing we didn't do was reinvest the money. Once we had it, we spent it on ice cream. Similar to what I'd do in the future with my earnings, but unfortunately it wasn't ice cream that I was spending it on.

CHAPTER 2

KIDDING AROUND

'I meant to behave but there were too many options'

Anon

WHEN I was born, apparently I was the darkest-skinned baby in a ward where they were all bright white. My mom looked at me and said, 'Oh my God. He looks purple!' Then my mom's grandmother said, 'He looks like you,' referring to her Native American roots. Mom replied, 'He looks Asian.'

Out of my two brothers and sister, I'm the one who has the darkest skin and the most prominent Hispanic features. I look different to them. It's like the Mexican genes travelled strong to me.

From as young as I can remember, because of the way I looked, everybody was mistaking me for being Asian. One of my uncles, especially. When I was about six or seven years old, in the early 1970s, he came back from Vietnam. One day, we had a gathering round at grandma's house and there he was holding a white can with a red label. It was a Budweiser. Every time he drunk the beer, he changed.

This day, after a few, he looked at me, paused, then shouted, 'Viet Cong, Viet Cong.' He then started running after me, trying to grab me, six, seven, eight times, while everyone else was shouting, 'No! That's Pauli!' I ran around the corner of the house in the end. That happened a number of times with him. It is funny now looking back, but that didn't make me laugh too much at the time!

There was always a bit of racism wherever we went because of our Mexican roots, but that was part of life you had to accept. Every neighborhood we moved to had a different mix of people. Blacks, whites, Hispanics, Asians, you name it. Everybody was in the same boat. However, no matter what insults got thrown your way, mom would never allow us to be racist. If we mentioned a black person with the 'N' word, you were in deep trouble. It was taken out of the Banke vocabulary. I'm not even kidding. That's a line you didn't cross and that taught us a lot growing up. Treat others the way you want to be treated yourself.

By the age of six, we had moved from Blythe to San Ramon, and from there to Fairfield, where we stayed with Tim and Becky's dad, as they had a different dad to me and Steve. Over the next few years, I was all over the place. Napa, Santa Rosa, San Marino, Phoenix, Arizona, Utah, you name it. I lived all over and probably averaged about three or four months at a time in any one place.

Moving houses all the time meant I also went to a lot of schools. For some people, moving schools was a big thing. They'd be quiet for two or three weeks, trying to get to know everyone. Me? I broke in with everyone right away. Having lived in five different states and all over LA, moving was a natural thing.

Although I fitted in at school, I wasn't what you'd call a confident kid. I was more of a follower, never a leader. But that's not to say I was a walkover. You've got to remember that when we grew up, the Mexicans and Asians didn't get on very well and due to the fact that many people thought I was Chinese, this caused a lot of problems. Sometimes, you had no choice but to stick up for yourself.

The funny thing is, though, back then one of my biggest idols was Bruce Lee and back in the late 60s and early 70s, everyone wanted to be Bruce! Me and my brothers would be practising the kicks and punches, and making all the noises pretending we were in the film *Enter The Dragon*.

If I'm honest though, I never liked fighting as a kid, but I soon realized I was naturally quite good at it and that's before I started boxing, even though I also had my fair share of ass-kickings. I tended to do better with bigger guys, because they underestimated me. The guys who gave me trouble were my size or smaller.

After a while, me and Steve started to get a reputation as two kids who could handle themselves in the barrio. My younger brother Tim used to tag along with us and when he looks back on those times now, he says, 'They didn't take no crap. They never went out looking for trouble, but they'd find it – and when they did, it was bad for the other guys.' Just to say, where we grew up, back then, it wasn't known as a barrio to us, just a poor area. When we got to Azusa a few years later, that's when we got to understand more about being around barrios.

On the whole, though, my memories as a kid were happy. Of course, me and my brothers, Tim and Steve, we were typical boys. We had strollers and turned them into race carts, that sort of thing, but also got into a bit of trouble. Take for example the time me and Tim stole this bike. We hid it in our garage and our brother Steve decided that it was going to be his bike. We stole it from someone, now he stole from us.

One morning, when Steve was getting ready to take the bike out, me and Tim loosened bolts on the front tyre because we were pissed off. We knew we couldn't take Steve on in a fight because he was stronger than us, so this was our way of getting him back.

Steve took off and somewhere between school and the house, he tried to jump off a kerb and the front wheel fell off. He went head over heels and knocked his front teeth out. Let's just say Steve was pissed with us for a long time after that.

Me and Tim also managed to piss off a few of the neighbors. This one particular neighbor hated kids. I don't know why, but he did. His property was a shortcut to school and he didn't allow anybody on it. It was a large piece of land and the edge of the property was about 300 yards from the house. If he saw you crossing, he would shoot salt rock pellets at you out of a shotgun. We didn't care, though, and always cut through. We never got caught, then one day, me and Tim were cutting through and he saw us. We started taking off, running like crazy, laughing, when all of a sudden, you heard this scream, followed by me yelling, 'He got me! He got me!' He'd hit me with that damn salt rock. While I was complaining about being shot, Tim could hardly stand up because he was laughing so hard.

Another time, me and Tim decided to have some fun by the freeway. The house we rented backed on to it, but also had this apple tree in the backyard, so we loaded up on these rotten apples. We then climbed up on the side of the embankment next to the freeway and lobbed these apples at the cars. One day, I thought it would be a good idea to grab a rock and do it. Oh man. This truck drove past and I let this big rock fly. Boom. Right through the windshield. We took off straight away and ran home.

This guy pulled over in his truck, but somehow found out where we lived and came knocking at the door. I'm not sure if he knocked on the neighbors' doors and asked about a couple of kids matching our description, but either way, he found us. We could hear him banging and screaming at the door.

Shortly after he arrives, the sheriff shows up and speaks to this truck guy with the blown-out window and a rock sitting in his front seat. We kept quiet and didn't allow them in, but it didn't blow over. Our mom wasn't there at the time, but she found out what had happened and we got in a bunch of trouble for that.

We tried to pull the wool over our mom's eyes on a few occasions, but she always had a way of finding out. Take the time I thought I was being clever playing hooky from school. She was never home early when we got home, but this day she was there. What happened was, she'd received a call from the elementary school saying that I was skipping class. So when I walked into the house and saw her there, I was like, 'Oh my God.' She asked, 'Did you go to school today?' I replied all upbeat. 'Yeah, I went to school today,' trying to play her off.

Here's the thing. Anybody that knows me well knows that I'm not a good liar. Then she asked again and I said, 'Yes' again. Then she asked one more time and I said, 'Yes mom. I went to school! Gees.' I thought she might turn around and accept it, but she picked up her car keys and said, 'We're going to drive to the principal's office.' As we got to the front door, she asked one more time and I kept to my story. She replied, 'OK. Let's go.' We drive all the way down there and just as we're getting close to the principal's office door, I said, 'Mom. I didn't go to school today.' I never expected her to go that far to shake the truth out of me. But she did!

Looking back, I should never have doubted her. Mom, after all, was president of the school's parents' association, who for the record gave her hell for sending out bilingual leaflets in Spanish and English. She was faced with racism from the school when she listened to some of the other mothers who said, 'Well, I'm from Poland, Italy etc.' Mom replied, 'Fine. Write it out in your language and we will print it.' Needless to say, she was only president of the association for one year. So when I played hooky, she went above and beyond to show there was no favoritism for her kids. I got a good spanking for that. I soon understood that lying don't pay.

As tough as mom was, if you kept at her, or maybe, when *I* kept at her, she'd eventually cave in. One time, when I was in sixth grade, everyone was getting their costumes to wear for Halloween. Mom said, 'I'll make you one.' I said, 'I don't want one homemade, I want one from the store.' Mom said, 'I can make you whichever one the store has.' I didn't budge and started to throw a bit of a tantrum. 'I want one from the store. I'm tired of looking poor. I need one from the store.' This went on for a while and then she said, 'OK. We'll go to the store.'

So here I was, happy as hell that I got my outfit. I got to school, and I swear to God, I was the only one wearing an outfit from the store. Everybody else in my class had a homemade costume. I felt so damn embarrassed.

In all honesty, I was lucky to get that Halloween outfit, simply because mom never had a lot of money to spare and that outfit was without doubt a luxury. Most of the time, we had to be creative with getting what we wanted or take what was on offer from whoever offered it. For example, back in the 1970s, mom was between jobs during the holidays and couldn't afford to buy a Christmas tree. On the last day of school before the holidays started, the teacher asked, 'Do any of you students need a Christmas tree?' I raised my hand.

I dragged that big tree home all on my own for three blocks and was so excited to show mom. 'Mommy, mommy! Look what I got!' as she opened the door. She was over the moon. We lived in a diverse working-class neighborhood and there was no shame in dragging a tree through the streets. Nobody judged you. Totally the opposite. They were happy for you that you had a tree at Christmas. That attitude thankfully wouldn't change, as we soon moved again.

CHAPTER 3

BOXING BUG

'Once he'd visited his first boxing club, that's where
it took off. Paul had his calling'

Yolanda Miranda

AFTER moving from Fairfield to Napa, we moved to Santa Rosa, northern California in 1975, where my mom was working. We stayed here long enough for me to complete my third to sixth grades in school, but I also got introduced to a sport that would eventually change my life, although I didn't fall in love with it straight away.

As a ten-year-old, new to Santa Rosa, I played a bit of baseball and football, but nothing serious. I was just a kid having fun. At the time, mom had a friend called Eugene Myers, who was the director of the YMCA's youth program for the neighborhood, so we used to go down there just to hang out. We'd play pool, backgammon, that sort of thing. YMCA had put together an outreach program for the kids who were living in the Windsor area, and boxing was part of it. The man who hosted the sessions was called Eddie Pagan.

The town of Windsor allowed Eddie to use the basketball hall at Windsor Junior High School as a training facility for the kids, under the banner of the YMCA. Although Santa Rosa was about eight miles south of Windsor, me and Steve were allowed to attend because we were part of the wider Windsor community.

The hall was about 4,000 square feet and back then there wasn't a proper boxing ring, just a load of mats on the floor to mark out the perimeter. There were also two heavy bags and one speed bag. Eddie had focus mitts and used to catch pads with the kids, and spar with them, as he was still very active as an open fighter in the amateurs. It wasn't a traditional boxing gym as you'd know it, but it was achieving the same results in terms of training and discipline.

You have to remember, Santa Rosa is a retirement community and more so back then. Many people didn't think that boxing was a safe thing to do or that it was a sport worth taking up. Eddie did, though. When he set up the program at the YMCA, he wanted to reach some of these kids who were getting in trouble. He specialized with at-risk adolescents and when he started the program, he took on all the kids nobody else wanted. To an extent, that included me and Steve. We weren't bad kids, just mischievous.

Boxing can reach all kids. What Eddie realized was, when they started doing the program, they started getting in shape and then into boxing matches. With that discipline in their lives, their attitudes at school positively turned around. He used to say, 'Here's two things you have to do if I work with you as a kid. You have to behave at home and you have to maintain at least a C average at school.' We were able to do that. And if you couldn't afford to pay for the boxing classes, you came for free. And that's still what he does now with his current gym. He never closes the door to no kids. A true gentleman.

Even though I attended a few evening sessions with Eddie, the truth is, I was basically following Steve. Yeah, I worked out a bit and learnt a few moves, but I just wasn't that interested. However, when we moved to Phoenix, Arizona in early 1977, that changed.

And all because of a trophy that wasn't even mine.

* * *

When we first got to Phoenix, me and Steve started training at Willy and Nettie Borchert's gym, which was called 'Willy's Boxing' at the time and had been open since 1970. The gym was behind their house in the backyard, all on one level, and looked like a garage transformed into a boxing gym. It was basic but had everything you needed. A full-sized ring, heavy bag, speed bag and some weights. It was very well put together.

The other thing they had, which was great for me and my development, was the heat. Training in those temperatures pushed me to my limits and helped me develop a mentality that nothing was impossible. Go that extra mile. Talking of miles, stamina was a big thing. Willy used to tell us that we had to run to win. It was a philosophy, so that's what we did. We'd be up very early every morning running five to eight miles, depending on how you were feeling. When I was under the big lights in years to come, those runs paid dividends, no doubt about it.

As for Willy, he had a couple of fights as a pro in 1976. The first he won by KO in the first round and then a week later, he lost in the first round against Roy Jones Sr. By 1977, Willy was still only 33 but had served five years in the Marine Reserve, so he brought the discipline to the gym, but in a good way. It didn't matter how many years you'd be training there, how talented you were, once you walked through the doors, you treated everyone with the same degree of respect and politeness.

He also had a few other rules. No guns, knives or weapons of any kind, no swearing, no drugs, and if you came to the gym thinking you could bully, you'd be out pretty quick. Willy wanted to get the best out of everyone and if you followed his rules, that's exactly what happened. He went on to train a great bunch of fighters, including the late, great Diego Corrales, who I'd later spar with. Back in 1977, without a doubt, Willy was a big influence on making me choose boxing as a way of life.

Willy wasn't a tall man but he had a very catchy voice that dominated the room. He was an old-school trainer who was demanding, but knowledgeable, supportive and a great teacher. There was a genuine love, care and concern from Willy and Nettie for the boxers training with them. They wanted everyone to become the best they could be. His students had good skills and that didn't happen by accident.

However, when I first started at Willy's, it was similar to when I trained with Eddie at the YMCA. It just wasn't a big passion for me and like before, I was simply going to the gym and following Steve. As a 12-year-old kid, I was very active and had a lot of energy to burn. I was the one child in our family who everybody would say, 'Do something with him!', but I just hadn't clicked with boxing at that stage.

Then something happened. I'd been playing football for three months and didn't have one trophy. When you're a little kid, you want a trophy! Then one day, I went to see Steve in his second ever amateur fight and he won the state championship at the Junior Olympics in Phoenix, Arizona in the 95lbs class. In fact, he beat a guy who had won it three times previously.

Steve was given a trophy, medal, flowers and a sweatsuit. I thought, 'He's only been boxing for one month at this club. This is his second ever amateur fight and he's already got a trophy.' That's when I said to myself, 'I'm gonna box, man!'

I just want to say something about my brother Steve. Like me, he was also a premature baby. He was in an incubator for three months due to a lung disease he picked up as a result of his lungs not being fully developed. But that didn't stop him in life. He was a born fighter and a great one at that.

In the years to come, Steve clocked up an amateur record of over 150 fights, losing only 14. He fought all over the world for the United States boxing team, but due to circumstances in his own life, he never turned pro. I'm sure if he had, he would have become a world champion, without a doubt. I've always maintained he was a better boxer than me. Thankfully, he stayed in the boxing game and has been training fighters since 1990.

When I told Steve I was going to fight, he said to my mom, 'I don't want my brother going with me. He ain't gonna train properly.' I didn't listen and started training at the gym straight away. I sparred once, maybe twice, then seven days after deciding to make a go of it, at the age of 12, I had my first amateur fight.

I couldn't tell you nothing about the fight or what the guy looked like, I just remember my hand being raised as the winner after the fight and being over the moon. Willy and Nettie were also really happy and that was a great feeling and memory.

Willy's gym was the perfect place for me to fuel my enthusiasm for boxing and sharpen my skills. It wasn't the biggest gym, but there was some major talent in there. For example, there was Louie 'Sharpshooter' Espinoza, who was a couple of years older than me and went on to become a two-weight world champion. Another guy most people have forgotten about was Chuck Walker.

When I walked into Willy's gym, Chuck had just got back from the 1976 Olympic Games, alongside stars like

Sugar Ray Leonard, Leon and Michael Spinks and Howard Davis, who sadly passed a few years back. Although he didn't progress past the first round at the Olympics, rumor was, legendary trainer Cus D'Amato was sitting ringside with Chuck's dad and wanted to bring him over to the Catskills in New York to train him. Although Chuck never took Cus up on the offer, that shows you the level he was at.

Back at Willy's in 1977, Chuck walked around with a white Team USA sweatsuit and I was like, 'Oh my God.' I only saw him a few times, but he had an effect on me. His presence, the way he moved. I didn't even know what a world champion was back then. All I knew was that people were crowding around him. I thought, 'That must be a great feeling.' I saw him wrapping his hands, hitting the bag and he looked special. I was impressed. My aim back then, as a result, was to fight in the Olympics.

It wasn't just the seniors who inspired me, though. There was a little nine-year-old kid called Paul Vaden who turned out to be something special. Very special. He would go on to have an incredible amateur record of 337 fights with only ten losses and in 1995 would become the IBF junior middleweight champion of the world. We're still good friends to this day.

Paul was, and still is, from San Diego. Part of his development was to go to different clubs and train with other fighters and coaches. That's how we met. Willy was friends with his coach Robert Coons and they would train at Willy's gym, stay at the house and get treated to Nettie's world-famous breakfast every morning they stayed. There was a tournament in Mace, Arizona called the Mace invitational. Robert and his fighters used to come to this tournament a lot from San Diego and even though his fighters were fighting in Willy's home state, Willy would always root for them in the competitions, as they'd be doing for us.

Having fighters from different gyms helped us in competitions. We adopted the mentality of 'hit and not getting hit' to get as many points as possible in our amateur bouts. That was a philosophy that Robert and Willy shared.

Back in Willy's gym, Paul used to observe me when I was on the bags or sparring and whenever I had the chance, I would be supportive of his own efforts as an up-and-coming amateur boxer. I don't say it to all fighters, but if I see a fighter has skills, I tell them straight up, and Paul Vaden had skills. No doubt about that. When I saw him working with Robert Coons, I'd say after, 'You're fast and you're only nine. You're doing these moves already. You're going to be good. Really good! When you grow up, you'll become world champion.'

Me and Paul won a tournament together in 1979, in Del Mar, California. I was in the 95lbs division and Paul was in the 70lbs category. There was a bunch of good fighters there, including Byron Lindsay, who tragically died in the plane crash of 1980 – more on this later. I remember seeing Paul warming up with Robert Coons for his contest and the way he threw punches was cute. He was a great little fighter at that age already. My brother Steve ended up working with Robert Coons years later. He adopted that European style. What I mean by that is their hands are up all the time behind the firm jab. Paul fought that way.

But let me say this. I'm impressed with every fighter out there. Anyone who puts those gloves on impresses me. A champion is a champion. I'd never disrespect them after everything they had to go through to get that far.

Sparring was something I got introduced to at Willy's gym and I was very fortunate to spar some great guys, such as Johnny Vasquez and Pete Solarez. I'd end up fighting Pete in the pros. They were tough and definitely better than me, but Louie Espinoza was probably the toughest of the lot. He wasn't called 'Sharpshooter' for nothing.

One guy who pushed me in sparring was an 18-year-old pro who had already fought about a dozen times and was being called a lightweight contender. They wanted sparring for his next fight, so they brought me over.

I was only 14 at the time and Willy took me to Arizona Boxing Club to spar with this guy. The trainer who used to run the place was called Pablo and always made us feel welcome. Even though this fighter was four years older, he didn't take no liberties. He was tagging me, but I was tagging him too.

The name of the fighter? Freddie Roach. I ended up sparring Freddie twice, about two or three rounds each time. In years to come, we remained good friends and he jokes now about how many selfies I take and post on Facebook whenever I go and see him at the Wild Card Gym.

Around the same time, I met Ray Mancini as I had a part-time job as a glove boy. Here's how the job worked. The boxing commission would hand you the gloves and then you'd take them to the trainers of the fighters. Then, after the fight, we'd pick up the gloves and take them back to the commission. We'd get paid about 20 bucks, which back then was good money for a kid.

At the time, I was Ray's glove boy for his second fight as a professional against Lou Daniels, which took place at the Civic Plaza in Phoenix on 13 November 1979. I think his dad was also there. I brought him the gloves and I was like, 'Wow! Ray Mancini.' Then, years later, when I was 26 and became world champion, I went over and told him the story and he was like, 'No way!' Ray would be a great inspiration and support to me when things weren't going so well in my life in years to come.

* * *

As an amateur, I wasn't a brawler, because I had good footwork. As opposed to later when I was fighting in the pros, it was all about getting in and out and bagging those points. Pop, pop, pop, pop, pop, as opposed to sitting down on your punches to make them harder.

My sister put my footwork down to my dancing. I used to love it. I was always winning these dance competitions at school and when we were at home, me and Steve would be practising to oldies, while Tim and Rebecca would be there watching us. One track we used to play over and over again was *Night Fever*. Everybody wanted to dance like John Travolta. We even had the lights on to create the disco atmosphere and everything. That's how we entertained ourselves. Also, being a good dancer was a great way to meet girls!

Even though Rebecca didn't come down the gym she still had to box, but in a different way. Our mom was one of 14 kids from a Catholic family and soon learned not to be pushed around. I think there was a bit of that in Rebecca, too. Despite us trying to be protective of her as kids, there was never really any need as she was probably the toughest of the four of us.

Rebecca's never boxed a woman in her life, but when we used to come back from the gym, she had to box us. What happened was, we used to box over who would do the dishes, and whoever lost had to do them. Let's just say she learned how to fight real quick. She could have been a good boxer, you know. She was pretty strong and fast but by the time she started to get into it, she had to move away. Here's what happened.

After Santa Rosa, we moved to San Bernardino, then to Phoenix. The next move to Azusa, California wasn't by choice. In 1979, mom was diagnosed with a brain tumor. She never let on that she had any health issues, but apparently she was having problems with her eyes and it turned out that the tumor was affecting her sight.

By the time we got to Phoenix, she became pretty sick and had to be hospitalized several times as an emergency because of the tumor. She started having spinal taps, 14 of them in fact, which caused her a great deal of discomfort. Mom was a 60s hippy and when the tumor hadn't cleared up after all that treatment, she decided to go to Connecticut on the East Coast and try natural therapies – herbs and stuff like that. Incredibly, over time the treatment worked and the tumor went into remission. When she did return home years later, her neurologist was shocked that it had disappeared. But that was in the future. At this point in time, things weren't great.

When mom went sick, it had implications for me, my brothers and sister. Rebecca went to our aunt's house in Phoenix and then eventually our grandmother's place, while Tim went to live with his father and stepmom in California. Me and Steve stayed at the house in Phoenix.

We were only teenagers and had all grown up together. To now not be able to see them that much was really hard. All we did was worry about each other. These were not the days of video calls, the internet and smartphones. When someone moved away, you were limited in terms of how you could keep in touch.

In the meantime, me and Steve were only 14 and 16, and were left at home on our own in Phoenix, starving. All we ate was potatoes. Steve got a little side job and we did the best we could without any adults in the house for a couple of weeks, but it wasn't easy.

When Willy and Nettie could see that me and Steve were struggling, they took us under their wing and for the next few months we ended up living at their house. They were actually thinking about adopting us because they knew we were living by ourselves. They were great to many kids there. There's certain things you don't forget as a kid and that's generosity and support.

They used to take the whole team out for breakfast. I don't remember if it was Denny's or whatever kind of restaurant, but they made sure each and every one of us were fed and happy. As someone who was poor, seeing what they did for the kids, again and again, taking us travelling, feeding us, I couldn't believe it. That was their nature, to take care of people, and I'll always be eternally grateful for their help, support and guidance to me and Steve at that difficult time in our lives.

Not seeing Tim and Rebecca was sad. We'd see them here and there, but not like before. It did have an effect on me. What helped at the time was boxing. It kept me busy. It filled a gap in my life. Thankfully, Willy and Nettie acted as teachers and mentors of how to take our lives forward. They taught us well and kept our heads straight.

There were a lot of homies and wannabe gangsters in our neighborhood and they influenced us to live a different life and not make positive choices. For example, a lot of the kids were wearing baggy pants to look like a 'Cholo'. Steve liked that look back then! Ironed baggy pants, 'wife beater' tucked in, shirt on top, with only the top button done up. Nettie especially used to make sure I dressed correctly. She didn't want me looking like some little homie gangster and said, 'You dress proper.' They took us out and bought us new outfits. Levi 501s, new shirts, basically giving us a clean-cut look.

I remember one of the girls came over to the house once and said, 'Oh. You look cute, Paul!' I was thinking, 'Dressing proper makes you look cute. I'll dress proper!' But it didn't stop at schooling us how to dress. They taught us manners. When to say, 'Yes sir, no sir. Pleased to meet you. My name is', how to act in front of people and how to shake hands. They were instrumental in our lives. Our mom brought us up on her own and was trying to put a roof over our heads, while also dealing with the union, so she never really had an opportunity to do what Willy and Nettie were teaching us. They gave me schooling as a teenager to become a good adult and taught us right from wrong.

Willy and Nettie's influence never left me. In years to come, when I started to get more and more recognized as a boxer, I realized I needed to dress in a certain way. Sporty. Very clean and very classy. I needed to carry myself like an athlete, not like a thug or gangster.

Thankfully, my move to California provided me with all the discipline I needed for all future moves.

CHAPTER 4

AZUSA

*'I had Paul at Azusa Boxing Club from about
1979, when he was 14, until pro. He had the desire
to fight in the nationals, be on the Olympic team
and train hard to be the best he could possibly be'*

Victor Valenzuela

AFTER three months of living with Willy and Nettie,
our mom shipped us off to her sister Olga and her
husband Don Wren, while she continued to get
treatment for the tumor. They helped us at a time in need
and never once made a fuss about it. I'll never forget that.

Thankfully, I knew aunt Olga and uncle Don well, as my
mom used to sometimes fly me out there during vacation to
hang out with their son, my cousin Donnie. They're good
people. Just to put it in perspective, I have 49 cousins, so we
used to do a lot of road trips to see family.

Once again, me and Steve had to go to a new school and
once again it had no effect on me. However, we were now a

bit older and school came with issues and distractions that could have easily led us down the wrong path. I thank God for my uncle Don. He was a former marine drill sergeant, so he taught us a lot of discipline, like getting up early in the morning. He acted as a father figure.

Everything had to be in order with Don. If you picked something up or used something, you had to put it back where you found it and God help you if put it down sloppy. And your bed had to be done to military standard. The sheets had to be dusted and the bedspread tight and tucked in like a trampoline, without a single wrinkle.

We also had chores such as washing the cars and cutting the grass, and if my friends came round asking for me, he'd say, 'He can't come out yet. He needs to clean his room before he leaves. He's not going anywhere.' Even in years to come, if we woke up with hangovers, we still had to do the same shit. That went on until I left at the age of 20! When my friend Louie Valenzuela comes to my house now, he says, 'It's not as clean and tidy like when you lived with your uncle Don!'

Uncle Don was a morning person because of his military background and maybe some of that rubbed off on me. In fact, I'm sure it did. I loved the discipline and army routines, and that's perhaps why I enjoyed boxing so much, because it came with a similar structure.

Like Nettie, Don wanted us to look presentable. Don's son, our cousin Donnie, who was like a big brother to us, was more of a sport jock kind of guy and Don wanted us to have that clean-cut look about us, to generate less attention with the wrong crowds. However, that meant the Chicano gang members could tell that we were not part of their neighborhood from the way we dressed.

Nowadays, Americans understand the Mexican-American concept. Americans are proud of their Mexican heritage and vice versa, but back then Chicanos were going around saying, 'Chicano power'. They felt marginalized. Nowadays, Chicanos get mad at me because I don't speak Spanish, like I'm not down with my race. I'm very proud of my race, but I was born here in the United States. I wish I did know how to speak Spanish, though.

Wherever we moved to, there were always issues with kids from the local neighborhood and Azusa was no different. In fact, Azusa was one of the most challenging areas. The homies would hit us in Spanish and were like, 'De donde eres homeboy?' I didn't understand what the hell they were talking about and looked at them confused. Then they'd repeat in English, 'Where you from homes?' I replied, 'We're not from here, man,' and they'd jump us. This happened a few times.

We had issues with a group of kids from a different neighborhood who said we were disrespecting their signs. We had a problem with them for a while and had got into a few scuffles. As a result, Steve used to walk me to class almost every day, because there was always somebody waiting by the school doors trying to get us. We knew how to box at that stage, so we were confident, but it was still scary nonetheless.

Then one day we had a big scuffle with them. Me and Steve were in the locker room at our high school and our lockers were close to the wall, mine at the bottom and Steve's on the top. From the corner of Steve's eye, he could see about seven or eight guys coming in and turned to me and said, 'OK Paul. Get ready.' Steve had just opened his locker and this guy came right up to his shoulder and said, 'Hey man. What's up?' Next thing, we're all fighting. While we're throwing punches, I kept thinking, 'We need to get out in the open. We're in a small little area.' So we got outside and were exchanging blows, when the security guard came over and stopped it. This happened for a short period of time, but during that time, it was a regular thing. If my cousin Donnie was around, he'd always have our backs and would jump in.

Uncle Don also used to teach baseball, so a lot of the kids in the neighborhood knew him. One time, we'd had a scuffle with this kid who my uncle taught and he decided to take me and Steve to the kid's house to sort the matter out once and for all. He knocked on the door and very politely said to him, 'Can you come outside, please?' 'Sure Mr Wren,' he replied. Everyone respected uncle Don. 'I hear you got a problem with my two nephews?' 'Yeah,' he replied. 'If you got a problem with them, we're going to take care of that. Pick one of them and handle business right now, then it ends tonight. Which one do you want?' In the back of mine and Steve's minds, we're thinking, 'I really don't want to fight, but if we've got to fight, then that's what I'll do.' Don continued. 'After you've had the fight, if you beat him, that's cool, if he beats you, that's cool. But then you shake hands and it's over. OK?' Thankfully, the kid didn't want to fight either, so we shook hands and squashed the whole deal. Thank God!

As time went on, we were boxing a lot in Azusa and many of these guys we had scuffles with got to know that and they began to recognize us as boxers. In fact, we got to become friends with them, which was much better than the other way round.

* * *

By this stage mom was now healthy, back into her union work and was involved in new campaigns all over the place. She was living in Venice Beach and we'd see her maybe four or five times a year. Me and Steve were already winning amateur titles in Azusa and I guess she figured that staying with aunt Olga and uncle Don meant we had some stability in our lives. She was right.

The only thing I was concerned about was that boxing would not be a part of my life. Luckily for me, it was. My Uncle Don took me to the Azusa Boxing Gym and that's where I met Victor Valenzuela. Little did I know, but in the same way I would end up living with uncle Don and aunt Olga until I turned pro, Victor would become my trainer throughout my amateur career and his family would become very close friends.

Like Willy's gym, Victor's had character. The place was a couple of miles from where we lived, but back then it felt like it was far away. It was a really old, small gym that used to be a bar and was in a barrio right in the heart of the neighborhood. The gym is still there to this day, in fact. Back then, it had wooden floors, old bags and equipment, and the ring was small, as it still is – 12x12 ft. We had fighters from other gyms who used to come over and see the conditions we trained in and would say, 'No wonder you guys are tough. There's no place to run in your ring! You have to fight.'

Victor was ten years older than me, one of six sons, and had started boxing at the age of nine, alongside three of his brothers. He was real quiet, but could be outspoken, yet strict and always in charge. He was a great trainer. Another level up from anything I'd experienced before.

He had over 80 amateur fights but never turned pro, instead becoming a trainer in 1977 at the age of 23. I'm so glad he did. He would eventually go on to become the head coach at the USA National Championships. Victor's dad Tony also used to teach at the club and, like the rest of the Valenzuelas, was a great guy, but it was the youngest of the brothers, Louie, who would turn out to become a lifelong friend, attending all my fights and sticking with me through thick and thin.

Back then, though, Louie didn't go to the gym every day and it was out of school that we became friends and started to hang out. Although we went to different high schools, I'd bring him to my high school to meet my friends and he did the same, and we'd start attending dances and party together. There was always a joke between us two when we'd go dancing. I'd say, 'I do it better than you.' Louie would reply, 'What? Are you crazy? Nobody can hang with the Lou-dawg on the dance floor.' It's still an ongoing joke and to this very day there's never a dull moment when we're together.

As I started boxing at the club, I soon started to pick up trophies. When you play sport, you're lucky if you travel the next town over, but I was going to Arizona, California, Texas, New Mexico. It was fun and a great experience, but more than anything it helped to maintain some form of extra direction in my life.

My brother Steve only hung around at aunt Olga and uncle Don's for a year and then left for my grandmother's house in San Bernardino. We kind of drifted apart after that for a number of years, which was a real shame, but thankfully our brotherly bond was strong enough to bring us back together in later life. In the meantime, my journey in boxing was about to move to another level.

I was determined to make it to the top.

CHAPTER 5

GYM ADDICT

'Rhythm is everything in boxing.
Every move you make starts with your heart, and
that's in rhythm or you're in trouble'

Sugar Ray Robinson, P4P boxing legend

T HE main reason I'd say we didn't get involved in gangs in our early years is because we were always in the gym. About four or five in the morning, we'd do our runs, then after school we'd head straight to the boxing gym. That was our life Monday to Saturday and if we had a fight coming up, we'd be there Sundays also. If you didn't have a fight, you'd be running instead to improve your stamina.

Sparring at Willy's gym was full on, but as I was getting more experienced, older and stronger, those spars moved up another level when I got to Azusa. You came in, worked hard and competed. If you didn't, you were out of there pretty fast. Those were Victor's rules.

The more I trained, the more I wanted to fight. So much so, that Victor used to say, 'You can't hold him back!' Literally. My character inside the ring was different to what it was outside. When I was with my friends and family, I was always laughing, joking around and was shy, but the second I stepped through the ropes, I changed. I was an aggressive fighter who always wanted to get the first punch in. After the referee broke me and my opponent from a clinch and told us, 'Get back to your corner', the second he looked away, I was straight back at the fighter. I couldn't wait to start exchanging blows again.

Back then, it was a rough neighborhood in Azusa, so we had a lot of hungry fighters. Take Zack Padilla, for example. When me and him were together in the gym, we were hilarious. Always having fun and joking around, but the moment we got in the ring, it was work time. All-out fighting.

Zack was a year older than me and fought a few weight divisions above me. His style was brutal. Seek and destroy. With the small ring we boxed in, sparring with Zack taught me how to cut someone off in the ring from an early stage. That's why few fighters got away from me or Zack in both that gym or in any other ring.

He liked to spar with me because I was shorter and a southpaw. His theory was that taller guys take longer to throw punches and it takes them longer to pull the punches back. Guys with shorter arms and reach like me could keep on throwing punches without giving someone like Zack a break, and he appreciated that.

One of Zack's main sparring partners for a number of years was Sugar Shane Mosley, who I also sparred once. It was a Saturday morning and he was getting ready to fight in some national tournament out east. When he turned up at the gym there was nobody to spar, so I jumped in with him. The way you saw him fight as a professional was exactly the same as he was as a kid. He was a machine.

Zack and Shane used to have ring wars. You'd think they were pissed off at each other, but they weren't. That's just the way they worked. Monday, they'd do ten rounds, Tuesday the same, Wednesday maybe even 12. They tore each other apart and the way I used to see Zack train and spar was inspirational. He'd train as hard as he could in the gym, because he didn't want to get tired when he fought. He knew from experience that if he got tired in a fight, he'd get knocked out or hurt. Seeing the way he trained, and being able to train alongside him, pushed me that bit further.

It came as no surprise at all that he eventually became WBO super lightweight champion, defended the title four times and retired as champion with a record of 22-1-1. Zack had a lot of good fights left in him and would have still been champion for years, but he discovered he had an aneurism, and that unfortunately stopped him from boxing ever again.

* * *

Victor left nothing to chance when it came to improving your fighting. Despite having a great stable of boxers, he always made sure we visited other local gyms to get quality sparring.

I sparred Richie Sandoval, who was very skilful. Richie went on to achieve great things in boxing, including qualifying for the 1980 Olympic team, although he never got to compete because of the boycott. Instead of waiting for the next Games, he turned pro, became WBA bantamweight champion in 1984 and only lost one fight in 30.

I also sparred Joey Olivo, who was a great fighter. He turned pro in 1976, was about six inches taller than me, six years older, strong, but gave me respect. Joey became WBA light-flyweight champ in 1985, but in my opinion he never got the exposure he deserved. He still works with the kids now as a great coach and I'll always be grateful for how he improved me as a boxer in the spars we had.

Incredibly, the most brutal spars people remember me having at Azusa Boxing Club were between me and my brother Steve. We would really get into it. Not mad at each other, but we'd get lost in the moment and at times it looked like a street fight. On occasions, Louie and Victor were seconds away from jumping in the ring to separate us.

Someone else who caught everyone's eye sparring back then was a little kid being trained by his dad. Victor would take me and some of the other fighters to the Johnny Flores Gym, which used to be the old county jail. This kid was beating the other kids up. He was probably around seven at that point and he'd be in there going pop, pop, pop, and the other kids would be down. He already had those fast and hard hands and we'd eventually be sparring partners many years later. His name was Oscar De La Hoya.

For now, though, it was all about my journey. Boxing was about to introduce me to new places and people I would never have had the chance to meet or see otherwise.

CHAPTER 6

WANDERLUST

'He was insanely good as a boxer. His fights were punishing. I can remember him pummelling people, but take a really good shot also. I think the opponents knew from early on that when someone stepped into the ring with Paul Banke, they were in for a brawl'

Tim Munz, Paul Banke's brother

BEING able to travel was a great luxury for a kid from my background and I never took anything for granted. I'll always remember the people who made these things happen, namely Victor, Willy, my uncle Don and aunt Olga, but also a few other key people. Take, for example, Danny Lugo, Zack's uncle, the president of the Azusa Boxing Club. If we ever needed shoes, gloves, anything, Danny would work with Victor and go out and get funds to make it happen. Danny took care of us.

We went to New Mexico a few times, Oregon twice, all these trips were down to him. He worked in construction, but helped out with the boxing gym for free. He had a very big heart and gave a lot of his time back to the kids in the community.

In fact, the gym was on his property. Danny didn't box any more but it was like he was boxing with us by being a part of it. He did a lot for the kids and never made a fuss of it.

In 1980, I turned 16 and it was a very memorable year on the boxing front for me. However, there's one particular event, just 13 days after my birthday on 14 March, that stunned the boxing world. Me and my brother Steve were close to being part of the headline. As described by apnews.com:

> The Polish Lot airliner on a flight from New York crashed two miles from Warsaw airport, March 14, 1980, killing all 87 people aboard, including 14 top U.S. amateur boxers and eight of their coaches, doctors and referees.

It's almost 40 years since that happened and it still brings chills down my spine. Coach Junior Robles wanted to get me and my brother Steve on the USA team, but in order to do so, we had to qualify. This competition in Poland was going to give us that opportunity, but God had other plans for us that day.

We spoke with our uncle Don and he felt that our priority needed to be school as we were not doing so well and we'd only recently moved into the area. However, he didn't force his opinion and said it was up to us if we felt it was an opportunity that might never come again. Me and Steve listened to uncle Don and knew that there would be other opportunities, as we were still young. If anything, I felt I was too inexperienced to fight for the team.

When the news hit the television on 14 March, all I remember is our aunt Olga hugging us and saying emotionally, 'We would have lost you, boys.'

Many of those fighters who died would, without a doubt, have gone on to be world champions. Steve's stablemate David Rodriguez was on that flight. I saw him box when he was about 12 or 13 and he was real good. His dad would eventually train me as a pro for a bit. Carlos Palomino lost a loved one and many years later said, 'There was a few fighters I knew who were supposed to be on that flight, but who didn't end up boarding it. Paul Banke was one of them. My brother Paul [Palomino] unfortunately did. He had only just turned 18 and was only a couple of years older than Paul [Banke].'

RIP everyone who was on that flight.

* * *

Later in my 16th year, I did eventually get a chance to represent the USA team. In addition to wearing the USA sweatsuit, I flew overseas to New Zealand, which was a massive thing for me. I once fought in the border town Mexicali with Willy Borchert when I was about 13 years old, and thought I'd travelled the world at that point. Then I started flying all over the United States: Ohio, Frisco, you name it, but this was the first time outside of the US. New Zealand was a big step for me.

We did the first leg, Los Angeles to Honolulu, which was five hours from LAX airport, and stayed there for about two hours while they refuelled the plane. It's no secret that I like to talk a lot, but remember back then I was a hyper teenager, so multiply that by 100 and that gives you a good idea of what I was like.

When we boarded the 747 for the last leg to New Zealand, I started to explore. I went up to the top deck of the plane and started talking with everyone. 'Hi, I'm Paul Banke. I'm a boxer fighting on the USA team.' I then worked my way around the other cabins to the point where I'd made a bunch of new friends.

As we started to make the descent to Wellington, New Zealand, all you could see in the fields below were sheep. The country was so green and beautiful, like nothing I'd ever seen before. After landing, we got off and the coach was saying to the fighters, 'Everybody come over here. We're going to pick up our bags.' Then he stopped and said to the others, 'Where's Paul Banke?' Soon, they spotted me with all these people around me saying things like, 'Hey Paul, here's my address, look us up,' or 'Let's take a picture, Paul.' The coach said to the fighters, 'Who are those guys?' and they replied, 'Coach, he was talking to everybody on the plane and we mean everybody!'

The people in New Zealand were great. We loved them and they loved us. I'm not going to go into too much detail, but being confident, fit Americans, let's just say we were popular with the ladies. God bless New Zealand. I had three fights and won them all, so overall it was an incredible first trip representing my country and flying overseas.

Shortly after New Zealand, me, Ricky Romero and Zack fought in a tournament held in Albuquerque called the National PAL [Police Athletic League] Boxing Championships.

Now's a good time to properly introduce Ricky. First time I met him was when I fought him. I was about 15 at the time. Ricky was a really good fighter and over the years he fought my brother nine times, beating him in eight of those fights. However, when we boxed, it was a different story – according to him and me anyway. We boxed in El Monte in the San Gabriel Valley, California and neither of us let up. It was a war. After three crazy rounds we got awarded a draw, which neither of us agreed with as we both thought we'd won.

Anyway, they had two trophies to hand out to the boxers but hadn't banked on a draw, so there was one big trophy for the winner and a smaller one for the loser. In order to decide who got which trophy, they flipped a coin. I guessed correct and got the bigger trophy. To this very day, I still tell everyone I won the fight because I got the bigger trophy. Through boxing, me and Ricky ended up travelling all over together and 40 years later, we're still close friends. When I call him, he still makes me laugh my ass off.

Back to Albuquerque. Victor was our coach and Louie tagged along for the week. I got as far as the semi-finals, but Ricky got to the finals and was fighting the legendary Johnny Tapia. Once I was out of the competition, I probably wasn't a great help to Ricky, as I was sharing a room with him, and from the moment we arrived I wanted to go out and party all the time. I didn't feel so bad, though, because I went out one night without Ricky and when I got back to the room, he said, 'Where were you last night?' and I replied, 'At a party.' He then said, 'I was at a party too, man!' We laughed. Albuquerque was a blast.

Ricky and Johnny had an almighty battle and Johnny was given the decision, but the fight was real close and I felt that Ricky did enough to win it. They never stopped throwing punches and ended up getting fight of the tournament. Johnny gave Ricky a lot of praise after that fight and whichever competitions Ricky took part in after, people would say, 'Look. That's Ricky Romero.'

I'd actually first met Johnny when I was about 12 or 13 and gone with Willy to Albuquerque to take part in a competition. Johnny was three years younger than me and weighed about 68lbs. I was fighting at around 85lbs. I just remember everyone looking at him and hearing people say, 'Damn. Look at this kid go!' That was Johnny Tapia. We became good friends over the years and I was devastated when he died in 2012.

RIP champ.

* * *

I met some great fighters that year through competitions, guys like Ronnie Essett, Henry Tillman and Mike Tyson. I first met Ronnie at the National Amateur Boxing Federation championships in North Carolina. He was fighting at 147lbs. Ronnie was a nice, funny guy and we quickly became friends, and started training and travelling together a lot in the next couple of years.

When Henry joined the team, he'd only been boxing for a short time and had never been on a plane before. I made him feel at home, told him to believe in himself and to look forward to the international travel and all the adventures that come with being on the road.

As far as Mike goes, everyone had heard about him. He was this short, stocky heavyweight banging people out. Everybody on the boxing circuit knew he was a bad boy in that ring and people faked injuries not to fight him. However, the first time I met him properly was at the Olympic Training Center in Colorado Springs at a national tournament in 1982. We were all warming up in the dressing room with the music on loud, dancing, talking bullshit, and Mike was walking around in circles not saying a word, with his head down, headgear and gloves on, like a little bull getting ready for his bout.

I walked up to him and said, 'What's going on, bro?', trying to break the ice. He pointed his glove to his trainer Kevin Rooney, who said, 'Leave him alone. Let him concentrate.' 'OK,' I replied. Me and Mike became good friends and years later he showed me that friendship when I needed it most, but on that day everyone steered clear of him.

You could already tell at that stage that Mike was going to make it as a boxer. His attitude was serious and mature, but unfortunately his style wasn't what the judges were looking for in the amateurs. My friend Henry Tillman ended Mike's dreams of getting to the Olympics, but I think it's fair to say Mike did pretty good when he turned pro. I was knocked out of this tournament by a boxer called Michael Collins, whereas Zack won the gold medal in his category.

The last tournament of 1982 for me was the national US Amateur Boxing Championships in Indianapolis, Indiana. I was up against Tracy Harris Patterson in Charlotte, North Carolina in the quarter-finals. Back then, he was known as Tracy Harris. The Patterson was added when he turned pro, which was a nice touch as he was the adopted son of former world heavyweight champion Floyd Patterson. Tracy went on to become a two-weight world champ later.

Funnily enough, when I was looking to make a comeback towards the end of my pro career, I almost ended up fighting him. I'd heard that he didn't want to fight me and I said, 'I didn't want to fight him, either!' Tracy was tough. Back to our fight as amateurs. It was a close fight but I beat him and that got me a place in the semis against Robert Shannon in December 1982.

Shannon dropped me twice in the first round and Victor threw the towel in. I'm not going to lie, I was hurt. Robert was a very good fighter and gave me a whole heap of problems as an amateur. I'd have to wait six years before I got my revenge.

For now, it was all about chasing my amateur dreams as a boxer.

CHAPTER 7

GLOBAL DEVELOPMENT

*'Keep your dreams alive. Understand to
achieve anything requires faith and belief in
yourself, vision, hard work, determination and
dedication. Remember all things are possible for
those who believe'*

Gail Devers

IN 1983, I moved one step closer to my dream of fighting in the Olympics. I was at my aunt Olga and uncle Don's house when a letter arrived addressed to me. I opened it up and it had the Olympic rings and the USA flag design at the top.

'Dear Mr Banke...' I'd been asked to try out for the US Olympic boxing team. I can't describe how excited I was. At the time, I was in 11th grade at school and looking to stay for another year to become a senior, but instead I got that letter and I didn't attend that senior year. I went straight to Colorado Springs.

The training center was beautiful, like you'd see in the photos with the flags flying, but actually being there was something else. It was surreal. You'd be walking around and bumping into the likes of Carl Lewis, Greg Louganis, Michael Jordan and Mary Lou Retton, thinking, 'Wow!' In terms of boxers, there were some incredible fighters. You had the likes of Vinny Pazienza, Pernell Whitaker, Robert Shannon, Ricky Romero, Mike Tyson, Meldrick Taylor, Evander Holyfield, Tyrell Biggs and many more. I soon learned the value of camaraderie because we ate, trained, lived and fought together. Over the next 18 months, there would be many times when we fought in a different country and the only people we'd talk to were each other. It was essential to get on.

Everything was new to me going to Colorado, including the stipends they gave us to live on. It was something like a hundred bucks every two weeks, but you've got to remember we had free breakfast, lunch and dinner at a café, along with free accommodation. That cash went far. Most of us came from humble beginnings, so we had more food than we ever had before and money in our pockets. Life was good.

It was great having as much food as you wanted, but I was getting fat there. Ronnie Essett tried to reassure me by saying, 'Food isn't a big issue trying to make weight as we have the discipline nagging on us all the time to make the team.' That might have been the case for Ronnie making 147lbs, but I was making 112lbs! It probably didn't help that we were also ordering Domino's Pizza and Popeyes Chicken late at night. That's not saying the food at the buffet wasn't good, it was great, but we wanted something different.

Thankfully, the training kept you on track. Whether it rained, snowed or shined, you'd be up at 5am going for your run, doing three miles around this lake at the training center. Sometimes they'd wake you up at 11pm to go for a run and we'd be like, 'What? Now? We've got to go jog?' But that all helped to give us the winning mentality. You'd think, 'My opponent is probably training now. I'm gonna train.'

Training alongside these big names was a huge motivation and I picked up tips from some of them. Me and Ricky used to run with Henry Tillman and Tyrell Biggs. Tyrell was kind of like a big brother to me and Ricky, which was something else because everybody knew Tyrell was a special fighter. Whereas I was on the B-team squad, Tyrell was on the A-team along with the likes of Evander and Henry. Tyrell went on to become the first person to win an Olympic gold medal in the new super heavyweight division in 1984. I also remember having a conversation with Meldrick Taylor. I'd had about 90 fights at that point and he was younger than me and had had over 200 and was boxing pretty much every weekend. It made me think whether or not I was fighting enough or if he was fighting too much. Either way, every person you spoke with had some knowledge to share with you.

Despite Robert Shannon beating me in the semi-finals of the nationals a few months earlier, we became good friends. Boxing apart, he's one of the nicest guys you could meet and he knew how to cut hair. I'm not talking about as a hobby, but as a proper barber. He went to high school in Colorado Springs for the first semester then for the second semester went to barber college. When he went home, he continued to attend barber college in Washington and got his licence there. His full-time job these days is still in the barber shop, but the difference now is he owns it. Tuesday through to Saturday you'll find him there and people still ask him questions about boxing and the Olympics.

Back to the training camp, Robert was in demand. He cut Evander Holyfield's hair and many of the other guys' and when it came to me I said, 'Can I get a buzz cut?' Robert said, 'Are you sure?' 'Yeah. I want a military cut,' I replied. The second it was done, I regretted it. I've always hated really short hair and have no idea why I decided to do that. Lesson learned.

* * *

My first big competition in 1983 representing Team USA was on 19 February in Yugoslavia. I had two fights; the first was against Redžep Redžepovski and was aired live on TV. I lost 3-0 according to the judges and when the result was read out, I thought, 'That's bullshit, man!' You could see a lot of people shaking their heads the moment the scores were announced. When you're in someone else's backyard, it happens sometimes. My good friend Jeff Fenech later fought him in the Olympic Games and also lost a controversial decision to him. Redžepovski would go on to win the silver medal at light-fly in LA a year later. Thankfully, three days later I fought against Nager Rugidi and won 2-1, so at least I finished off my trip to Yugoslavia on a high.

My next fight overseas was in London on 18 July, against Stephen Nolan, who was a tough kid, but I beat him. Then, on 15 October, the USA squad took on the Irish team in a competition in California and I was in against a really strong southpaw called Gerry Duddy. We had a very good team, including Michael Nunn and Mark Breland, but the Irish were tough.

I was wearing headgear for that fight. Duddy wasn't because it wasn't obligatory for the Irish like it was for us. Some fighters liked it, others didn't. For me, I saw nothing wrong with a little bit of padding around the head.

The first half of the first round it was even, then I tagged him and Duddy took an eight count. The second round was close, but I felt I was applying the pressure and landing more and the last round he came on real strong. When the final bell went, the crowd stood up and started cheering like crazy, just in appreciation of the fight. I won by split decision, but I think the fans won that day.

Not long after, I was back on a plane to fight in a competition in Calgary, Canada. I went out with my coach Bob King, who's a great guy and I'm still in touch with him now. Bob had his own club in LA called The Central City Boxing Club, which fought against Victor Valenzuela's fighters a few times. Right now, the LA Lakers arena is right where his gym used to be.

In 1983, Bob received a call to select a team to fight against the Canadian squad, all expenses paid. He said, 'That's fine. Just tell me what you need.' They were all open fighters, all really experienced, so he just needed to select the weights.

Although we were representing the USA team, it was with a California squad. The legendary world champion Archie Moore, 'The Mongoose', was with us as one of the coaches. I was young at the time and didn't fully appreciate the great fighters back then, which was a real shame. I was like, 'OK. That's Archie Moore.' People were going over and speaking with him, getting autographs and having pictures taken. Now I'd be like, 'Wow! It's Archie Moore! The legend,' then I'd run over and want to speak with him and without a doubt take a selfie. What I do remember about him was his relaxed manner and the way he came across as being a very wise man. You'd see him looking at the fighters and then making small comments after, which made total sense.

The Canadians treated us very well, took us places to visit and gave us all the food we wanted to eat. Then, when it came to the day of the weigh-in, it was no surprise that I couldn't make weight. I took some drastic measures, which then backfired on me when I least expected.

On the night of the fight, I said to Bob in the dressing room, 'Coach, I don't feel great. I'm having a problem.' Bob looks at me a bit strange and says, 'What's wrong?' 'I have to go to the bathroom.' 'What do you mean you have to go to the bathroom? You're about to fight in a minute.' 'I couldn't make weight, so I took an Ex-Lax.' 'Why the hell did you do that?' Let's just say I had to go to the toilet a number of times. Thankfully, I managed to make it to the ring and went on to win the fight.

I had some great trips that year with Bob. Never a dull moment. Another time, a Puerto Rican team came to fight us. They had a group of pretty good boxers, like John John Molina, who became super featherweight champion of the world a few years later. They had us lined up in weight order at the Olympic auditorium in Los Angeles, with the Puerto Ricans on one side and the Americans facing them on the other. When I was in front of my opponent, I started shadow boxing and talking to myself, saying, 'I'm gonna get me a Puerto Rican. I'm gonna get me a Puerto Rican!' Everybody started laughing. I ended up beating my opponent, which would have been very embarrassing if I hadn't after all my cockiness!

By the end of 1983, I was listed as number eight in the overall national amateur rankings, with Todd Hickman first and Steve McCrory second. I'd clash with Steve in the not-too-distant future. Thankfully, my international travels continued and my next outing overseas would turn out to be my most memorable.

CHAPTER 8

COLD WAR

*'Paul was a real good guy who was always
smiling, trained hard, tough as nails
and fought like the devil'*

Henry Tillman

BEFORE heading off to Moscow, me, Ricky and
Joey Belinc decided to go to the shopping mall
looking for odds and ends to take with us for the
trip. We always had problems with the military guys near
the training center because they were jealous of the US
Olympic team. On this day, there was a small group of three
who were much bigger than me and they started talking
shit. Ricky and Joey walked away and carried on with their
shopping, but in the meantime, it got heated with me and
these guys. We ended up having a long argument and one
of the military guys said, 'Let's step outside,' and I said,
'Yeah. Let's go.' Before we got to the door to go outside the
shopping mall, this guy started throwing punches at me and

talking more shit. I said, 'Fuck you,' and started to fight. Ricky's now appeared again and next thing this military guy pushed me and I went through this big-ass shop window behind me. This guy shouts, 'Oh shit' and runs off scared, while I'm lying on the floor covered in glass. Ricky says, 'You OK?' I said, 'Yeah, yeah, I'm good.' He then says all angry, 'We're not going to get to go Russia now because of this, you son of a bitch!' Somehow I didn't get hurt, but people were walking past trying to make a buck and say that they got cut from the glass, so they could sue the Colorado training center.

The police then turned up and straight after our Olympic assistant coach from the training center, Roosevelt Sanders, appeared. He was a former marine. We told him what had happened and we felt bad because he had this look of disappointment on his face. He said, 'Come on. Let's go back to camp.' To be honest, though, we were more worried about the grilling we'd get from lead coach Pat Nappy when we got back to the center, because he was even more disciplined than Roosevelt.

Next day we flew to Russia. Moscow was real cold, the food was nasty, but the people were cool and very polite to us. One thing I took for granted back then was that America had blacks, whites, Mexicans, Asians, a variety of cultures and nationalities, but they were all American citizens who'd grown up in the US. But in Russia, it was just Russians with no mix. Funnily enough, though, they all thought I was an Asian guy wearing a Team USA sweatsuit.

Asian, Mexican or American, that didn't stop me being popular with the ladies. I met a very pretty red-haired Russian girl at a club and when I say she was red-haired, I mean all over. Hairy arms, hairy legs, hairy armpits. Hairy! We had a kiss and a cuddle in my room and I remember her saying, 'My papa, if he find out', then she did the knife across the throat sign. I remember telling people, if I'd have got her pregnant, that would have been the only red-haired Mexican, Russian, American kid out there at the time and I would have been dead. That's when I replied to her straight away, 'OK! Time for you to go!'

* * *

Back then, it was billed as the USA versus the Soviet Union. My fight was on 27 January 1984 and I was facing Rashid Kabirov, who'd won the bronze medal at the 1983 European Championships. At that point, Russia's record against the US was 26-5, so the pressure was on me to bag a win in their own backyard. The added pressure was that 1984 was an Olympic year, with the Games being held in Los Angeles, so winning would get me one step closer to that dream.

After the weigh-ins, I did an interview and then me and Ricky walked to the elevator to get to the room. Next thing, Kabirov comes around the corner with his coach and now the four of us are walking to the elevator. I turned to Ricky and said, 'I think this is the guy I'm going to fight.' I then looked at the Russian and said, 'What weight you fighting?' 'Fifty-one kilos,' he replied. I then shouted at him, 'That's my weight. I'm gonna kick your fucking ass!' Kabirov looked at me a bit stunned and I don't think even understood what I'd said. Ricky started laughing really hard and didn't stop even after they'd jumped out of the elevator.

The Olympic Sports Complex Arena we fought at was built specifically for the 1980 Olympics boxing tournament, which the US boycotted. Three and a half years later and here we were making our first appearance for the US team. Incredibly, when the Olympics came around a few months later, Russia, along with 17 other countries, including Cuba, boycotted the Games, which was a real shame as those two countries alone had some of the best fighters on the planet.

Back to Moscow and the day of the fight. The complex was incredible. Even later, when I fought as a professional in Vegas and at the Inglewood Forum with full capacity, it was nothing compared to this. There were 17,000 people and while I was being introduced in the ring, I looked up waving and thought, 'Wow. That's a lot of people.' It was a huge, hostile crowd and it didn't help at the time that the US and Russia weren't getting along so good.

I felt I was robbed in Yugoslavia, so I wanted to be busier in this fight and not leave any doubt in the mind of the judges. There was also the added pressure of the fight being broadcast live on ABC's *Wide World of Sports*, so I knew there would be hundreds of thousands, if not a few million, looking at me.

From the opening bell, Kabirov was on the back foot trying to get me with his jab, counter punches and fancy footwork, but my aggression took him over and didn't allow him to get into the fight. By the second round, the Russians started booing their homeboy because he was not doing enough, whereas my coach, Bob Sanders, was using that to push me even more, shouting, 'Don't wait on him, Paul.' In the third and final round, I could hear the crowd screaming, 'U-S-A, U-S-A.' I managed to force Kabirov to take a standing eight count in that round and won the fight overall 3-0. Oh my God. What a rush.

Overall, the US team lost 8-3, with me, Todd Hickman and Paul Gonzales winning our bouts. That was my favorite fight representing the US Olympic team, hands down. The atmosphere, the size of the event and winning away from home made it that much more special. In my post-fight interview with Don Chevrier, you'll see me with a peach-fuzz moustache and big mop of hair saying that I was looking forward to coming home, training hard and getting that Olympic gold medal. I was getting ready to move up to the A-team and achieve my dream.

Mike Tyson was watching the fight with Cus D'Amato on television back in the US and when he saw me later, he said, 'You throw a lot of punches, man, a *lot* of punches!' That was the great thing about the camaraderie in that team; we all loved and supported each other. There was no social media back then, so if one of your team was on television we all watched and we all got excited. If one of your team won, we made a huge fuss, but if they lost, we made sure we were there for them to pick them up.

Zack liked Moscow so much that he went touring around the place and ended up staying after the trip to explore some more, but I just wanted to fight and get out of there. We stopped over in Sweden and Denmark on the way back and then headed to Los Angeles for the last leg of the journey.

After landing at LAX airport I looked out for Louie, who was my ride home. As I walked out of the arrivals gate, there he was with his brothers Juan and Danny, his friend Joe and Victor's brother-in-law, Gus – about seven or eight people in total. They all came over and made a real fuss, hugging and cheering me like I'd won Olympic gold. We then walked out of the airport, I said my goodbyes to the guys on the team and then the rest of us followed Louie as we all walked over to this big gold stretch limo. He says, 'Here we go.' I said, 'Yeah, right. I've been on the plane all day, I'm tired, I smell, need to wash and I'm ready to go to bed. I'm not in the mood for jokes. Where's your car at, Lou?'

Next thing, the trunk opens and Louie and the guys grabbed my bags and threw them in. Louie's brother-in-law then steps out and opens the door for me. I said, 'Are you kidding me?' Louie replies, 'It's no joke. We got you a limo.' You got to remember, this was in the early 80s. If you took a ride in a limousine, you were a superstar. I said, 'What!' As we started to drive out of the airport, I stood up in the limo and stuck my head out of the sunroof, shouting at everyone from the Olympic team, like, 'Look at me, look at me!'

What I didn't realize was that Victor, Louie and all the trainers at the gym rented the limo to pick me up at the airport. I'll never forget the ride and their generosity. But it didn't finish there. Instead of dropping me home, when we got to Azusa, we went straight to a restaurant and I thought, 'Cool. Let's get some food. I'm hungry.' But when I walked in, there was a surprise party for me. Everybody was there from the city, the gym, Victor, Victor's dad, his brothers, aunt Olga and uncle Don and many others. I couldn't believe it. What an unbelievable end to an incredible competition. I couldn't wait for what my future travels held in store for me.

* * *

On 25 February 1984, I returned to Canada, but this time I was fighting in Edmonton. I fought a guy called Bill Dunlop and beat him 3-0, then shortly after I was off to Thailand.

April 1984, we headed to Bangkok to fight in the King's Cup tournament, which was attended by most countries from around the world. Russians, Danish, Swedish, Koreans, you name it. On the way to Thailand, we stopped overnight in Japan. People used to steal towels, soap and stuff from the rooms, but when I saw the robes they had, I was like, 'Damn! This robe is nice. It's coming back with me.' I took that sucker home.

We were in Thailand for two weeks and it was hot. Really hot. Felt like 120 degrees. I remember walking down the road with future two-weight world champion Reggie Johnson, and we took off our shirts because of the heat. Seconds later, the cops came running over to us and told us to put our shirts back on. Someone said it was against the law to walk topless, but either way we didn't argue. One thing that really stood out when you walked around Thailand was that they worshipped Thai boxing like it was a God. Every town we went to, Thai boxing was on the television 24/7. Walk through a market, they're watching Thai boxing. Go to a restaurant, Thai boxing. Walk into a shop, Thai boxing.

It was crazy. I distinctly remember walking around town with this guy from Bangkok and he pointed out this little kid to us who was eight years old. He said he was in charge of feeding the household and taking care of the family. I said, 'What do you mean?' The guy replied, 'He fights in Thai boxing and gets paid and that's what his family survives off.' I couldn't believe that.

I fought against a guy called Kuanmuang Klinchan and he beat me on points. Shortly after the fight, these three Thai guys at the arena came over and started speaking shit to me. I said, 'Fuck you.' I'd lost my fight and was already pissed off. Then one of the guys said, 'You guys like Thai boxing? You wanna go outside and Thai box?' I turned sissy! I was like, 'Nah.' Reggie Johnson turns to me and says, 'I thought you were gonna kick their ass.' 'Hell no. That Thai boxing is some crazy stuff. It's no joke. They'll beat the shit out of me,' I replied.

Something else that was no joke was the 1984 US Olympic boxing trials. This was the dream I'd been aiming for since I first laced up the gloves and now it was finally here.

CHAPTER 9

SHATTERED DREAMS

'When you suffer an attack of nerves, you're being attacked by the nervous system. What chance has a man got against a system?'

Russell Hoban

O N 6 June 1984, in Fort Worth, Texas, I was up against Ronnie Rentz in the quarter-finals. Ronnie was a big bad boy who had beaten me fair and square a few years earlier in a close fight. I think he may have even dropped me. However, this time round, I beat him 5-0. The day after, I remember looking at the papers and I got front page with a color picture. It was one of the first times I'd seen a color photo of me in the press.

I now knew I'd be facing Steve McCrory, brother of world champ Milton, on 9 June. Steve was a really well-respected fighter who had fought in the Pan American Games, the World Cup Games and was definitely the favorite. I knew

I would have my work cut out as the underdog, but that motivated me. Then something happened in that fight that never happened to me before. I choked. I choked badly because the pressure got to me. The night before, I was like, 'I'm fighting Steve McCrory tomorrow. Oh my God. Whoever wins gets the chance to get one step closer to fighting in the Olympic Games.'

First and second rounds I lost simply because I didn't do enough, which was the total opposite of a fighter like me who never stops. Third round, I knew I was behind and just went for him. I guess the pressure was off me now to an extent and I felt confident pushing him and came close to dropping him. Unfortunately, it was too little too late and I lost. My Olympic dream had been shattered.

That fight hurt me so much and I won't lie, I cried that night. When I went back to my room, I was so upset I wanted to commit suicide. I'm not saying I was going to, but that's how low I felt.

Steve went on to win the final and later that year won Olympic gold. I guess, if you're going to lose to an opponent, why not lose to the eventual gold medallist? In fact, take a look at the people who fought in the trials and the guys who eventually went to the Olympics. I think it's fair to say that 1984 had some of the best US boxers competing together at any one time. Look at what we accomplished at those Games and how many medals we got. Also, take a look at how many fighters in the team, from the trial stage right through to qualification, who went on to either medal or become world champions as pros. I was honored to have been a part of it all.

A month later, me and Louie decided to go to the Los Angeles Sports Arena to watch the Olympic boxing semifinals and give some support to our boys. My right hand was in a cast, though. Here's what happened. I started doing odd jobs and working in construction to get some cash. Zack Padilla's family, who were all big and tough, worked in construction making cement and I ended up working with him for about a year on and off.

Back then, it seemed like it was all Chicanos working in construction. Anyway, one day I was using this big air compression machine and bang. It came down on my right hand and chopped a third of my index finger clean off. I went to the hospital, but they didn't have the other piece of my finger, so they just stitched the end up and now I've got one short finger. I thought it might affect my boxing or maybe the way I'd need my hand wrapping or clench a fist, but thankfully it never did. The only thing it did affect was my ability to open beer bottles! You got to twist those suckers open and when you're missing part of a finger, it ain't that easy.

Nowadays, I joke and say my first wife bit it off and if I want to annoy Zack when we're talking, I'll stick the finger up my nose. Zack will look at me and say, 'Don't do that, man! It's disgusting.'

Back to the Olympic trials. As I was watching, it was hard to believe only a few weeks before I was fighting alongside these guys, looking to qualify, whereas now I was watching them one step away from getting a medal in the actual Olympics.

At the end of the fights, I was walking out when I bumped into former WBC heavyweight champion Ken Norton. I always respected Ken for the fights he had with Muhammad Ali and was proud that he even knew who I was. I was even more shocked when he handed me his business card and said, 'If you think of going pro, let me know.' At that point, I hadn't given it much thought as a lot of people kept saying to me, 'Stick around for the next Olympic Games,' as I was only 20. I never did call Ken, which is something I regretted.

As we walked from the arena, everyone was spilling out and there was traffic everywhere in the parking lot. Next thing, this Rolls-Royce pulls up and I hear this distinct voice. 'Hey Pauli, come here, come here.' Louie turns to me and says, 'Who's that?' 'That's Mike Tyson. He's a bad dude,' I replied. At that point, Mike was known but he had nowhere near the profile he was going to get as a pro. He made a big name as an amateur then started to fade because he didn't make the Olympic team when he lost out against Henry Tillman. After that, all the media focus went on the fighters who were boxing for medals. Boxing's a fickle sport at times.

I walked over, shook his hand and said, 'Hey Mike. This is my boy, Louie.' Mike says hello to Louie then says, 'Pauli. You gonna turn pro or stay amateur?' 'I'm gonna stay amateur for a little bit,' I said. 'I'm a go pro, man,' he replied. 'I wish you the best, Mike. Good luck.' We talked for a bit and then he took off. As it goes, we both turned pro the year after in 1985, within five months of each other.

I remained an amateur boxer for about another year and had more memorable trips overseas, one of which was in Venezuela. We flew into Caracas airport and were fighting in some small town called Barquisimeto. The competition was like a military tournament and I lost out there, but it was a great experience.

After the fight, we were hungry and all we wanted to do was go and eat. I was the only guy with Mexican roots on the team. Everyone else was white or black and, as always, the rest of the team assumed I spoke the language and said, 'Where we going to eat, Paul?' 'I don't know,' I replied. The only words I knew were 'pollo [pronounced poyo]', Spanish for chicken, and what I called 'papas' for potatoes. When we found somewhere that was serving food, I was standing there doing an impression of a chicken, flapping my arms like wings while the other guys were dying of laughter. In the end, the lady said, 'Ah, pollo y patatas!' I was like, 'Yeah, poyo and papas.' Either way, we ended up getting our chicken and French fries!

Barquisimeto was a tough little place. We saw a lot of people living in houses made from either plywood or cardboard and were told to not walk around certain areas, especially at night-time. On this particular day, it was getting late and we decided to explore. Next thing, this jeep pulls up and four soldiers jump out with rifles and grab a hold of us. We all had our team sweats on and were trying to be cool and said, 'We're the USA boxing team.' There was about six or seven of us and they had us with our hands up in the air, spreading our legs, checking us for God knows what. We were scared shitless. The guys said to me again, 'Paul. Say something.' I replied, 'For the last time, I don't speak Spanish!'

They wanted ID, but we didn't have anything on us. They started fucking with us, shouting while pointing their guns at us, which was scary. We went out thinking we might go to town and get laid, but we were now worried that we were going to get whacked. They let us go in the end, but that episode scared the shit out of me.

Not long after, I fought in the USA National Championships and lost to Eugene Speed, then in March 1985 I took part in a USA versus Korea competition in Vegas. As usual, I had good support and remember my uncle Don coming to watch me for this one.

I was up against Moon Sung-kil, who was a bad boy. He'd beat Robert Shannon in the third round of the Olympics in LA, then lost to Pedro Nolasco in the quarter-finals. As a pro, he'd go on to become a two-weight world champion. That night in 1985, Moon tagged me bad. Beat the shit out of me. I ended up losing in the third round when the referee stopped the contest. Something about those Koreans. They're tough! I'd meet another further down the line as a professional, but that contest would be far more memorable.

With the Olympics three years away, I decided it was time to go pro. I was proud of what I'd achieved as an amateur, but wanted to make some money from boxing. As opposed to the amateurs, where my goal was to win a gold medal, I didn't have any aims as a pro. Who knew what lay ahead for me?

CHAPTER 10

HIGH GROUND

*'I saw Paul fight a few times at the Inglewood
Forum. He was a warrior. He came to fight. There
was no trying to find him, Paul Banke was always
there right in front of you. He was an excellent
counter puncher and he had power in both hands.
His fans were standing on their seats going crazy,
cheering the action'*

Carlos Palomino, WBC welterweight
champion, 1976–79

AFTER nine years of amateur boxing, I'd fought 176 times, had 150 wins and 26 losses. I wound up ranked fourth in the US in my weight category, never won the nationals, but was always in the mix. My dream of fighting in the Olympics never happened, which is a shame, because that makes your stock rise like crazy as a pro.

Instead, I decided to re-establish myself to a new section of the general public – the fans who only followed pro boxing. I set off on my new journey with no expectations but to simply be the best pro boxer I could be.

When I decided to turn pro, I also moved out of uncle Don and aunt Olga's. I'll always be grateful that they took care of me for over six years. One thing I didn't realize was going to have a big impact on my life when I left that house was the discipline. Without that, I started to make choices and take risks I wouldn't have previously done under their guidance.

On 3 August 1985, I made my debut against a fighter called Elmer Mejia at the Pony Express, Phoenix. It was my opponent's first fight also, so I was kind of confident, but this is pro boxing, so there were differences. The hand wrapping, the gloves were smaller and there was no head gear. There was a bit of pressure but I thought, with my amateur experience, I'd be OK, especially as my style as an amateur was very similar to how many of the pros fight – aggressively.

I won the fight by second-round KO and I'll be honest, it felt good. Then, three weeks later, I knocked out Mike Perez at the Pride Pavilion, Phoenix.

Three months after Perez, I fought Miguel Rodella for $1,500 and knocked him out in the second round. I don't remember much about Rodella, but what I do remember on the night was there was a timing problem and the rounds were only 90 seconds. Instead of investing my money, I bought cocaine with that purse.

I was also still working construction because I needed a steady income. You'll find a lot of boxers still take on the same kind of work. Construction, working the fields, postman, because many don't have an education and many come from deprived areas. But what little money I did earn went straight back into drugs.

Three days after Rodella, I beat Juvenal Molina over four rounds on points. After clocking up a further three wins, on 5 August 1986 I was up against Pete Solarez, who I was odds-on favorite to beat. I knew Pete before the fight as we used to train out of Willy Borchert's gym as amateurs and had sparred many times. Despite being the underdog, Pete beat me on points. I didn't take my first loss well and decided to retire. What I did over the next eight months wasn't great.

* * *

When I fought Pete, I was having problems outside the ring that were affecting me badly. That's not taking anything away from Pete as we're friends today and I respect him as a good fighter. It's also worth pointing out that my problems didn't happen overnight, either.

Stability in my pro career was nowhere near as good as my amateur days. I started out as a pro being coached by Tony Serda, who was training Richie Sandoval, then I moved on to Dave Rodriguez for a few fights then went through a number of other trainers throughout the rest of my career. There was one main reason why, or should I say one word. Drugs.

I'll be straight with you. When I lost against Pete, it hurt bad and I hit the drugs. Cocaine mainly at that time.

The thing is, drugs weren't a new thing in my life at that point. Far from it.

When I was about 14 or 15, I experimented with some marijuana but the summer of 1985, just before my pro debut, was the first time I stuck a needle in my arm. I'd moved back to Blythe and started seeing my little brother, and that's when it started.

Everyone thinks you start using drugs at a party, but it wasn't like that. I was just round at someone's house and there were a few people there getting high, so I thought, 'Let me try this.' I wanted to experience something new back then, but I never once thought how this could jeopardize my career as a professional boxer. Never once. If I could go back in time and change one moment, that would be it. That first needle, that first taste of hard drugs, would eventually wreck my life, my family and my boxing. Who knows how my life would have turned out either way, but I'm sure it would have been better without drugs in it.

Heroin was the first thing I injected, but I didn't like the high that came with it. I could never do heroin back to back as it messed me up too badly, too quickly, so I used crystal meth. That became my drug of choice for the coming years.

The thing is, I used to hate needles before I started drugs. Really hated them. But then I started to slam heroin and coke into my arms. On the streets they don't say 'slamming', they say 'mainlining', which means, straight into the vein. When you smoke hard drugs you're high for maybe a couple of hours, but when you inject you're high for about six or seven hours.

As I injected it, it made me cough. You hit the vein, and I don't mean to glorify it, but when you hit it through your veins, it makes you feel like you're having an orgasm. Many times I used to walk away from other people, because I thought I'd come in my pants after injecting.

Snort it, smoke it, it has its effect, but mainline it and your heart starts pumping and it's a rush. A big rush. Do I miss that feeling? Hell no. I don't like thinking about it because there's still that appeal. It takes everything that's good in your life and then takes it away from you. That's the bottom line. But back then, I wasn't looking that far ahead. I wish I had, though.

The drugs not only had an effect on me physically. As a fighter, I was going through a lot of managers and trainers because they were struggling with my behavior and lack of discipline.

My mom summed me up perfectly back then.

> The gym was a second home, the ring was his playground, the other boxers were his playmates. He was constantly trained and told what to do. But outside the ring, and outside that environment, he lacked the skills to live life. He was very, very sheltered. For him to come out and socialize, it was like a candy store. *(Thecomeback.com, 12 September 2011).*

Around this time, I reconnected with my little brother Tim. I was only 21 and we hung out in Venice Beach. Venice has everything there. There's no discrimination, anything went. Transexual, drag, gay, all races, Rastas, you name it. We lived in a one-bed apartment that you could see right into from the street, and sometimes I'd be lying on one side of the bed and he'd be lying on the other as we both watched television. People would look through the window and because I was dark, he was white and we were both in bed, people in the area assumed we were a couple.

If I was looking to focus on my boxing and steer clear of the drugs, this was the wrong place to be. We're all products of our environment and this was without doubt the wrong environment to be wrapped up in with the drugs available.

Me and Tim, being young, decided we were going to be bums and started doing drugs daily. Whatever we could get our hands on. Our mom said, 'I'm not putting up with this, you need to get out of the house.' Tim said, 'Where we going?' and I said, 'Blythe.' I called my dad and then we got on the bus and headed to his and my grandpa's house. We stayed there for a couple of months and got fucked up most days.

I hadn't seen my dad much at that point, maybe ten times, and although he wasn't Tim's dad, he was cool with us staying. My dad and grandpa were good people. I miss my grandpa and I wish I would have listened to him more, found out more about him and the Banke heritage from the Basque country, but all I did was get high. In the end, it was my late aunt Aimee who asked us to leave. She used to walk in the house and see us getting high, and after a while, enough was enough. We ended up going over and staying at my cousin Willy's house.

Thankfully, boxing helped me to get back some focus in my life, even if I wasn't living the true life of a fighter.

CHAPTER 11

CAREER BLOW

'First time I met Paul is when I fought him.
I heard a lot about Paul Banke going into that
fight and knew he was a great fighter from the
amateurs. On top of that, he was a southpaw.
That night, he fought a great fight. He put a lot
of pressure on me and came at me from all angles.
He threw punches in bunches and he could take a
punch. I could tell from that performance that he
was going to be a great champion – which he was.
He's very humble, inside and outside of the ring.
He never bad-mouthed any opponent. That says a
lot about him as a person and a boxer'

Hector Lizarraga, IBF featherweight champion, 1997

THE problem with Vegas was that the drugs were far too easy for me to get, so after the Solarez fight I went back to Blythe, California. However, after an eight-month blowout, strung out on drugs, I fought Andre Smith in Santa Monica. My comeback didn't go as planned.

Smith had an unbeaten 9-0 record at the time with eight knockouts and was a natural super featherweight, a 130lbs fighter. I'd just come off a loss, went off the rails for a few months and was a 122lbs fighter. Maybe this wasn't the best fight for me on my return.

That said, I got myself in good shape for Smith and lost a really close majority decision over eight rounds, which many thought I'd won. My main recollection of the fight wasn't Smith, though, but the fact that O.J. Simpson was in the crowd that night. I didn't know it at the time, but it turns out he was a friend of Smith's.

In the next ten weeks, I had three fights. The first two I won by knockout, which was a big confidence-booster, and the third one, against Hector Lizarraga, I won comfortably on points over the distance. It was the first time, in fact, that I'd gone ten rounds.

After that fight, me and Hector kept seeing each other at different shows and kept in touch. We earned each other's respect in our fight and became good friends. I'd like to say a few words about Hector. When I fought him, his record was 5-6-3 as a professional. On paper, he was a journeyman as he'd lost more than he'd won, although some of those losses were debatable.

Then he did the unthinkable after we fought. In his next 33 fights, he only lost one and ten years after our battle, he became IBF featherweight champion of the world. How's that for a comeback? Four weeks later, with short notice, I was back in the ring against Jesus Poll, who was unbeaten in

14 fights. For the sake of a few grand, I should have turned down the fight. But that was never me.

Poll was a good boxer. I'd seen him in the amateurs and knew he'd come to fight. The vacant USA California State featherweight title was on the line over a scheduled 12 rounds. I only had ten days to prepare and, even worse, I did dope in the locker room before the fight that night. I'd put some dope in my sock and just before I put my gloves on in the bathroom, I took the crystal meth out and took a little snort.

I was really not in any condition to be in a boxing ring, or any other place that required any thought or co-ordination. I did dope twice before fights, in that one and in my very last fight against Juan Francisco Soto. That's crazy. I was behind on the scorecards by round six, then in the seventh Poll caught me. I went down, got up, went down, got up, went down, got up. After three knockdowns, the fight was over.

My professional boxing record now stood at 10-3, with three losses in my last six fights. This is not the way I intended my pro career to pan out. In the end, it wasn't a 'how' but a 'who' that got me back on track.

CHAPTER 12

ALL HEART

*'I knew he had a drug history, I went in with my
eyes open. But I also thought he had a lot of talent,
that he could go places if he was guided right. And
I knew that deep down he wanted to put his drug
problem behind him'*

Bob Richardson, *Los Angeles Times*, 30 March 1989

FOUR months after the loss to Poll, I was back in
the ring against Ramon Rico. I hadn't cleaned my
act up. I was always slamming dope and don't even
remember the fight if I'm honest. All I know is that I won
a points decision over ten rounds in San José.

Then, shortly after the Rico fight, I was given an
opportunity, a serious boxing opportunity that could move
me up the world rankings. I was asked if I'd like to fight in the
Stroh's tournament at the Forum, Inglewood, California. All
the fights were going to be shown live on national cable TV,
which meant huge exposure and the winner would move up in
the world rankings. Here's how the opportunity came about.

I was living in Blythe and getting high all the time, which was obviously messing with my boxing. This guy called Bob Richardson brought in me and Eddie Rodriguez to spar with some boxer, basically to keep this guy in shape. I forget the name of the fighter we'd been brought in to spar, but the second I arrived at the camp, I remember thinking, 'Wow. This is nice. Really nice.' Me and Eddie beat the crap out of this guy and after the sparring was done, Bob said he wanted to keep me on in camp.

However, if I stayed, it came with conditions. I looked at Bob's set-up and thought, 'This guy's got a nice house by a lake, they're good people, he's got it going on. Time to get my shit straight.' Bob was aware that I was doing drugs and said, 'Do you really want to be in this tournament? You need to get off the drugs. Then we can show everyone the real Paul Banke. Stay with us and we'll take care of you.'

That's where my nickname, 'The Real' Paul Banke, came from.

By living on site, Bob tried to keep me clean whether I had a fight coming up or not. He wanted to keep me in check at the weekends because he couldn't trust me. He wanted to change my mindset of doing dope when I wasn't training, which had become a natural thing by now. In addition to having drug tests every week and being confined to the camp, I had to attend rehab in Redwood. On top of that, Bob made sure that I was tested a lot while at the camp. I couldn't tell you how many times exactly. Thirty, maybe 40.

The problem was, I couldn't stop taking drugs. I failed all the tests apart from one. I owe a lot to Bob because even though I kept failing these tests, he never gave up on me. He wanted to see me clean.

From the time I started smoking marijuana, I'd end up smoking too much marijuana. Started doing coke, too much coke. Same with speed and crystal meth. I knew I had an addiction problem from early on but just couldn't and wouldn't stop. I had to be an actor around people. In the gym, outside, wherever. I kept having to say to myself, 'Play it off like you're not high.' I'd keep repeating that to myself again and again. If you look at some of my photos back then, my face looked all sucked up because I was that high.

I remember everyone asking, 'How do you get speed while you're at Bob Richardson's camp?' I knew a girl who lived at the top of the hill and she'd have speed in a can for me. She'd drive by and put it by the side of the road and after my runs, I'd go back and pick up the can. You have to remember that this was a very rural area, so nobody was around to see me pick up the can. I also got people to mail it to me. I'd give them money and they'd mail me. In general, though, I could always find drugs. Wherever I was, anywhere in the world, I could walk into a place and instantly tell if someone had anything to sell. You become tuned to that.

* * *

Not many people know this, but Bob did the gym as a labor of love. Bob Richardson owned a successful roofing company with over 350 employees, and sunk hundreds of thousands of dollars into the gym, not even knowing if it would ever break even. Who knows if it ever did? He certainly didn't do it for the money. When he took a fighter on, he did it with his heart and with good intentions.

In addition to housing, feeding and keeping me away from the temptations of the city, Bob also gave me a hundred bucks a week, which back in 1988 was a lot. With all that, I basically didn't need to spend any money. It was similar to the Olympic center in Colorado.

Bob Richardson kind of became my new uncle Don. A true father figure. In pro boxing, he was the man who made me. Bob was straight up with me about how the drugs were taking over my life and constantly gave it to me both barrels if I didn't listen. I loved Bob.

However, it wasn't all smooth sailing. We often had a love-hate relationship, hugs one minute and blazing rows the next, but it was no different to how fathers and sons would be. Bottom line is, I used to listen to him. He was a smart man. He used to tell me things like getting involved in real estate and told me how to carry myself. He told me to dress respectfully and not like a homeboy or I'd get treated like a bum. To make that good first impression and look like a clean-cut athlete. Short hair, no goatee beard, no stubble or anything like that.

The camp itself was incredible. It was called 'All Heart Boxing' and set in five acres of beautiful grounds. We had some great fighters working out there like Al Long, Levi

Billups, Russell Mitchell, Greg Haugen, Tyrell Biggs, Carl 'The Truth' Williams and Juan Laporte.

One thing I'd always been good at as an amateur was running, but at Bob's camp I took it to another level. Nobody could beat me on that camp. Everyone knew I was getting special treatment from Bob, but nobody trained harder than me. I remember at the time doing an interview for *The Ring* magazine and they asked how hard I was training. I said, 'I'm training harder than Mike Tyson,' at a time when Mike was in his heyday.

We used to do this 6.2-mile hill course near Canyon Lake and I'd often do it in 36 minutes or slightly under. That's sub six-minute miles. There was a group of about five or six boxers who'd do the run with me and I ran my ass off to make sure nobody beat me up that hill. I had this truck in front of me, which was like my rabbit. When I was running, I used to tell the driver to step on it to help give me a good pace. I used to see him looking behind like, 'How the hell is this guy keeping up?' I loved those runs.

I said nobody could beat me on that run, but that was until this group of fighters from Kenya, Africa came over. Whoa! They kicked my ass. I was running under six-minute miles up this hill and they were leaving me standing. I thought I was badass and cocky, but these guys could run. Fast!

Those runs would provide me with extra stamina and that's exactly what I needed going into LA's biggest boxing competition of 1988.

CHAPTER 13

NO HORSING AROUND

*'I enjoy competition. I enjoy challenges. If a
challenge is in front of me and it appeals to me,
I will go ahead and conquer it'*

Conor McGregor

I N 1988, if you were looking to climb up the world
rankings and also bag some cash, the Stroh's tournament
was where you needed to be. If you won all four fights,
there was a chance you'd be a few steps away from fighting
for a world title. Three or four days before the tournament,
I met this guy at the hotel I was staying at and I got some
dope off him. Not a lot. A line of speed. I stayed up all
night. Not ideal, but I had to deal with it.

My first fight was against Lucilo Nolasco from the
Dominican Republic on 7 March 1988. For the Stroh's
tournament, every fight was televised and getting huge
media attention, so one of the things you could really pick
up on was my staredowns of my opponents. There wasn't

any! I never liked to look the other fighter in the face when the instructions were being read out. When I got in the ring, I always stared down at the floor. That was throughout my amateur and pro career. I just didn't have a poker face.

One routine I started doing when I boxed professionally, which I didn't do as an amateur, was the need to be hit first. My mom used to say, 'In order for Pauli to get off in the ring, he had to be hit hard by the opponent. That then set something off inside of him and he went for it. But until he was hit, he couldn't fight.' That was so true. As an amateur, I had boxing skills. I was never a banger, so I didn't need to get hit to get going, but as a pro, it made me relax and loosen up. When I got in the ring, I was like, 'Hit me. Get those cobwebs off me now instead of later.' Once my opponent did that, I was ready to mix it up. That broke the ice. Never mind throw the jab, slip, slip, slip. Bullshit. Let's land that first punch, boom, and we're off.

Another thing I did during the pros was to never allow anyone to touch me when I walked to the ring. I'd put my hood down on my gown, put my hands on the trainer's shoulders and lower my head. I was in my zone and wanted to get into battle. I came out firing and never backed down or quit.

Back to Nolasco. He was really respectful, but he was no joke. The fight turned into a war. His record might not show it, but he was world-level material. He had much better skills than I did and also had hurtful power, but I used my boxing ringcraft to beat him over the full ten rounds.

Straight after the fight, the owner of the LA Lakers, the Inglewood Forum and the organizer of the tournament, Dr Jerry Buss, came over by the ring, grabbed my hand and said, 'Awesome fight! You gonna be my fighter!' For the next few fights, he became my promoter. At the time, I was well known, but not a household name. Having Dr Buss on board more than helped in that direction. I think he loved boxing more than basketball. The basketball made him money, but if you saw the way he was around the boxing, it was another level of excitement.

After the Nolasco fight, Bob Richardson bought my pro contract for $1,000 and officially became my manager, which I was really happy with.

Not many people would have taken the risk, time and genuine interest in me the way Bob did, and I'll always be grateful for that.

I've been asked many times before if I've ever had my nose, teeth or jaw broken. The answer is, never. In over 200 fights as an amateur and pro, that's not bad going. However, six days after the Nolasco fight, on 13 March 1988, I had a nose operation because I couldn't breathe through it. Although I hadn't broken my nose before, the area around it had taken a lot of punches and that had caused damage. They removed my cartilage and I was good to go.

Two months after Nolasco, I was up against Alberto Mercado in the quarter-finals. My training for this fight went really well, but I almost pulled out because of something tragic that happened only a few days before.

When I started training at Bob Richardson's boxing gym, Ray Luna became my trainer. I'd grown fond of Ray as he'd put his heart and soul into making me a better fighter from day one. Then, a few days before the Mercado fight, I walked into Ray Luna's room in Bob Richardson's house on the lake and found him dead. His face was purple and he was laying in bed sideways completely motionless, with his arm out, almost like he was reaching over for something. Perhaps his heart pills. I'm not sure, but that's how I found him. I shouted out to him, 'Ray, Ray!' But he didn't raise up. I ran out of the room screaming, 'Ray's dead! Ray's dead! Help!' I made a big old scene. I was scared.

I decided that I was pulling out of the fight. I was so stressed that I temporarily started to lose my hair. A couple of fights later, you can actually see I had a bald spot and had to see a dermatologist to help make the hair grow back. Thankfully, my friends convinced me to get back in the ring, telling me that Ray would have wanted me to fight on. So that's what I did. I fought for Ray that night and dedicated the rest of the tournament to him.

Ray would always be a tough act to follow for any trainer, but the man who stepped in, Steve Rosenzweig, was a natural successor and did a great job. Steve had actually been a high school teacher for over 30 years, so here's how he got into becoming a boxing trainer. Ray was pretty much retired in boxing when Bob convinced him to make a comeback and be the principal trainer at All Heart Boxing Club. This was long before I'd started to train there. I don't know what Bob offered him, but it worked.

Ray would be in the boxing gym three or four hours a day and he would teach Steve. He taught him about the fighter's mentality and things that would have taken Steve a lifetime to learn. Ray had connections in boxing that shortcutted All Heart Boxing's development by 30 years. At first, a lot of stuff Ray taught Steve, he thought, 'I can't buy this.' But he learned over time that he was right. Bob moved Ray from Palm Springs to his house at the lake and the gym was built at the back of Steve's property. In Steve's words, 'He taught me 90 per cent of everything I ever knew. He was a hell of a man.'

With Steve in my corner, I knocked out Mercado in three rounds on 9 May 1988. The Puerto Rican had fought 39 times as a professional by this point and won 30, with 26 beaten inside the distance. He had only been stopped three times himself. He was 27 years old and was still a big threat. Beating him made a statement, but stopping him made an even bigger one.

One thing I'd noticed by now was the level of support I was getting at the Forum. When I started out as a pro, because I looked Mexican, they'd always cheer for the other guy. Then I started winning, I made a name for myself and everyone in Cali became very loyal to me. It's the same with any sport. If you're a baseball player and don't score home runs, you ain't going to be too popular, but if you start scoring those home runs, the second you get up to bat, they'll start cheering you. When I started to win, people started to realize that I was an exciting fighter and that I was a crowd-pleaser.

Next up was Robert Shannon, the man who'd stopped me as an amateur in the semi-finals of the ABF National Championships and then went on to compete in the Olympic Games in 1984. So here I was in the semi-finals of the Stroh's tournament up against Shannon again, and I won't lie, the moment I found out I was fighting him, I was scared. That stoppage defeat in the amateurs was at the back of my mind. He was also now trained by Angelo Dundee, the man behind a long list of great boxers such as Muhammad Ali, Sugar Ray Leonard, Willie Pastrano, Wilfredo Gomez and many others. That got me even more nervous.

However, this time, my head was straight and the nerves helped to push me to my limits. I ended up beating him over ten rounds in what turned out to be a great fight. The tactics weren't very scientific. I knew he had power, but I did what I did in all my fights. Took it to him, kept busy and kept in front of him. My defence was to keep coming forward. A memory from that fight was when I caught him with two consecutive low blows, right in the nuts.

Even Johnny Carson mentioned it and played the tape on *The Tonight Show*. To this day, Bob jokes that he couldn't have kids because of those punches below the belt. Thankfully, we've remained friends. It's a sport, the same as when we're playing baseball, basketball or football. We were friends before getting in the ring and remained friends after.

Beating Bob was a big boost mentally and gave me the confidence I needed going into the final on 13 September 1988 against Carlos Romero, from Venezuela. It was my fourth tough fight in six months. You wouldn't see that happen these days in tournaments at this level. You'd be lucky if they have four fights in two years.

For the Romero fight I was training in a gym in Utah for a month and a half, did some sparring with about five or six guys, altitude training, got my timing on point and was in great shape. Then I got the news that my grandma, Consuela, had passed away a week before, which was tough as we were real close. I wanted to go back for the funeral, but my family told me to stay where I was and stay in shape for the fight, which is what I did in the end.

Between Ray and my grandmother passing away, I was still suffering from hair loss and even 'Chick' Hearn, who was doing the commentary for the fight, mentioned my bald spot and how it had happened.

The fight against Romero was tough, man. I've used the term 'war' in many of my fights and this was no different. I guess the way I fought, my style, brought that out in me and my opponents. We stood toe to toe in the center of the ring, working inside the pocket. It was like fighting a mirror. I'd hit him to the body, he'd hit me to the body. I'd hit him to the head, he'd do the same. Neither man backing down and both working a similar game plan. The ref was hardly needed. In round six, we went for it. There were big exchanges that could have knocked either fighter out. As the bell rang for the end of the round, the crowd were cheering and whistling. Then, in round eight, he caught me with a body shot that hurt like hell. Bam. The second it landed, I had to hold on to see the round out.

In the tenth round, I must have landed over 70 power punches to his head. How he didn't hit the canvas, I don't know. But the attack hadn't gone to waste. In the 11th, I caught Romero with a straight right that literally spun him around. I knew I had him hurt and changed it up to the body, chopping him with three hooks. Next thing, 43 seconds into the round, Romero shook his head to say he'd had enough and turned away. He'd done a 'No Más', but what I didn't realize was that I'd broken his ribs. The fight was over. What a relief and what a fight.

The crowd loved it so much, they started throwing coins into the ring out of appreciation. So much so, they provided the commentators with hard hats. Straight after the contest, in an interview with *KO Magazine* (January 1989), I said, 'I can still fight better. The Romero fight took a lot out of me. The guy was tough. I got hit with too many jabs. Got hurt a couple of times.'

Something that helped with that hurt was the money. I'd received $25,000 for getting to the finals and was then presented a check in the ring, live on cable television, by comedian Arsenio Hall for $75,000 for winning. Arsenio had been sitting ringside with Rob Lowe watching the fight and had just made the movie *Coming to America* with Eddie Murphy, so he was a very big name. As he handed over the check, fans went crazy cheering for me – a moment I'll never forget. I made a point of thanking Bob for pulling me out of a hole and for giving me the opportunity to fight in the tournament. Once again, I dedicated the win to Ray Luna.

I even got love from the UK. Graham Houston wrote in *Boxing News* magazine, 'Banke, a southpaw slugger from southern California, stormed to the Inglewood Forum super bantamweight title with a series of sizzling wins at the Los Angeles arena.'

After the fight, we partied hard. Back then, Dr Jerry Buss would have parties at his house, which were crazy. His house was huge. Even the 'Brady Bunch' could have got lost in there. There I was, this cheeky little Chicano kid, being introduced to the likes of Sylvester Stallone, Magic Johnson, Jack Nicholson, the late, great John Candy, and many other guys I'd only ever seen on TV. For me, the whole lifestyle thing was all new. Dr Buss was taking me around introducing me to these guys, saying, 'This is my fighter, Paul Banke. He just won the Stroh's tournament.'

It was surreal, but a blessing to have had the opportunity to mix at that level.

* * *

A hundred thousand bucks was a lot of money back then and thankfully I had a clear enough head to spend it on something other than drugs or booze. I bought a motor home trailer, which I parked up on Bob's five-acre plot. I love my animals and also bought a horse and pigs. People think having pigs or horses is easy. No way. You gotta be there for them every day and it costs a lot of money. You've got to water and feed them every morning and evening, pay for vets, new horse shoes. It's no joke.

Something else that was not a joke was just around the corner in my professional boxing career. The moment all contenders dream of having.

CHAPTER 14

FIRST TIME FAILURE

'I met Paul Banke when I was doing commentary for Prime Network at The Forum on 7 March 1988 and Paul was fighting Lucilo Nolasco. That's when we became friends from there on. How I rated Paul Banke? He reminded me a lot of Bobby Chacon. A heart bigger than his body. Paul was quick and could crack a bit! I compare him to Carlos Zarate, Ruben Olivares, Alfonso Zamora – he was that kind of hitter. They don't make fighters like that any more!'

Ruben Castillo

FOUR months later, on 9 January 1989, I was back in the ring against Texan tough man Ramiro Adames, fighting for the vacant WBA Americas title. In all honesty, when I was asked to fight him, I didn't want to. He'd been in with some big names like Daniel Zaragoza and Roland Gomez, and had never been stopped before. He had 16 wins in 20 fights, 15 of those victories by stoppage, so he was known as a hard puncher. He was also ranked fifth in the world by the WBA at the time, whereas I was ranked 18th by the WBC. The media were already looking beyond me, saying how Adames would be fighting the WBA super bantamweight champion Juan José Estrada straight after me. I knew that I was going into the fight as the underdog, and as with Mercado and Romero, if I could stop him, I could make a statement. And that's exactly what happened.

Adames was a raw slugger, so I intended to box him behind my jab, keeping my distance until I felt an opening was available. At the end of the first round, my strategy paid off when I dropped him with a right-left combination. The next three rounds were brutal. Although I was in control, Adames was still looking to take me out with one big, clubbing shot and managed to land it in the fourth, cutting me over my right eye.

When I got cut, I'll admit, I was a little nervous. However, every time I threw a punch from then on, I caught him and cracked him. I cracked him good and just kept cracking him. Before the fourth round was up, I let loose with a combination of about eight punches and floored him again. His left eye was a mess and almost closed by now.

I could tell Adames was getting tired as he was missing a lot of punches. When you punch into thin air, it's worse than connecting in terms of losing energy. By the sixth, I knew he was there for the taking and I landed two left hooks to his head on the bounce. The moment the second one landed, he hit the canvas again. Although he wanted to carry on, his eye was completely shut and the referee did the right thing by stopping the contest. That fight gave me a really big rush, but the best part was that me and Adames became good friends after that fight.

KO Magazine wrote soon after, 'The 121lb weight class is among boxing's hottest, and Quail Valley, California's Banke may be the hottest junior featherweight in the world.' The *LA Times* also showed me some love on 21 January 1989, reporting, 'Banke, setting up in the ring, looks like a mini-Tyson, with his fists carried high against his jaw, his feet flat and spread apart. He wings in blows like cannon shots. He also has a set-up punch that collapses defences.'

At the time, the media were saying that the winner of my fight against Adames would fight the winner of the Juan José Estrada versus Jesus Poll fight, for the WBA 122lb title. That's a fight I really wanted. More than anything, I was hoping Poll would win because I wanted to get my revenge. I said on live television, 'I dare Poll to fight me if he wins... I owe him one.'

As it goes, Estrada stopped Poll in ten rounds and I never got the chance to fight either of them. However, every cloud has a silver lining and some luck was about to come my way.

* * *

Beating Adames moved me up in the world rankings and would help me get those bigger fights with bigger pay checks. Believe it or not, though, I only earned $4,500 for that fight, but that didn't matter. I was hungry. One week after the Adames fight, I was back in the gym.

I was now ranked second in the world by the WBA and fourth by the WBC, but the man everyone wanted to beat was WBC champ Daniel Zaragoza because that was seen as the most recognized belt and Zaragoza had beaten Carlos Zarate to get it in the first place.

Then came the call from Dr Buss. 'You're fighting Daniel Zaragoza for the WBC world super bantamweight title.' Oh my gosh. I was so excited. Money apart, Zaragoza was a legend and I couldn't wait to get in the ring with him. The fight was originally set for March 1989, but it had to be delayed until 22 June because Zaragoza burst an eardrum in sparring.

I went into training camp real confident because Zaragoza was seven years older and I thought his style was custom-made for me. That was probably my downfall, though, being over-confident. You always need to retain an element of being scared, being the challenger and being hungry. Step away from that mindset even just a bit and that can cost you the edge in a fight.

The training camp lasted six weeks and I had a great group of guys training me, consisting of Steve Rosenzweig, Sherman Henson and Mack Kurahara. Sherman used to box in the army and with that military discipline he used to push me that bit further and harder. Years later, a lot of that rubbed off on me when I started training fighters myself. I now make a person bust their ass in training, making them throw a lot of punches, keeping them busy and fit.

Sherman worked the mitts for this camp and one session I accidentally dropped him with a hook to the body that slipped past the mitt. He told me, 'I hold the body bag for Levi Billups and he's a heavyweight, but you hit a lot harder than Levi.' That was a big compliment because Levi was a good heavyweight who went on to share the ring with some great champions like Vitali Klitschko and Lennox Lewis.

However, it was Sherman's strength and conditioning training that was really valuable because we knew that Zaragoza had the engine to fight 12 full rounds at high speed and pressure. Sherman got me in the shape of my life and worked on me constantly moving during the fight, using my footwork while throwing combinations and working under pressure. He improved my overall work ethic.

What Sherman showed me made sense and I knew I could use it in the ring. The strategy was to put pressure on Zaragoza, let my hands go and counter with him. Sherman would say, 'When he lets his jab go, you jab with him and then you come back with a combination behind your jab.' Sometimes we'd still be in the gym working long after everyone else had gone home. Then, after we'd finished training, we'd sit down and talk or go out and eat, just to keep our boxing minds going.

It wasn't all serious with Sherman, though. One time, after one of my fights, we were travelling from Quail Valley to Utah and we stopped in Vegas at this Mexican restaurant. Sherman's African-American and I'm Mexican-American. We walk in and the people inside are speaking Spanish.

Sherman said, 'Paul, you understand what he said?' 'No. I was born here and raised here, man! I was going to ask you.' We both started laughing.

Mack Kurahara also worked the mitts for me, as well as being my cut man. In training he'd tell me, 'Remember one thing when you're in with Zaragoza. Kill him!' Obviously he was just trying to get me pumped up, not literally saying to kill him, just beat him up. 'Do the combo. Up and down, then to the side, one shot to the body, then move to the other side and do the rock 'n' roll and take him out and kill him.'

I knew Mack originally when I was an amateur, but got to know him well when I turned professional and was staying with Bob. Mack was one of those old-school people who didn't give a shit and I liked that. He went on to train six world champions and at the age of 86, he still trains fighters now.

Mack came with a great back story. He boxed in the US air force in the 1950s and went on to be inducted into the California Boxing Hall of Fame, received the Joe Louis humanitarian award and was inducted into the WBC Hall of Fame. He came with a wealth of knowledge. He also looked like the twin brother of the old guy from *The Karate Kid*, Mr Miyagi (played by Pat Morita).

Funnily enough, they were born in the same year and were very good friends. Whenever they were out together in big crowds and would walk away in separate directions, autograph hunters wouldn't know which way to go. Mack would point at Pat saying, 'That's the real Karate Kid, not me! I'm not Mr Miyagi.' Even when Pat died in 2005 and Mack was at his memorial, Ralph Macchio, who is Daniel-san in the film, said, 'Damn, you look like Pat!'

I had a good relationship with Mack and even after I finished with boxing and had my problems, we still kept in touch. To this day, once a week we call each other and it's a standing joke that whenever we speak he'll say, 'You in jail? Stay out of trouble!' and we both laugh.

Back to the team. Each person had their important role in my training camp but Steve was the principal guy. Nobody could motivate you like Steve. During a fight, he'd say things like, 'Knock this motherfucker out,' or 'I'd bet the house on you.' I'd get so pumped up listening to him.

The training camp went real good. The only problem going into this fight was me. I wanted to beat Zaragoza so badly to become world champion that I was too cocky and too ready for him.

* * *

On the night of the fight, I was interviewed live on television and they asked me how I saw it going. I said, 'I don't predict no knockouts. It's going to be 12 hard rounds.' And that's exactly the way it went. As Jimmy Lennon Jr was doing the announcements in the middle of the ring, I was bouncing up and down, but looking at the floor while shadow boxing. Zaragoza just stood there staring at me. I had a lot of nervous energy and just wanted the first bell to go.

The commentators on television, who included my good friend Ruben Castillo alongside the late, great Chick Hearn, said the worst thing I could do was try and trade with Zaragoza in the early rounds, but that's exactly what I did. For the whole fight, in fact. It seemed to work. He had a three-inch reach advantage, so by staying on him, it negated that advantage.

By the third round, you could hear chants of 'Ban-ke, Ban-ke, Ban-ke' from the 5,000-strong crowd, which got me really pumped up. If that didn't, then hearing Steve shouting, 'Head and body, Paul,' and 'Don't wait, Paul,' certainly did.

In the fourth round, I opened a cut over Zaragoza's right eye and it started streaming down his face, then 30 seconds later I caught him with a big left hook that almost took his head off. Somehow he didn't go down, but there was a massive roar from the crowd. I kept catching him with straight lefts and hooks on the cut for the rest of the round and bullied him up until the bell. At the end of the round, we had a staredown and started speaking to each other. The referee had to split us up.

Chick Hearn said in commentary, 'Banke's getting a little over-excited now,' and Ruben Castillo added, 'I just think he's trying to let Zaragoza know that he's the conductor of this orchestra.' At the press conference before the fight, I kept calling Zaragoza an old man, but let me tell you, he impressed the fuck out of me. Next round, I kept peppering the cut over the eye at every opportunity, but what spoilt the round for me was that I was getting cocky. Every time I dropped my hands or said something in front of Zaragoza, he'd unload and catch me and that gave him a clear round on the judges' scorecards. In fact, the first three rounds I was talking too much, then the next three I was posing too much. If I'd have kept my mouth shut and kept fighting, I might have impressed the judges more. At the end of the sixth, Steve said, 'Keep busy. You don't need to stand in front of him,' then Mack added, 'He's the champ. You gotta go get him.' In other words, stop showboating.

Seventh round, my footwork had become much slower and I was trading more. When I had good footwork in the first three rounds, I won them clearly, but now Zaragoza was winning rounds on his distance, jabs and his own footwork as I walked into punches. Just as things weren't going my way, in the last minute of the round I caught him with a left hook and his gumshield went flying. Seconds later, we clashed heads and it opened a cut on Zaragoza's head and I went for him, finishing the round strong. So strong, in fact, that I only sat down for about 30 seconds and walked over to the middle of the ring, eager to fight. The referee told me to get back in my corner. Just like my amateur days!

Round eight, I was all over him, in close, moving my feet again. That gave Zaragoza problems because of my speed and volumes. My corner kept shouting, 'Up and down. Up and down,' and that's exactly where I kept throwing the punches. I reopened the cut over his eye and that made Zaragoza even more cautious.

Halfway through round nine I tagged him with a right hook, then a left hook to the chin. About five seconds later, I repeated the same combination and Zaragoza was down. The crowd was going crazy as he got up on wobbly legs. I'd also opened up a new cut by his nose, under his left eye. His face was a mess. Big round for me. At the end of the round we did the staredown again, but this time he looked away first.

I talked a lot of shit before the fight but seeing how he got up when many other fighters would have stayed down impressed the shit out of me. He was still ready to fight and was very strong. He old-manned me and came for me in the next round. He'd been headbutting me the whole fight and was good at disguising it. For this fight we had thumbless gloves but I wish I hadn't, so I could have poked his eyes out!

The last round, I came off the stool really early and was standing in the center of the ring jumping up and down, waiting to go. In the last minute of the round, Chick Hearn said, 'A man who has beaten the drug habit and now many people think is on the verge of beating the WBC super bantamweight champion Daniel Zaragoza.'

When the final bell went, the crowd was cheering, 'Ban-ke, Ban-ke, Ban-ke'. Then, when they started reading the scorecards and the first one was 115-113 in my favor, I was thinking, 'I'm about to become world champion.' Then the other cards were read out, 116-110, 117-110.

My mom was in the ring with a bunch of flowers when they said, 'And the winner, and still world champion.' I was devastated. It was a close fight and everyone was shocked by how wide they'd given it to Zaragoza. I threw too many punches, maybe overshot many and Zaragoza's experience took over, but no way did he beat me by six or seven rounds, especially with the knockdown.

I went from jumping up and down, thinking I was about to be crowned champ, to falling on my knees. My mom shouted, 'You stand up and take it like a man,' and that's just what I did. I was just so hurt and angry with myself that I didn't get the win. That split decision made it even harder to accept because if I'd been beaten by stoppage or a wide points distance, it would have been easier to swallow, but having one of the three judges giving me the fight made it tough.

Zaragoza came over and tried to talk to me and put my hand up, but I kept blanking him, which I'm sorry for. I have nothing but respect for Zaragoza, he's a legend and one of the most polite men you could ever meet. I was just caught up in the moment and the hype.

When we got back to the dressing room, Sherman said, 'I thought you won the fight. It's no problem, though, because we'll get back there, get the rematch and next time we'll beat him.'

At the press conference afterwards, we talked about how Zaragoza had beaten me mentally. When I dropped him in the ninth round, most guys when they get dropped try to move away from you to recover. Zaragoza didn't do that. With the smart boxing brain he had, he came forward to let me know that he wasn't hurt. That took something from me mentally in that ring. I reacted by taking my foot off the gas pedal, which let him get back into the fight.

The morning after, I bumped into Zaragoza after breakfast down the hallway of the Marriott Hotel in Inglewood, where we were all staying. He was there with his wife and his people, and he had his hands on someone in front of him because his eyes were almost swollen closed. Despite that, he was still really polite and came over to ask how I was. I have nothing but respect for him.

It was a good fight, it was close, but I knew that in order for me to take the title from a world champion, I needed to do more. The day after, I was already focusing on the rematch.

* * *

After the fight, I did what I knew best when I was down. Partied. By then, the drugs were easy to come by and were almost always free. As an amateur boxer I had a lot of TV exposure, including a little bit on HBO. But I loved it. Thank God Facebook wasn't around then because I'm all over it now! My girlfriend Angel always jokes with me, saying, 'Look at me! Look at me!' whenever I post another selfie with someone. But back then, I had no idea how much media I'd get as I started to box professionally, and more to the point how much I started to get when I started to climb the ranks. With more media and wins came more parties – and drugs.

I'm ashamed to say it, but throughout my professional boxing career, I never strayed far from a needle. I'm surprised I passed my dope tests as a pro boxer. I can only imagine they were a bit looser back then because on occasions I was injecting in the week before the fight and sometimes on the day of my fights in the dressing room. I still have needle marks on my arms and ankles from the scarring where I used to inject. I also used to inject in my hands a lot and sometimes in between my toes, but the marks there have pretty much gone. On occasions I'd also do it in the neck, because you have the main veins running through there and you'd get the biggest rush.

Bob Richardson knew that the best way to keep me away from drugs, or at least reduce my usage, was to keep me in the ring. He also knew that if he could get me off the drugs, I would have a good chance of becoming a champion after my performance against Zaragoza. He sent me to Utah to stay with Steve for my next two fights hoping that drugs would be harder to come by, and he knew that Steve wouldn't leave me alone for long. Yes, drugs were harder to come by, but not impossible to find, unfortunately. However, by staying away from the city, that kept me away from more distractions than I would have had otherwise.

Four months after the loss to Zaragoza, I fought against José Luis Soto and knocked him out in the second round. That felt good, winning like that, and the media started talking about a rematch with Zaragoza, which is exactly what I wanted.

Before that could happen, though, I had one more test, going up against my old opponent and current-day friend, Lucilo Nolasco. Similar to the first time, we went the full ten rounds again, but this time it was a lot closer and I won by split decision.

Shortly after beating Nolasco, I got the news I wanted to hear. Dr Buss had organized the rematch against Zaragoza for 23 April 1990 at the Forum. It was my second chance to prove I was the best in the world. When I told the team, Sherman said, 'Let's go get him. This time we'll beat him. In fact, this time we'll stop him.'

CHAPTER 15

FIGHT OF MY LIFE

'When I was younger, I'd run to the gym every day to work out. My mom would shout from the window of the apartment complex we lived in, "Why don't you take your brother Pauli?" I'd say, "Why do I want to take him for? He ain't gonna work. He's gonna quit. He ain't gonna become nothing in boxing." Lo and behold. He became world champion.'

Steve Banke

YOU hear many boxers talk about how their dream as a kid was to become world champion. Well, that wasn't mine. I dreamt of being an Olympian soon after I started as an amateur and never looked beyond that. Never in my wildest dreams did I ever think that I'd fight for a world title, and here I was having my second shot.

For the first fight against Zaragoza, I got paid $15,000 and cleared less than half of that. Remember, that was for a world title fight. Have a guess how much I got for the rematch? The same again. But it wasn't about the money. This was now about pride and redemption. I wanted to show everyone that the first time was not a fluke and, in fact, it hadn't even been the best version of myself. This time, they were going to see 'The Real' Paul Banke.

Everyone knew the rematch was going to be something special. I was hungrier this time round, no doubt about it. I had this good feeling running through me. I knew it the night before. I knew what I was going to do and that I was going to win. I trained hard the first time round, but this time it was the belief, knowing that I could do it, which pushed me.

I bust my ass in training because if I gave it my best and didn't succeed, then at least I would know I gave it everything I had. I could accept that. To beat a great champion and take his belt, you have to train like a champion, so for this camp, we added Terry Claybon to the team. Terry trains all the movie stars, including most recently Jake Gyllenhaal for the movie *Southpaw*. Terry made me run that bit faster, punch that bit longer, train that bit harder. Alongside Steve, Mack and Sherman, I had one of the best teams in boxing at that moment in time.

After the first Zaragoza fight I trained really hard, but the difference now was my mental strength. I was more focused than I'd ever been before in terms of training and executing the proper gameplan, and having that focus in the Soto and Nolasco fights is what kept me going strong up to and including the rematch with Zaragoza.

To get prepped for the second fight, we moved from Quail Valley, California to Richfield, Utah, which was 5,500ft above sea level, giving us the benefit of altitude training. When I was running, my trainers would be driving right beside me in the car doing about 10mph. I was still running six-minute miles and that's uphill in the mountains of Utah.

I went into training camp with a champion's mentality. We watched videos of the first fight and knew that this time we needed to be busier and technically even better. Doubling and tripling combinations to the body, then up to the head, then back to the body and changing angles all the time. Basically, not being predictable and standing in front of him like I did in the first fight.

I can't remember another training camp where I trained so intensely. Every moment, I was thinking about this fight. I didn't want anyone around for weeks because I knew it meant so much to me. I was very bitchy and snappy before this fight and real tough to be around, but that was good because it reflected my hunger to be champion. In addition, I was making weight and that was always an issue for me. Like all fighters, I had issues making weight but I was never heavily over. I was fighting at 122lbs and walking around at no more than about 130lbs, but those last few pounds were always a real struggle, which made me more irritable.

* * *

The night before, I couldn't sleep at all. I was so nervous. All kinds of thoughts were running through my head. Many believed that I won the first fight, but did I really? How good was Zaragoza? Was this really my time? I had a lot to prove to myself on 23 April 1990.

Zaragoza, at this point, had a record of 40-4-1 and had defended his WBC title five times, four of which were against world champions. Also, he'd never been stopped in his 45 fights. I entered the ring with a record of 18-4 and was the clear underdog. That really motivated me. I also kept reminding myself that I was in with a legend, just to create that added pressure to push me harder in training.

Come fight night, I was physically and mentally in the best place I'd ever been in my whole boxing career. In the changing room a couple of hours before, I was calm and loose. I love my coffee and back then I'd ask Sherman if he could get me some. I drank loads of it, but used to drink it with lots of sugar, which is not great when you're trying to make weight. Around this time, I got introduced to Sweet'N Low and Diet Coke, and haven't looked back since.

When Sherman got back with the coffee, I thanked him. He replied, 'My theory is, you treat a champion like a champion, before they become a champion, and they will become a champion. You're ready to be a world champion. They just didn't give you the belt the first time.'

When it came to the ring walk, I didn't want anyone touching me or getting around me. I was too focused and very bitchy. However, the moment I got in that ring, everything felt different. I was more serious, more aggressive, more pumped up, more focused. Not relaxed, just ready.

If there's one thing I'll always be grateful for, it's the support at my fights. This time, even more people turned up. Just under 6,000 to be exact. My close friends and family especially were always there and I'll never, ever forget that. I might not have had the chance at the time, but I thank each and every one of you from the bottom of my heart.

Dr Jerry Buss was there with a number of Lakers players and other celebrities to support, but my number one cheerleaders were my sister Rebecca and my mom. You'd think they were in the ring, they were so loud. 'He's not anything! Beat this guy!' they'd be screaming. Then, if someone in the crowd said anything about me, Rebecca would usually be the first to turn around and shout something like, 'Don't you talk about my brother like that.'

You had to really hold her back, especially when at the Inglewood Forum with the home support. The whole family, in fact, couldn't sit in their seats as they were always on their feet. That night particularly, they were all that bit louder and crazier. It was as if they knew something special was going to happen.

Then came the moment that reminded me why I was here. Ring announcer Jimmy Lennon Jr got on the microphone and said, 'The rematch main event you've all been waiting for. The WBC super bantamweight championship of the world. Welcome the challenger known as "The Real" Paul Bankeee.' When he said that, I was covered in goose bumps.

This time, I wasn't talking to Zaragoza from the corner or trash talking, I was far more serious. He was looking at me while I was looking at the ground bouncing up and down on my feet.

Zaragoza was a southpaw like myself and many people asked me if that caused any problems. The answer is, no. I used to come straight at you, so it didn't matter if you were southpaw or orthodox, and that's exactly what I did that night. First round, I went out and just took it to him. From the first fight, I knew he was tough, smart and had boxing skills, which explained why he'd survived so long in the sport, but tonight that was changing. I started chopping away at the body and then following it up with hooks to the head, staying on him constantly. About a minute in, I caught him with a lovely left hook that instantly reddened his left cheek and made him hold on. When Zaragoza fought back and unloaded on me, instead of showboating and talking to him, I threw bunches of punches back, which proved to be far more effective. Lesson learned.

In the third round, Zaragoza started unloading with straight power punches and caught me flush on the nose a few times, which had blood streaming down my nostrils. I then unleashed on him, opened a cut over his left eye and we both started trading punches non-stop on the ropes. The crowd was going wild, everyone standing on their feet.

I started to throw a serious number of hooks and in the fifth round opened a cut over Zaragoza's other eye, which started to bleed down his cheek heavily. His face was starting to look a mess, but he came back firing and even had me rocked at the end of the round. Shortly after, the doctor was looking at the cuts and swelling around Zaragoza's eyes and seeing if he was going to call it a day.

Knowing the fight might get stopped, Zaragoza came out hard in round six and we had a war. I re-opened his cuts and he opened a cut over my right eye. At the end of the three minutes, the crowd was going crazy again, but for both of us.

I wasn't looking for the stoppage in the first fight, but when I knocked him down in the ninth, I was pissed that I didn't get it. This time, if he went down, I wasn't leaving him alone. When I came back to the corner at the end of the eighth round, Steve told me, 'It's real close on the scorecards. You can't take your foot off the gas.' Then, just before I was getting ready to come off the stool, he shouted, 'Knock this motherfucker out!'

We both went to war again in the middle of the ring and I opened another cut on Zaragoza's face, but under his right eye this time. Two minutes in, I landed a right hook to the body, then a right uppercut to the chin followed by a left hook to the jaw, and he went down. Zaragoza took the eight count and came back at me firing shots. He even started showboating, shaking his head as if to say, 'Is that all you got?'

At that point I knew he was badly hurt, so I kept on hunting him down and then managed to land a right hook on his chin, followed by a left hook, and this time he crumbled to the floor. The referee didn't even start the count, he just waved it off after two minutes and 51 seconds of the ninth round.

When the ring announcer said, 'And the *new* WBC super bantamweight champion of the world,' it's hard to describe that moment. It's like my ears blocked. The fans were cheering like crazy, but I couldn't hear them and everything seemed to be in slow motion. When people came over to talk to me, I couldn't hear most of them and didn't understand what they were saying. It was like being in a dream or a state of shock, but positive shock. To this very day, I still get excited when I think about that moment.

After the fight, I'm in the changing room pretty much naked when about 20 reporters walk in and start asking me questions about how I feel, who I might fight next, that sort of thing. As I'm putting some clothes on and answering more of the questions, my good friend Louie Valenzuela walks in unannounced and quietly stands behind the reporters. What happened was, his brother Victor had someone else fighting on the undercard and somehow Louie had got himself a pass and snuck into the dressing room. Louie basically came in to congratulate me, but wasn't expecting a room full of reporters.

Right in the middle of a sentence I shout, 'Hey Louie! What's happening?' Everybody turned around and Louie got so embarrassed as I started laughing. I then carried on with the interview while Louie stood there laughing. I didn't do it to embarrass him, I did it out of love. Whenever I fought at the Forum, no matter how strung out on drugs I was, I'd always keep Louie and his family tickets and I'd always call for them once I arrived. I never forgot where I came from.

* * *

Without a doubt, that was the performance of my life. From the training camp, the people around me, the stoppage, everything went as planned and more. Years later, Zaragoza conducted an interview with *The Ring* magazine, talking about the best opponents he'd ever faced, and he had this to say about me. 'He never stopped throwing punches from all angles. He didn't care if he received some in return as long as he got his shots off.'

That night, I didn't go partying after. I went back downstairs and saw my friends and family, had a couple of beers, but didn't go crazy, because I was so sore from the fight. I owed it to them because when I won, they won with me. They meant so much to me and their support always made me push that little bit harder when I maybe sometimes didn't want to.

It's a shame I didn't have them with me for my next fight because it was without a doubt the toughest I'd ever been in.

CHAPTER 16

KO IN KOREA

*'In a boxing match, sometimes a fight breaks
out. When Paul Banke was in the ring, a fight
would always break out'*

Ivan Goldman, journalist and bestselling author

MARCH to May was a busy time for me. On 3
March 1990 my first child, Paula, was born
then on 23 April I won the world title and
five weeks later, on 29 May, I got married. I could have
done with longer breaks in between all of that, but all three
things were very significant and positive episodes in my life
back then, so who's complaining? Boxing-wise, I definitely
could have done with a longer break after Zaragoza, but
four months later, on 18 August 1990, I was defending my
title against Ki-Joon Lee in his own backyard, South Korea.
Why was I fighting out there? Simple. I was getting paid
$185,000. Mind you, after deductions I walked away with
60 grand. Still good money, though.

Lee was undefeated with a record of 14-0-1 and being the underdog in his own country, I knew he'd put on his best performance ever. I saw videos of his fights and thought, 'He's OK, but he doesn't throw that many punches.'

Training went well but nothing can prepare you for actually being in the ring. In fact, Steve used to say that I was a constantly improving fighter at All Heart Boxing Club, but I was never a gym fighter, which was very true. I came alive whenever I was in front of an audience. In the gym, I didn't do well in sparring and that included the camp for this fight, even though I'd become world champion. I remember this little amateur kid came from Quail Valley to our camp and he wanted to spar because there was no one else available. He asked if he could spar with me and I said, 'Sure.' There I am a world champion, nice and relaxed, and I was overwhelmed as this kid, about the same weight, came at me throwing all kinds of punches. He was all over me!

Me, Steve, Mack, Bob and Marty Dickens from the boxing commission went to Korea two weeks before the fight to get used to the altitude and get the jet lag out of my system. Sherman also helped with the training for this camp, did his homework on Lee and got me in the best physical condition of my life. Unfortunately, he couldn't come over because he was training Juan Laporte, who was also in the camp and was one of my sparring partners.

Juan's a good man and was very ring savvy. He used to stand on my feet in sparring, like Vasiliy Lomachenko does, and then throw a punch straight after. If you weren't paying attention, he'd pick up on that real fast, step on your feet and bang, you were nailed. Very crafty. Juan was getting ready to challenge 'The Professor', Azumah Nelson, for the WBC super featherweight title a few weeks after my fight, so Sherman needed to be with him in those essential last few weeks of camp.

From the time we landed, you could tell the Koreans wanted to give as much advantage to their man as possible. The gym we were going to was 15 minutes from the hotel, but they would drive us for four hours, trying to make it difficult for us to train. Then, the second day, after we went running, cleaned up and had breakfast, I went for a walk with Mack in downtown Seoul, where we were staying.

As we were walking, there were about seven punks across the street looking at us, calling us names and throwing pebbles at us. Mack got pissed off, got to a phone and called a friend of his, Henry, who he'd trained in the USA. Henry answered the phone and Mack said, 'Some punks across the street are picking a fight with us.' 'Where you at, Mack?' Henry was fuming and said, 'Stay right there,' and came down right away from his apartment block and met us. He then walked over to this other big block and called the ex-middleweight champion of South Korea, who also came down.

Without hesitating, they both went over across the street and gave all these punks a slap. I don't know what he was saying in Korean, but when he came back Henry said, 'I told them that when these two guys walk down the street, you don't even look at them. If you act like that again, I'll throw you in a garbage can and throw you in the river.' Funnily enough, they never bothered us again.

We knew that they were going to tamper with the food, so we had our guard up. There were five of us at dinner and we used to switch up our meals to make sure they didn't drug my food or give me something that would give me food poisoning. And if they weren't trying to get you sick, they were trying to hurt you in sparring.

We were asked if we could do an exhibition with one of their fighters, which would be filmed on Korean TV, and we agreed. The idea was to move around the ring a little bit with someone roughly my size and put on a bit of a show. Next thing, their man walked in, who was at least 160lbs. Steve went crazy. 'No, no. He's not sparring this guy. This is strictly a photo opportunity now.' I told Steve it was OK, assuming the guy would dance around, but after a minute this guy went crazy on me and took the shot of all shots at my body, trying to break a rib. The second it landed, Steve jumped in there and started yelling, 'What the hell are you doing? This is a fucking exhibition.' He grabbed me by the arm and pulled me out of there.

One thing I didn't mind in their favor was the trunks. Soon after I got there, this guy came round with these boxing trunks and said, 'We'll pay you $10,000 to wear these trunks,' which had Korean sponsors and writing all over them. I said, 'OK, but they've got to be blue and you gotta put "Banke" and "USA" on the front of them.'

The guy said, 'Yeah. No problem. We can do that.' Easy ten grand.

* * *

I'll never forget the weigh-in. When Lee walked in, he looked like a ghost. Really pale, skinny and staggering. I turned to Mack and said, 'What's happened to this guy?' Mack said, 'They drained the shit out of him to make weight.' I even felt a bit sorry for him. Back in those days, there were even rumors that fighters would sometimes take out blood before the weigh-in to help them make weight and then put it back in after. I'm not saying that was the case here, but this guy looked like the living dead. The day after, on fight night, he'd pumped back up and looked huge. He must have put on 15–20lbs and had muscles bulging everywhere. I didn't feel sorry for him any more.

We were staying in Seoul but the fight was in Incheon, which was miles away. The place looked like a farming town. It took a couple of hours to get there normally, but they drove us all over the place. In the end, it took us a little over four hours. We went past all these rice paddy fields and then finally there it was, this small arena, in the middle of nowhere, which looked like a dorm. It was weird.

When we eventually got inside the arena, the first thing that hit you was the heat. It was hot enough outside, but inside it was suffocating. Air con? Forget it. Everyone had fans and pieces of paper in their hands to cool themselves down. That was crazy.

When we got to the changing room, Steve looked around and said, 'Where's the ice?' This Korean guy replies, 'We don't have any.' Steve flipped. 'What? No ice? Get me some ice!' 'We don't have any,' the guy said again. Steve totally lost his temper and shouted, 'No ice, no fight.' Suddenly a load of ice appeared. You didn't mess with Steve.

When I stepped through the ropes, which were in the colours of the South Korean flag, the crowd was only cheering for him. A total contrast to being at the Forum, but it had no effect on me at all. I'd fought in 12 countries as an amateur and was used to travelling and being in front of hostile crowds. I also knew that if it went to points, there was a good chance I'd get robbed in his home town and that made me want to fight that much harder.

Marty was in the crowd somewhere and passed a message to some guy, who came up to Steve. 'Marty says to tell you, if this fight goes to a decision, you grab Paul and get out of the ring as fast as you can. Don't even wait for the decision because if they don't win, they're going to riot in there. It's going to get very, very dangerous.' Thankfully, Steve didn't tell me about that until after the fight, as I had enough to think about.

From the first bell, this guy put his chin down, worked out of a crouch, stood flat in front of me and loaded up on every punch, looking for the knockout. There was no holding on, just non-stop exchanges of punches. I also noticed in that first round that he kept going in with his head and the referee was letting it slip. I was butted about three times in the first three minutes. Unfortunately, that would continue for the whole fight and would get worse.

By the second round, he was low-blowing me to my balls, my thigh and anywhere he could get away with whenever the referee was on the opposite side of him. Third round, I worked nicely behind the jab to start with and caught him with some solid left hooks to the chin, then he hit me with a low blow that the referee pulled him up on. Moments later, the referee had to warn him for using his head. It was already a real tough fight.

Five rounds in and Lee's left cheek was swelling up from my jabs and right hooks, but he was not letting up. In the eighth round, seconds after it started, he caught me with a big uppercut to my chin, which stunned me. Seconds later, he headbutted me and had a point deducted. That was a real messy round. By the end of it I had a big swelling under my right eye, but Lee's face was now turning into one big purple swell. Unlike the first half of the fight, he was now holding on a bit, while his punches were more looping swings than crisp shots. By the end of the next round, his eye was almost shut.

In the tenth round, I was in so much pain. This guy was still using his head, elbowing and hitting me in the neck. He hurt me so bad, I wanted to cry in between rounds. Both my eyes were starting to close and I was thinking, 'How much more can this guy take? I'm throwing my best shots and this motherfucker won't go down. In fact, he's still firing back at me.' I was in his country, I was scared, frustrated, almost blind and I was getting hurt. I didn't want to be in that ring. I didn't know what to do. I was hoping that somebody would pass me the kitchen sink so I could hit this guy in the head with it. Thank God I was in great shape because that's what kept me standing.

Towards the end of round ten, Steve was looking across the ring while Lee was putting a pounding on me. He rested his arms on the ring apron and yelled out to me, 'Don't quit.' When I got back to the corner, Steve did what he was best at, motivational talking. 'Listen Banke, don't you fucking quit on me. You'll never go back to America and you'll never have a wife or kids again. You'll be done. That will be the end. So you go out there now and you take it to this fucking guy. Get on to his body, work that head and you do not stop. This is the round that I want him knocked out.' In the meantime, Lee's corner were giving him smelling salts, which I'm pretty sure weren't allowed.

When Steve told me to knock him out, it triggered another gear in me. My adrenaline started pumping, I was excited and I went out there with the intention of finishing Lee off, which very nearly happened. Towards the end of the round, I caught him with a right hook and straight left. He wobbled and I immediately tagged him with another big left hook. This time he hit the canvas. As he was on the way down, I tried to throw more shots, but got tangled in the ropes. If I'd connected, the fight could have been over there and then, but instead he made the eight count, which took him to the bell.

Going into the 12th and final round, I knew I had him and went for the stoppage again. Steve was shouting, 'Go get him, Paul,' and I went out there, bam, bam, bam. When I landed that final one-two combo, he staggered and then the referee jumped in. I was so happy. I'd beaten this guy who I was starting to think was indestructible and kept my world title. I wanted that world title more than anything when I beat Zaragoza and keeping it was just as important to me, especially against a tough opponent, because it showed I wasn't a one-fight wonder. Without a doubt, that was the toughest, most brutal fight I'd ever been in.

After I knocked him out, it suddenly went very quiet in the arena as their man had just been defeated. They were pissed off and started throwing water and stuff at me. We got out of there pretty quickly and headed back to the dressing room, where they had police waiting inside for our protection.

The WBC walked in and asked me for a piss sample to check for drugs and I told them, 'I can't piss. I've got no fluid in me.' I was drinking a lot of water, but I got hurt so bad and I was so dehydrated because of the heat that it took me two hours before I could piss. When I was finally able, it came out raw blood because of the body shots I'd taken to the kidneys. Just imagine taking a knife, cutting your finger and letting it drip. That's what the sample looked like.

Soon after, we grabbed our bags and headed back to the hotel, with police protection all the way back. My head was swollen, hurt and felt like it was about to pop. Mack stayed with me most of the night because he was scared for me. He didn't want me to go to sleep in case I had a brain injury and didn't wake up. Thankfully, that wasn't the case and the next morning we went to the airport and headed back to the USA.

* * *

A few days after getting back from South Korea, Bob Richardson paid for me to go on a fishing trip in Alaska, which cost him about $500 per night. That was a hell of a lot of money back then. We flew from Anchorage to this incredible retreat and I was there for two nights, three days, hanging out with about 40 or 50 people, including baseball player Steve Garvey. Bruce Jenner (now Caitlyn) and Kris Kardashian, who had just started going out at that point, were also there. When we got to the resort, in front of television cameras, Steve says to the guests, 'Let me introduce you to the world champion, Paul Banke, fresh off his world title defence in South Korea.' That was cool.

About a week later, I was back in the gym. After the two toughest fights of my life, I should have taken some time off. Instead, I was getting ready to defend my title on 5 November 1990 against Pedro Decima from Argentina, less than three months after having fought Lee. Rumor was that I would have a showdown with the WBC bantamweight champion Raul Perez after Decima. The Argentinian was only getting paid $7,500 compared to my $60,000. My next payday against Raul would be real decent, so I was already focusing on that, which was a big mistake.

In all honesty, I didn't want to fight Decima, but I needed the money. Why? I had money, but I'd blown a lot on dope. Being world champion really didn't help. After my defence, my profile rose even more and I got invites to parties all the time, which meant more drugs. Girls came at me, guys came at me. It was crazy. Everyone looked at me different now. I was like, 'So this is what it's all about?'

In the meantime, I got ready to fight Decima and defend my world title again. What could go wrong?

Age 15. Hungry

June 1983. I was No.8 in the USA as a flyweight. Check out some of the names out there at the time

Proud to be a part of the USA boxing team. 1984

1984 – King's Cup tournament, Thailand

Holding my own against Steve McCrory, 1984 Olympic trials

Olympic trials, 1984. My dream shattered as Steve McCrory has his hand raised.

With Mack Kurahara and Steve Rosenzweig standing behind, covered in my blood

Straight after defending my title in Korea against Ki-Joon Lee. My face was a mess.

4-23-1990. In the changing room getting ready to beat Daniel Zaragoza and become world champion

Trading blows with the legendary Daniel Zaragoza in the last of our trilogy

Promo poster for the Antonio Ramirez fight

When I beat Antonio Ramirez on 28 August 1993, but the records say I didn't!

My last fight as a professional against Francisco Soto, 6 December 1993

Last fight against Soto. The tattoo on my arm said 'Champ', but I was far from

Supporting my mom on one of her rallies

With the ring announcer Jimmy Lennon Jr and the late, great Diego Corrales. I look terrible. I wasn't in a good place

With Jeff Fenech and Jose Sulaiman

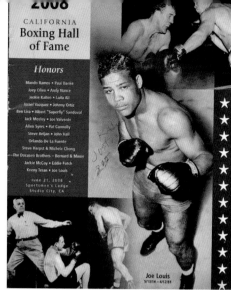

The roll of honour for the 2008 California Boxing Hall of Fame inductees

2010 – trying to make out everything was okay. I was still strung out on dope

Saying a few words at being inducted into the West Coast Boxing Hall of Fame in 2017. Happy times

Never turned back after writing this

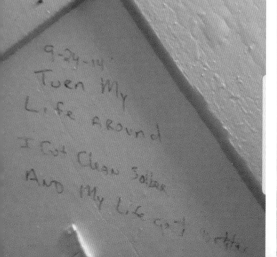

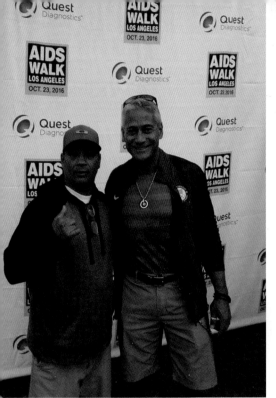

Taking part in the AIDS walk in 2016

Attending the 9th Experience, Strength Hope Awards, 2018

Fun times with my friend and sportswriter, Michele Chong

With my beautiful girlfriend, the one and only Angel

With my friend and old sparring partner Freddie Roach

With Mauricio Sulaiman

With my old sparring partner and friend, Robert Garcia and his brother, four weight world champion, Mikey

With Mack Kurahara and my brother Steve. I've still got that shirt!

2018 – Still very proud to wear my belt. (Photo Pepe Sulaiman)

CHAPTER 17

SLAM DUNK

*'He put his hands up and let himself be used as
a punching bag. That was not Paul Banke in
that ring that night'*

Steve Rosenzweig, 2018

I'D just beaten and stopped Ki-Joon Lee and Daniel
Zaragoza back to back, but my toughest opponent at
this point was the dope. By now, my sister Rebecca
was working for Bob, along with my brother Tim. They'd
come and watch me train, but I was already out of control
and they could see that. I was training but I wasn't
concentrating on boxing any more and didn't want to stay
inside Bob's grounds. When I first went there, I didn't
have structure and the camp provided that, but by the time
I did have it I was out of control and started to rebel. I'd
always been very strong-willed and outspoken, but when
I was high, that was even more the case. Looking back, it
upsets me to think how I repaid Bob with the way I was

behaving. I wanted to party but Bob didn't allow it. He kept saying, 'I want you to do good. I know you can do good.' But I didn't listen.

Two days before the fight, Earl Gustkey from the *Los Angeles Times* said, 'Paul Banke will show up fit and primed for battle. If he goes down, he will get up. Win or lose, fans will cheer his name when it's over.' Three or six months earlier and Earl would have been very accurate, but unfortunately not this time round.

They were referring to the guy who beat Zaragoza to win the world title and who beat Lee in Korea. That was 'The Real' Paul Banke. On 5 November 1990, that version of me was never going to show up.

I had a lot on my mind at that time. Things weren't going well with my wife, I was getting jealous of her and tripping because of the amount of drugs and partying I was doing. I only sparred twice for that fight, which was crazy. You *have* to spar for a world title fight and that's coming from someone who didn't spar a hell of a lot.

On 3 November 1990, me and Steve left Utah to go to LA. I was staying with Steve and later that day was walking down the hallway in his house when I threw my arms around him and started weeping uncontrollably. I was crying so much, I could barely talk. Steve was saying, 'Talk to me. Tell me what's wrong.' Finally I said, 'I'm scared. I'm really scared. I'm afraid of this fight.' 'Why?' Steve replied. I explained that I wanted to fight, but I couldn't because my head was that fucked up on dope.

A day went by and Steve couldn't get my spirits back up, so he called Bob and said, 'I want to cancel this fight. Paul's not ready for it.' He then explained what I'd told him. 'If he's physically not right, that's one thing, but if he's afraid, we can't pull out,' Bob replied.

* * *

Even if I'd been in good shape, Decima was always going to be a tough fight. He was ranked the number one contender by the WBC and I knew his style would give me trouble all day long. He was awkward. I was supposed to fight him in the Stroh's tournament, but thankfully didn't have to. Now, three years later, I'm up against him and not looking forward to it.

A couple of hours before the fight, some guy came into my dressing room who worked for Don King and said, 'Sylvester Stallone's come to watch you fight.' That got me even more nervous. He'd just finished making the film *Rocky V*, which featured real-life heavyweight boxer Tommy Morrison.

Unfortunately, me and Tommy would have more than boxing in common a few years later. Then he mentioned the CEO of HBO [the US subscription TV network] was also watching and he hoped I'd put on a good show, which got me even more nervous. That's when I started to choke.

When I came out for the ring walk, Chick Hearn was commentating and said that I wasn't perspiring. In other words, I hadn't warmed up in the changing room. He was spot on. I didn't want to be in this fight.

By the second round, my mouth and nose were already bleeding from the uppercuts, jabs and straight right hands Decima was landing, punches I would have dodged and countered six months earlier. In the dying seconds of the round, Chick Hearn said on television, 'Banke doesn't look like Banke.' When I got back to the corner, Steve shouted at me, 'Why aren't you fighting back?' 'I don't know,' I replied.

In the fourth round, I got caught with a solid right hand and hit the canvas. The moment it happened, Steve was saying to himself in the corner, 'Thank you, sweet Jesus. That's what we needed. Now when he comes back to the corner, I'll kick his ass so far he'll go out and smash this guy.' Unfortunately, that was never going to happen.

Before the fight, you could decide if you wanted the three-knockdown rule and we decided to go with it. If either fighter got knocked down three times in a round, the fight was over. That decision turned out to be a tragedy. Twenty seconds after the first knockdown, I got hit with a four-punch combination that left me with a cut under my right eye and major swelling.

Straight after, I was down again. Two minutes and 35 seconds into the fourth round and the fight was over. I was no longer world champion, while Decima had become Argentina's only world champion at the time. At the Stroh's tournament, Miguel Diaz, Decima's trainer, told me, 'You'll be world champion one day.' Three years later, guess what? I lost the title to Diaz's fighter.

You know, I watched the second Zaragoza fight maybe 30 or 40 times, the Ramiro Adames and Carlos Romero fights quite a few times, but the Decima fight I watched once, twice maybe. It hurts me even now to watch it knowing the opportunity I threw away. I should have been world champion for a few more years but I was robbed. By who? Me. My addictions robbed me of that opportunity.

After that fight I retired again, partied hard and started slamming dope all the time. It got crazy and crazier for me, and things went from bad to worse very quickly in the next few years.

CHAPTER 18

LOSING THE BATTLE

*'Losing a game is heartbreaking. Losing your sense
of excellence or worth is a tragedy'*

Joe Paterno

DECIMA walked away with a handful of dollars as
world champion and then three months later got
beaten by Kiyoshi Hatanaka in Japan. He never
won the title back. The belt makes you the money and if you
don't have it, you've got nothing to bargain with. Boxing is
a very tough sport at times.

It didn't take long for Zaragoza to jump in against
Hatanaka and by June 1991, he was world champion again.
In the meantime, because I'd retired and gone off the rails,
I no longer had my team around me and wasn't training
at Bob Richardson's camp any more. I had no structure,
no discipline and was fighting purely for money, which is
not the mindset to have when you walk into a ring and get
punched in the face.

I'd like to say a few words about Steve Rosenzweig. Steve was with me from the Ramon Rico fight until Pedro Decima. He was a great trainer and I'll always be grateful to him. If I had been in a better place in my life, we could have gone on to defend the title many more times.

Shortly after Zaragoza beat Hatanaka, people started crying out for me to fight him and win back the title. So I decided to come out of retirement to finish off the trilogy. Norman Kaplan, Don King's lawyer, and Dr Jerry Buss became my managers.

Before going in with Zaragoza, I had a warm-up fight against Antonio Ramirez on 26 October 1991. Billy Smith trained me for the fight. Not taking anything away from Ramirez, because he was a tough guy, but my last fight was at world title level and this was his US debut (although he'd reportedly had 12 pro fights with 11 wins and a draw in other countries). Either way, I got ten rounds in the bag and beat him easily on points. Now it was time for Zaragoza again.

After our first two fights, everyone assumed that the rubber match would be just as exciting as the first two. It had only been 20 months since I beat Zaragoza to become world champion and many were saying that I had just had a bad day against Decima, or that his style was all wrong for me. Either way, on 9 December 1991, we were back in the Forum, Inglewood to deliver the last fight in the trilogy.

I hardly trained for this fight and was really strung out on dope. I was off it for maybe a week during the camp, but I was getting high all the time. What a wasted opportunity.

On the night, my footwork had gone to shit and I found it difficult to move out of the way of anything that Zaragoza threw. Even though he hurt his hand early on in the fight, I still couldn't capitalize on his injury. As opposed to the first two fights, where I ran over to Zaragoza from the first bell and unloaded, this time I was on the back foot and mainly attacked with single shots. Sometimes I'd throw the double jab, but my combinations were non-existent. It looked more like one of my sparring sessions.

After 12 rounds, I lost the fight on the judges' scorecards by four rounds, 116-112 (twice) and 117-113. Incredibly, they saw this fight closer than the first one, which many thought I'd won clearly. However, this time there was no dropping to my knees being upset with the result. In fact, I was clapping Zaragoza when the scores got read out.

The third fight against Zaragoza was my last competitive fight. From here on, there was a guy who looked like Paul Banke stepping through the ropes, but had nothing to do with the guy who beat Daniel Zaragoza to win the world title. It was just a matter of time before I threw the towel in as a professional boxer.

* * *

After somehow managing to last the distance with Zaragoza, I went in with 1988 Olympic gold medallist Kennedy McKinney on 20 March 1992 at Caesars Palace,

Las Vegas. The headliner was Tommy Hearns against Iran Barkley and Tommy Morrison fought Jerry Halstead in the principal undercard bout.

A few days before the fight, I'd got delayed on the way over to the press conference. I don't remember how or why, but I was like, 'Damn it.' Remember the referee Mills Lane? His catchphrase used to be, 'Let's get it on!' Anyway, Mills was one of the judges for the fight and as I'm walking in, he's walking out. He comes up to me and growls, 'Hey Banke. Where in the fuck you been?'

Kennedy had been saying a few things about me in the conference and Mills basically wanted to let me know. I knew Kennedy from the amateurs, so we were friends and knew he meant nothing by it. Me and Mills still laugh about that moment to this day.

This was Kennedy's last tune-up fight before going for a world title, whereas I was fighting purely for the payday. Again, I was strung out on drugs, speed to be exact. Drugs react different on people, but for me speed actually had a calming effect. It annoyed my wife because the week before the fight, we went to church and nobody could tell I'd been hitting the dope. I remember walking in with the kids and chatting to everyone, and my wife said, 'I can't believe everyone thinks you're so damn nice and you've been up all night on speed.'

More regrettable than the drugs was the fact my son Bobby Jay had only been born a few weeks earlier, on 28 February 1992, and I wasn't in the state a father should be when their son is born. My wife brought my son over to the hotel and stayed for the week of the fight, but didn't go to the fight itself. They stayed in the room when it was fight time.

On the night, the commentator mentioned how both fighters had drug history, but both were now clean. I can't speak for Kennedy, but I certainly wasn't. Despite not being in great condition, I still went into that fight thinking I could win. In the first round, I brought the fight to Kennedy and was landing well, but by the second, there was no snap in my punches. In the last few seconds of the round, I was knocked down with a flurry and was dazed. When I got up, the bell saved me.

Round three was definitely Kennedy's, but four and five were good for me. I was landing well and throwing good volumes. When I started round six, I felt like I was coming back into the fight, but then in the last minute he cracked me. I got up and started trash talking to Kennedy and with about 20 seconds to go, he cracked me again with a right hand and down I went. Referee Richard Steele walked over to my corner and said to my trainer, 'Your man's taking a beating.' The doctor then came over and took a look at me and next thing Steele had called it off.

Even when I look at that fight now, it hurts me. Not because of the result, but because I knew I was strung out and wasn't at my best. I could see my feet weren't the same, I looked like an old man against a very good kid who was coming up. Kennedy was a good fighter, very smart, and I wish we'd have fought when I was in my prime. I think we would have had an incredible fight. Everybody has their time and that was no longer mine. Kennedy, on the other hand, became IBF junior featherweight champion in his next fight and had five consecutive and successful defences.

* * *

Next morning, we have breakfast and I leave the restaurant and grab a handful of Sweet'N Low and put them in my pocket. My buddy Victor says, 'Paul. You got a house in Utah, a house in California, 20 grand in your pocket and you're stealing Sweet'N Low. What the hell's wrong with you?' 'That Sweet'N Low is some expensive shit, Victor.' He started laughing. Despite what Victor said, the truth is that the money had pretty much gone.

I was eating it like crazy getting high all the time.

CHAPTER 19

CURTAIN CALL

'To fight someone like Paul Banke, a WBC champ, would have been incredible. Even though we were in training together, had become friends, we were still going to fight each other. That's just the way the boxing world works'

Wayne McCullough, WBC bantamweight champion, 1995/96

MY professional boxing career pretty much ended after the loss to McKinney. I didn't fight for another 17 months, but it wasn't the loss of a fight that kept me out of boxing, it was something much more valuable. To this very day, it deeply upsets me to even think about it.

I was injecting every week and getting high all the time. I even missed Christmas a couple of times and holidays because of the way I was. Then one day my wife said to me, 'Don't come home.' Shortly after, on 15 August 1992,

I was divorced from my wife, separated from my kids and wasn't able to have access to them. It's a day I'll never forget and still hurts badly. I've got pictures of all my babies and I can't look at them any more because it upsets me so bad. To this day, it's my biggest regret, not being able to go clean at that point of my life. I can't say I raised them. Instead I abandoned them and that still eats me up.

I felt real low after that split and decided to have a tattoo on my arm that said, 'CHAMP'. I actually wanted to have the WBC belt tattooed on my arm, but couldn't afford it. I don't know why I had 'champ' done because that's not like me. I felt like I was bragging having it on my arm. At the time, though, I wasn't thinking straight. The first opportunity I had, I got it covered up with a tribal tattoo.

Splitting from my wife, not seeing my kids, that increased my drug use. My life became one big downward spiral. I was living in Vegas, working in construction, taking drugs and selling them at the same time. It was a vicious circle I couldn't break. Buy, sell, use, buy some more, sell some more, use some more.

As crazy as it sounds, though, I wasn't a bad guy and had morals, even though I knew what I was doing was damaging the people who took it. When I was selling on the streets, I'd have two small plastic baggies in my back pocket. One would contain speed and the other had Sweet'N Low in it. The intention was to show them one bag, then hand them the other. I'd make $40 with that scam and then I could buy more dope later.

I was 28 years old and this guy came over to me who must have been 25, maybe 26. I don't know where he lived or worked, but he was real polite and asked, 'Can I buy some shit from you?' 'Yeah yeah,' I replied. Remember, I'm going through the divorce, living in Vegas, working in construction again, trying to get my life together and having my own issues. I pulled out the real dope and said, 'Nah. You don't need this.' Then I put it in my back pocket, trying to make out I wasn't going to sell it to him. He said, 'What you doing? I wanna buy it.' I then pulled out the Sweet'N Low and said, 'OK.' He hands me the $20 and says, 'Thanks man.' I'm thinking, 'I've ripped this guy off with the fake dope. I'll make another $20. Cool.' He then says, 'I'm going through a bunch of shit, man.' He starts telling me how he was going through a divorce and how he's lost his daughter as a result. I heard the pain in his voice and I started getting real sad. I thought, 'Oh my gosh. He's going through what I've been through a few months ago and what I'm still going through now.'

I heard it in his voice, the hurt, the pain, and felt bad for him. I understood what he was going through and that bothered me. I then said, 'Hey man. Give me back the dope.' He says, 'No man, I need this shit.' I replied, 'Listen bro,' then pulled out the other baggie from my pocket. 'This is the real dope. I was trying to rip your ass off, man. I swear to God. Keep both the bags.' I then gave him a hug.

Another time, I had half an ounce of speed on me and some guy comes up to me. I said, 'You want something?' and he replies, 'Yeah.' He handed me $20, but then I looked at his girlfriend and saw she was whacked out and gave him his money back. My heart told me no. I felt sad for her. She didn't need any more shit. He said, 'She's OK bro,' and I said, 'No. She don't need no more,' and I walked away.

The sad part is, almost everyone had a story. These were not people at a nightclub wanting to get a buzz, these were people at the lowest point in their lives who needed something to give them a short break from the pain. The dope did that, but once it wore off, the pain was ten times as bad. The comedowns were horrible. The only way you'd get rid of that feeling would be to take more dope. There comes a point when you naturally stop. It's when it kills you.

* * *

By late spring 1993, I'd been out of boxing for just over a year and had a few months to clear my head after the divorce. Then an opportunity came my way that got me back on track, or at least gave me a bit of focus. Oscar De La Hoya needed six sparring partners and I'd been asked if I wanted to be part of his camp for a week up in Big Bear, California. Oscar had won gold as a lightweight at the Barcelona Olympics the year before and at that point was getting ready to fight Troy Dorsey in his eighth fight on 7 June 1993. Troy had been world champion and was a banger, so they were looking for sparring partners who would bring the fight to Oscar. They were paying 500 bucks for the week, putting me in good accommodation and feeding me well, so of course I said, 'Yeah. Cool.'

I was told to go straight after Oscar and that he wouldn't manhandle me. First round I just started swinging at him, banging, like Troy Dorsey fought, while Oscar boxed me. Every time I threw something, he'd already moved and countered. He was quick. Really fast. He's probably the best fighter I've ever sparred with. Of course, I was washed up by then but I knew enough to know that this guy was incredible. His punches came in like, pow, pow, pow, in a split second. But people were clapping as I went for Oscar, shouting, 'Yeah. That's what we brought you in for. That's what we want!' They loved the way I was sparring and decided to keep me on for about the next three months.

I also sparred a fighter who would become a good friend over time, Robert Garcia. Robert was 5-0 as a pro at the time and would eventually go on to become IBF junior lightweight champion in 1998. His brother Mikey also boxed and didn't turn out too bad either! Back to the camp. Me and Robert had an exhibition bout at the Garfield High School, California, which was being televised by Channel 7 for the news and had been organized by Oscar's people. George Foreman was there, Oscar, Anthony Kiedis from the Red Hot Chili Peppers and many others. Robert always says I was really tough in that spar, but that's not true. He tagged the shit out of me and tore me apart.

I decided to use Oscar's camp as an opportunity to come back. If I failed this time, I'd hang up the gloves for good.

I had a fight lined up against Antonio Ramirez again, scheduled for 28 August 1993, so this was going to be my training camp, too.

I hate to admit it, but I was doing dope then. In fact, I was strung out most of the time in camp. I knew it was wrong, but I kept on doing it because the addiction had control of me. Despite that, when I used to run with Oscar in the morning, I was one of the few who kept up with him while all the other guys fell behind. We'd be together until the last mile and then, boom, he'd leave us. When I was training to be world champion, I reckon I could have beaten him!

This time I fought Ramirez at featherweight. For the life of me, I honestly don't remember losing, but the records say I lost a majority decision. I knocked the guy down and was in control of the fight, so I'm on a mission to get the result corrected as I'm certain I won the fight.

Four months later, I had my last fight as a professional boxer against Juan Francisco Soto, from Mexico. He had a record of eight losses and no wins. I didn't train properly and the night before I was up injecting crystal meth. Soto beat me on points over ten rounds and straight after I said to myself, 'I ain't ever getting back in the ring again. Ever.'

It was humiliating. Only three years before, I was a former world champion and I was now losing to a guy who finished his career with a record of two wins and 17 losses. I knew it was time to walk away from the sport. The paydays couldn't cover my embarrassment any longer. I didn't want the boxing world to see me like this again, so I went to Vegas instead and worked in construction.

The closest I came to getting back in the ring was about a year later against Wayne McCullough. I'd first met Wayne while training in Big Bear. We were staying in the same motel, log cabin-type accommodation, and he was in training for an upcoming fight. Wayne still likes to tell the story of when we went for a run together and he took off and left me standing. Wayne, if you're reading, I don't remember the story, but at my peak, you'd have had your work cut out!

By now, I was a laborer for a company up in Utah, doing cement work, shovelling. Wayne was a prospect and they wanted to use me, as a former world champion, to help with publicity. I think they offered me something like 20 grand for the fight, which was a lot of money for a broke man. At the time, I thought, 'That would be nice. Twenty grand!' It was almost a done deal.

I never actually retired because I was only 29. Getting myself into shape and making a comeback was not an impossibility, as long as I cleaned myself up. The problem was, I never did. I got three days sober but couldn't stick with the discipline. Instead, I said that I was working construction now and refused the fight. The truth is, I didn't want to embarrass myself any more. Wayne was real good and would have probably kicked my ass, but without getting clean and sober there was no way I'd have ever found out.

I'm really proud of what Wayne went on to achieve. He won the WBC bantamweight title and fought 11 world champions in his 34 pro fights. The best bit is we're still really good friends. We've become closer now because he's moved to California, whereas before he was living in Vegas, so I see him and his wife all the time at boxing and Hall of Fame events. His daughter is over 20 years old now, but when she was a little kid, I used to buy her cuddly toys every time I'd hook up with the McCulloughs. She still remembers that.

Unfortunately, my memories of what was going on back then were anything but positive. Finishing as a professional boxer was the least of my concerns. What was about to happen next was the start of a very sad story.

CHAPTER 20

BUSTED

'Every true hustler knows that you cannot hustle forever. You will go to jail eventually'

The Notorious B.I.G.

WHEN I was a teenager, I really wasn't a bad kid. I had the opportunity to join gangs and get involved with some bad people, but I chose to box instead and that discipline helped me out. However, I did get in a bit of trouble, but that was always going to happen in Azusa.

The very first time I got arrested and taken down the police station was when I was 12. I was caught shoplifting in California from Kmart or JCPenney, something like that. Next time was when I was about 15 and in high school. I was on the way to a dance and was trying to be a bit of a homeboy, so I got my mom to drop me off at the corner a block away, instead of in front of the school. So there I was hanging out with the homies and by now we were all drunk across the street from the school. Suddenly, one of the guys I was with threw a bottle just at the moment a cop came past and next thing I know, I was being arrested and ended up in jail for a couple of days. I was the only one who got pulled that night and it wasn't even me who threw the bottle!

Throughout my life, I'd be in jail about 20 times. A few times for 29 days, once in LA County and a number of times in Vegas. One incident that stood out was when I was 28 and going through the separation from my wife and kids. I was living in Pomona with my mom, tripping, getting high, and my wife was living back in her apartment, which was about a 20-minute drive. I went back and forth a couple of times that night, paranoid that she was with someone. I went there at 10pm and then 3am, tripping both times. I ended up breaking into her house and cutting my wrist going through the window. Someone called the police and they arrived almost immediately and put me in the back of their car. Bad memories.

Another time, I was on a bus on the way back from Utah and this homie was there with his girlfriend. He asked, 'Do you do dope?' I said, 'Yeah, I do dope.' His girlfriend didn't say shit, but she was looking at me. So we went to the back of the bus and I took out this little $20 baggie of dope and we did a line of speed each. What I didn't realize was that the girlfriend got pissed off, walked over to the bus driver and told him that I'd given her boyfriend dope. She snitched on me. We pulled up at the next stop and the cops were waiting for me. They took me off, while I was thinking, 'What the fuck is going on?' That was the first time I'd ever been busted for dope. I was supposed to attend court classes, like rehab, and also pay a fine, but I did neither. If I ever go back to jail in Vegas, I'll probably get put inside for a couple of months because there's still a warrant out there for me.

* * *

By the summer of 1995, I'd been in jail about 15 times. I'd been arrested for drugs, jaywalking, but never anything auto-related. Then it happened twice within the space of a few weeks.

Here's what happened the first time. I was staying with this girl in Vegas for about a week and she threw me out. I was pissed off, found her car keys and took off. I guess she didn't report it for a day and a half, but eventually the police caught up with me, busted me for joyriding and put me in jail for about three days. My brother Tim ended up bailing me out, then took me and my truck back to Utah.

About three weeks later, I was back in Vegas. Somebody took me out to a party on the other side of town, east of Las Vegas, and the next morning I took off, high as a kite, and headed for the bus stop. Buses were only coming by about once an hour because this place was in the middle of nowhere. One went by without stopping, then the same again. You have to remember, when you're homeless, sometimes the bus picks you up, other times, they open the door and you say, 'I don't have any money,' and they close the doors and take off. That's what happened that morning and I said, 'Fuck it,' and started walking.

I saw this building far away and headed for it. Turns out it was a car wash. As I got there, some guy got out of his car to get someone's attention to wash it, but he left the keys in the ignition. He got out, I got in and took off. Stupid, stupid. I had that car for four days.

The fourth day was strange and memorable on a few fronts. That evening, I went to the Mirage Hotel where my friend Sam, who worked there, spotted Dennis Rodman and said, 'Let's go over and talk to him.' We had a quick chat, talked shit and then left him to do his thing. Then, later that evening, I left the casino and I'm on the freeway when a couple of cop cars appeared out of nowhere and tried to pull me over. Stupidly, I kept on going and drove off to a different freeway with these cars in pursuit. After maybe five minutes I gave in, pulled over and got out the car.

As I did, the cops had guns on me and one had a dog with him. I put my hands above my head and didn't move. The guy with the cop dog said, 'I'm glad you didn't run when you got out the car. I hate to see these dogs going for people.' 'Me too!' I replied.

I got arrested, taken to the main jail in Las Vegas and was there for the next 20 days. Getting banged up wasn't that memorable, but what was about to happen as a result of it would affect me for the rest of my life.

CHAPTER 21

POSITIVE

'Let us give publicity to HIV/AIDS and not hide it,
because [that is] the only way to make it appear like
a normal illness'

Nelson Mandela

WHEN I got to the jail, they went through the usual drills. Name, date of birth, fingerprints and all the rest. They knew I was slamming dope and asked if I was sharing needles and I replied, 'Yes.' They then asked if I wanted to do a blood test to see if I had HIV and I said, 'Yeah. I'll do it.'

They don't give you the results straight away and as stupid as it sounds, I was more concerned about everything else. I was on the streets, living in my truck and wondering when I could get my next fix, so knowing the results was the last thing on my mind. I also thought, for sure, because of the number of offences I'd committed over recent months and years, I was doing prison now. As it goes, they kicked me out 20 days later. As I was leaving the jail, the police officer said, 'You could have got three years straight in prison. Clean yourself up.' The official court verdict was still in the balance, but in the meantime I walked out of jail.

A few days later, I called up for the results. The lady replied, 'We can't give you the results over the phone, you need to come down in person.' I didn't think anything of it and a few days later went down to the Martin Luther King Hospital. I'd been out of jail for a week by this point. The date was 10 July 1995. A day I'd never forget.

I walked into that clinic alone and expected them to say, 'Get out. We found nothing in your blood.' Eighteen months earlier I was in the ring as a professional boxer, so surely I couldn't be sick, right? In fact, in the last few months, I'd been thinking about making a comeback. I was only 30 years old and many friends and family thought that a return to boxing might do me a lot of good, to help me refocus. It would have because boxing always took care of me. I'd like to make a comeback right now if I had the chance! I had visions of walking back into the ring with everybody screaming like they used to do when I stepped through the ropes. That's the rush I wanted. That's the high I wanted again, not the one from a needle.

Instead, I walked into the waiting room, where there were about four or five other people sitting there anxiously waiting for results. I was called up pretty quickly, walked into the doctor's office and don't remember much of the conversation, apart from, 'Mr Banke. You're HIV positive.' I heard what she said, then a few seconds later it sunk in.

'You're HIV positive.' I replied to the doctor, 'That can't be. I've got babies at home. They need their daddy. I can't be. I can't.'

I walked out of the hospital, back to my truck and laid in the front seat. I then took a deep sigh and said to myself, 'Oh my God. You got the HIV virus.' That fucking blew me away. I then started thinking, 'How am I going to be able to tell everyone? How?'

Next morning, I called my mom and said, 'Mama. I'm coming home. I'll be back pretty soon.' I didn't tell her why, so she probably just thought I was strung out or down on my luck, but definitely had no idea of the news I was bringing home with me. I needed a few days to try and clear my head before heading back and spent the next few days in shock, walking the streets in a daze.

About a week after the diagnosis, I put my shit into my truck, got myself a bus ticket and headed back to 29 Brooks Ave, Venice, California, to my mom's little one-bed apartment, just off the boulevard, by the ocean. All I had with me was a paper bag with my things in it.

The bus journey was about four hours and I don't even remember it. I was in limbo. As I walked in, my mom and sister Rebecca gave me a big hug. I was living on the streets at the time, so I smelt like shit and looked like shit. That must have been hard for them to see.

We sat there on the couch in the living room and my sister started saying, 'Why don't you get back into boxing again, Paul? That will help you out. Get you some money, get you fit and healthy again.' 'I can't,' I replied. 'What do you mean you can't? Of course you can.' That's when I said, 'I've got something to share with you both.'

I hadn't intended on telling them so quickly, but within 15 minutes of walking through the door, I dropped the news. 'I got tested HIV positive.' My sister screamed, 'You liar,' not because she actually thought I was lying, but because she didn't want to believe it. They both started crying uncontrollably. I kept saying, 'It's OK, it's OK,' but it really wasn't. My mom was holding Becca back as she wanted to run out of the door, struggling with the news.

My mom then called my brothers within a few minutes and had them both on the line at the same time. Steve was in Texas and Tim in Utah. 'Hey, you guys. Your brother came home. I got some bad news.' Then she started crying, 'He's HIV positive.' They took the news real bad, which then upset me as I didn't want to hear or see anyone crying.

Unfortunately, the worst was still to come.

CHAPTER 22

DEATH'S DOOR

*'In 1985, Rock Hudson died with AIDS. I'd
only injected a few times at that point and wasn't
thinking about things like getting a virus from
needles. No different to a guy who gets in his car,
drives real fast and never thinks he'll have a car
accident. Or a 16-year-old girl who never thinks
she'll be the one who will get pregnant. You think it
will never happen. Let me tell you – it happens'*

Paul Banke

A T the time, I was staying in a Christian home as I was supposed to be doing time for prison for the grand theft auto, but instead I was here for the next six to nine months, where I was placed to recover and get clean from my addictions. The Christian home knew I had the virus and they were cool with me going for check-ups with my mom.

Getting checked for AIDS was purely my decision. After being diagnosed with the HIV virus, I'd kind of accepted that and wasn't expecting them to tell me I had AIDS. If anything, a part of me still thought they'd tell me they got it wrong with the HIV diagnosis. We did the blood work and then about ten days later, on 21 August 1995, my mom came and picked me up, and we drove to see a doctor in Carson to find out the results.

The doctor came out and explained the difference to us between HIV, AIDS and normal T cells. 'Mr Banke, anyone who has between 500 and 1,500 T cells is normal. Anyone who has between 200 and under 500 has HIV and anyone below 200 has full-blown AIDS.' Then I asked, 'What do I have?' The doctor gave it to me straight. 'You have a cell count of 80. You have full-blown AIDS, Mr Banke.'

The second I heard the word AIDS, I jumped up, opened the door and ran out into the parking lot. That scared the fuck out of me. My mom and one of the nurses ran out after me and tried to console me as I was kicking and screaming. Mom caught up with me and said, 'Pauli. Please. You got to go back and listen to what the doctor has to say,' which I did.

Part of me was thinking logically, maybe because I was really scared, I don't know, but either way, from the moment I had the news I wasn't in denial and was straight up with my wife.

I told her what had happened about stealing the car and then the drug test. She needed to know, so that she and the kids could then be tested. Thank God they were all clear. Thankfully, even though we were separated, she still accepted me when I told her. Some people didn't, which was tough to deal with, but I got used to it.

With the court case still open for my joyriding, when we discovered I had full-blown AIDS, me and my mom sent the report to the court in Vegas. Soon after they received it, they dismissed the case. It was cheaper for them not to press charges, as most people were dying from AIDS. They didn't want the medical bills. Basically, they didn't see the point of trying to keep me alive.

I also started to make funeral arrangements because being told I had AIDS in my mind was the same as being told I had a death sentence. Some of the people who had gone public with the virus by then included Arthur Ashe, Greg Louganis, Esteban De Jesús, Freddie Mercury and N.W.A rapper Eazy-E. With the exception of Louganis, the rest were dead. Eazy-E was born the same year as me, but had died five months earlier in March 1995. My future didn't look great.

There were few stories of people living and, in fact, a number of people were committing suicide after getting the diagnosis. That was fact. Back then, Bill Clinton was president and he had papers stacked ten feet high on his desk about people who were dying from AIDS. It was big news, but never happy news.

The ultimate dream for me now was to live to 40 as I didn't think I would. I was really worried about getting sick, as I am to this very day, because if you get sick, with a really weak immune system, that can take you out. I remember telling my mom to close the windows in the house or roll the windows up in the car because I was worried a draft would make me sick. I was paranoid.

Also, my kids were babies back then. Four and two. It was heartbreaking to have to think about funerals, but it had to be done. I organized a burial plot, ten pall-bearers, signed up for my casket and everything. My family were each going to contribute a piece towards the funeral costs. That was some horrible, weird shit for all of us.

From the moment I was told I had AIDS, I woke up in the middle of the night pretty much for a whole year, crying and real scared. All I thought about every day was that I was going to die, so my thoughts were, 'If I'm a die, I'm a keep getting high.'

I was living with my mom in Venice Beach now and as much as she wanted to help me out, I was a nightmare to live with because of the amount of dope I was slamming. I just wanted to bury my head in the sand, but unfortunately, that wasn't an option.

CHAPTER 23

OUTCAST

'Honesty is the first chapter in the book of wisdom'

Thomas Jefferson

P EOPLE often ask me, 'Paul. How did you get AIDS?' The answer is, I can't tell you that specific moment or who was responsible for passing the virus to me, but I do know that it was from sharing a needle or having unprotected sex.

The year I turned professional in 1985 was the same year I slammed a needle in my arm for the first time. Back then, the virus was called ARC [AIDS Related Complex]. AIDS stands for Acquired Immune Deficiency Syndrome, but what they didn't realize back then was that it was the HIV virus that was responsible for AIDS, so they went with ARC. Anyway, back in 1985, I was starting to attend parties and was becoming well known in the media, which meant getting women and drugs was very easy. I was only 21 years old and went crazy.

I got AIDS from living a certain lifestyle and making bad choices, but I was embarrassed to share that with anyone. At the time, apart from my family and wife, I don't remember who else I told. However, a month after I got the news, my mom suggested I speak to the media and helped me get in touch with them to let the public know. I really didn't want to do it, though. I was happy getting high as it took me to a place that stopped me temporarily thinking about the virus.

The media picked up on me having AIDS, so my mom decided it was time to release an official statement instead of letting the press come to their own conclusions. I would be the first US boxer in history to go public about the virus.

A month after the diagnosis, I read out a three-page statement to a guy from the *LA Times* and a photographer, while my mom and brother Steve were standing by me. I don't remember what was in the statement because my mom had written it for me, but she made me practise it over and over again to make me sound convincing. The basics of the content were explaining to everyone I had full-blown AIDS and how my life would now be different as a result.

After an interview with the newspaper guy, we went outside and the photographer said, 'Let's take a photo.' As I'm standing there waiting for him to snap the shot, he said, 'Do you always smile in photos?' I said, 'Yeah.' He said, 'Don't smile this time. Smile with your eyes instead.' In other words, don't smile. It was a sad story and he wanted a photo to reflect that, which in itself made me sad.

Soon after, the guys from all the news channels started getting in touch. Channel 2, Channel 4, Channel 7, Channel, 9, CNN, you name it, and they were all asking the same questions, about three or four times a day. It was tiring me out and I was getting even more depressed. Also, as everyone was finding out, people kept coming up to me saying, 'Oh, poor Paul. Poor Paul.' I didn't want that 'poor Paul' shit. I didn't want that sympathy because they thought I was going to die.

I was in the press, but the likes of Magic Johnson got major television publicity because they were in the limelight and were clean-living guys. Then, a year later, heavyweight Tommy Morrison announced he had it and all the media attention went with him. Maybe they didn't want to get involved with me to their level because I was strung out on dope and my face didn't fit. I was a faded name compared to these guys, but at least the big benefit was that they raised awareness of the disease at a time when a lot of people with AIDS, especially celebrities back then, were in denial.

Even when they died, they'd make out the heart attack or pneumonia was not related to any condition they had. There was a big shame that came with AIDS and I was trying to let the public know that having AIDS was not something to be ashamed of. It was more the lifestyle people lived that needed to be addressed.

One of the biggest stigmas connected to the virus back then was being gay. People came at me all the time asking if I was gay. You're a man, you have AIDS, you're gay. That was the stereotype. For me, I didn't and still don't give a shit if you're gay, straight, transgender or whichever background, because we still all gotta deal with it in the same way. We're all human beings. Whether it be from unsafe sex, injecting drugs, a blood transfusion, anyone could and still can get the virus. That was my reason to make some noise with the media.

I also had something else to contend with. Shortly after the diagnosis, I went to see a neurologist with my mom. He conducted some tests on me and told me that I had pugilistic dementia. I didn't know what it was, to be honest, and when I found out, compared to the AIDS virus, it really wasn't a big issue for me. I turned to the doctor and said, 'Cool,' then walked out as the doctor stood there a little shocked at how unconcerned I was. Even to this day, I know I might repeat things a few times and show some effects from the boxing, but it doesn't concern me. It is what it is. The AIDS virus, however, always has my undivided attention.

* * *

Despite raising awareness of AIDS in the media, I'll be honest, at first I didn't try to educate myself about the virus. I had a lot of people tell me stuff, but I didn't go and look for the information. It scared the fuck out of me. People were dying, so why would I want to read anything about that? My mom was great when it came to this, though. She went out and learned everything. Symptoms, effects of medication, came with me to see the doctors. Everything.

The main and probably the only AIDS drug available at the time was AZT (azidothymidine) and everyone infected had banked all their hope on it making a difference. It was mixed with a cocktail of other drugs and at the time I was taking 13 pills a day. A lot of people reported really bad side effects from the meds, but with me it was OK. At a time when I didn't have much to be thankful for, not having any side effects was a blessing.

Years later, after many tests, it turned out AZT was almost useless. The drug was kind of rushed on to the market to fight the HIV and AIDS epidemic, without having been tested properly. Everyone in the media was making out it was some kind of super drug, when it wasn't really. At the time of writing in 2019, I now only take two pills a day. Big old pills, though!

Back in 1995, I started off taking my meds as instructed by the doctor properly, with all the best intentions, but then I started hitting the dope, getting high and not taking them as I should. I was on and off for about the next ten years. There's no excuses. If the medication makes me live longer, then 'Hello!', take the damn things.

They say illness doesn't discriminate and that's true, but if you're poor and ill, then you've got added problems. I didn't have medical insurance and at the time people were dying because they weren't covered. Many on the streets also died because they couldn't afford the transportation to get them to and from the medical centers, things you take for granted when you have a few bucks in your pocket.

I was very lucky to have got on to the Ryan White program, which covered all my medical care and support that I needed. It had only been around for two years at the time and I thank God it was there to help me. I'd end up staying with the program for about eight years until Medicare took over. They still support me to this very day.

Unfortunately, at the time, I threw that support back in their face because my drug addiction once again messed things up. You have to remember that AIDS pills were, and still are now, very expensive. About a thousand bucks a bottle at the time. So instead of taking my meds, I'd sell them to these Russian guys I knew for a couple of hundred bucks per bottle. When you're trying to buy drugs, that was good money. A lot of people were doing that because the Russians back then wanted the medication as they didn't have access to the same stuff we had.

Probably the hardest part of having the virus in the 1990s was the rejection. Some people didn't want to shake your hand and others would literally step away when you told them you had AIDS because very few people understood how you could catch it. You'd see their facial expression change.

I remember going to a family christening party at my grandma's house and everyone knew I had the virus. She was about 70 and was handing out glasses for egg-nog, but when it came to me, I got a Styrofoam cup. I was the only one. That wasn't a one-off. It happened all the time. Back then, it was like, 'Don't drink from his glass. He's got AIDS.

Don't use the same spoon. He's got AIDS.' People didn't even want me kissing their kids on the cheek and I'm talking close family members. I'd be like, 'That's cool,' and smile, but actually, that really hurt. I still feel that pain when I think about it now.

One of the few people at the time who didn't step away was Mike Tyson. He showed me love. I will never forget one episode soon after I tested positive for the HIV virus. Mike was getting interviewed, not sure if it was HBO, but it was one of the big channels. He spots me, cuts the interview short, comes over to me and gives me a big hug. It made me feel like a million bucks. He told the interviewer, 'This is also a world champ. His name's Paul Banke.'

Unfortunately, not everybody saw it like Mike and that became obvious quickly.

CHAPTER 24

SCARED

'We think sometimes that poverty is only being hungry, naked and homeless. The poverty of being unwanted, unloved and uncared for is the greatest poverty. We must start in our own homes to remedy this kind of poverty'

Mother Teresa

FROM 1995/96, on and off, I was homeless for about a year. I stayed with my mom here and there for a few weeks, but then she would kick me out because I kept getting high on crack, speed and cocaine. I'd then go to rehab and repeat this time after time. It was a never-ending toxic cycle that I couldn't see myself getting out of.

I even started to run out of places to live. After my truck broke down I got strung out, went to rehab and what happened was, the state gave me a $6,000 pension. I gave my mom a couple of grand and put a deposit down on an Acura Legend car with the rest. The problem was that my money was going on dope and I couldn't make the payments on it. I went back to rehab for a number of weeks and my family said, 'Don't worry, we'll take care of the car,' referring to the payments, as I was three months behind. But they didn't take care of it and the car got taken away.

One of the few places I was still able to find a bed for the night was in jail and that wasn't by preference. I was still getting arrested for stupid shit. Sometimes I wished I was getting busted for bigger crimes, though, because it was embarrassing! One time I got picked up for jaywalking in Vegas and the police put me in jail with guys who'd done things like assault, armed robbery, domestic violence, that sort of thing.

Soon after I arrived, these guys were like, 'What you get put in for?' I didn't want to say jaywalking. They asked again and I said quietly, 'Errr. Jaywalking.' They started laughing. Other times people would ask, 'How long you in for?', and I'd say, 29 days. They'd look at me and say, '29 days? I can sit on my head for 29 days. That ain't shit.' But 29 days for me was a lot of time.

Thankfully, nothing happened with these guys but on other occasions, I'd see fights break out that simply never needed to. Even cops were beating people up; everyone was always ready to fight. It was scary in there, but you had to put on that tough face. I remember one time I was brought into court with this black guy, who was a manager for Starbucks and had been convicted of domestic violence. Because we were there early, we had breakfast together and got talking. I could tell he was very sharp. He was a businessman and started to talk to me about how to talk to people when getting a job and making the most of your money. He was a cool guy and we clicked straight away.

Now I don't have a problem if you're black, Mexican, Asian, whatever, but unfortunately that's not the case in jail. The cops, who were Mexican-American, grabbed this guy and put him in this cell with about 20 Mexicans on purpose, just so they could stand there and watch the Mexicans beat the shit out of him. That was bullshit.

Some things never changed, though. To some I looked Mexican, but to many, I looked Asian, which was not great as the Mexicans and Asians always fought in jail. The Mexicans all had last names like Hernandez, Rodriguez, Gonzalez, where's mine is Banke. They'd be like, 'What kind of name is that? You ain't Mexican. You Asian.' I'd be telling these people I was Chicano and they'd say, 'Prove it. Speak Spanish.' I obviously couldn't, so I had to get my mom on the phone to help. 'Mama. Can you speak to these people and tell them I'm not Asian?' She'd say, 'Put them on the phone,' then she'd be telling them, 'He's Yaqui. Native American. That's why he looks Asian. But he has strong Mexican roots.' Mom to the rescue.

One time, I was in jail and I'm sitting there with these Mexican guys who were from a big gang. I'm overhearing a conversation about boxing because I'm nosey, and the guys say, 'You listening to our fucking conversation?' The guys from Mexico stand up and start saying, 'You fucking with the wrong people.'

I was a fighter, but I was scared. I told them I was a former professional champion and that's why I was interested in their conversation. One of them then says, 'You box, homes? What's your name?' 'My name is Paul Banke,' I replied. The Mexican guys say all excited, 'Oh, Paul Banke! He beat Zaragoza!' One of them then points to me and says, 'You're the one with the AIDS. I saw your story on TV.' He jumped up and went over to the phone and said, 'I'm calling my uncle to check you are who you say.' Basically, this guy wanted to kick my ass if I didn't match who I said I was.

Zaragoza was a hero in Mexico, so my fight was a big thing over there, especially as we fought three times. The homie suddenly shouts all excited, 'Hey Paul! My uncle wants to talk to you!' I said with relief, 'Cool.' If there's something I learned from that experience, it's that you don't listen to other people's conversations!

Then there were other times when I was treated unexpectedly well in jail. One day, this Chicano cop pulled me over when I was in this crammed cell. He called me out, 'Come over here, Paul Banke.' I didn't recognize the guy and started to think the worst. He then says, 'You don't remember me, do you?' Now I was really getting worried. 'No I don't,' I replied. It turned out I used to go out with his sister. As we got out of the cell, he said, 'How you doing, Paul?' He showed me some love, kept me away from everyone else and put me in a cell by myself.

* * *

About a year after my diagnosis, nothing had changed in terms of the way people treated me as a person with AIDS. I was still a leper to most. Mike Tyson was one of the few who continued to go out of his way to try and pick my spirits up.

I went to watch Mike fight in Vegas in November 1996 against Evander Holyfield. Bob King very kindly picked me up, then I met up with my good friend Richie Rich (Richard Hansen) and a few others. We were there for the press conference, the open workout at the Golden Gloves gym and the weigh-in. There were a lot of boxing people in Vegas that week. A lot!

On the day of the open workout, me and Richie Rich joined a really long line of people waiting to get an autograph or photo with Mike. We're not just talking fight fans, but the likes of Bob Case from the IBA (International Boxing Association) and former world champions Lloyd Honeyghan from England and Jeff Fenech from Australia.

As we're waiting in line, Mike spots me. He was in the middle of an interview, I think it was with an Italian reporter, when he stopped talking to the guy and came over and held me tight, then kissed me on the forehead before talking with me for a few minutes. He wasn't scared of the AIDS but more importantly hadn't forgotten about me, the person. That was classy from Mike, especially at a time when my self-esteem was real low.

We also decided to crash the press conference, which was a closed thing with a big sign outside saying, 'Press only.' Me and Richie said, 'Fuck that. We're going in.' We snuck in through a side door and this security guard spotted us, so we ran and ditched him, but managed to sit down at the other end of the room without him noticing. The press conference was going on and me and Richie got split up. In the meantime, Richie had got into the whole press thing so much that he even pretended he was a journalist, got on the microphone and asked Mike about sparring with Holyfield at the Olympic training camp.

As the press conference was starting to wrap up, WBC president José Sulaimán spots me and calls us up on the stage for a chat. We started talking to him about the fight, but also if he knew how we could get tickets as we didn't have any. José didn't hesitate and said, 'Leave it with me.' He sorted us out with good seats. The next thing you know, we're standing with José, Don King, taking pictures on the stage. Crazy. Then, out of the corner of Richie's eye, he sees the security guard we ditched earlier and he's now spotted us. We didn't want him snatching us by the arms in front of José, Don and all these other guys, so Richie turns to me and says, 'We gotta go. Now!' And just like that, we ran out of there.

After that press conference, we hooked up with Jeff Fenech and one of his friends from Australia and ended up having lunch together at the MGM. After a long lunch, we left because Jeff wanted to take us to the Stratosphere and go on that rollercoaster at the top. As we're walking out, Richie sees Bobby Czyz, the former two-weight world champion, and says, 'Hey Bobby Czyz! What's up?' Bobby gave him a look, like 'Who are you?' and Richie went for him. Jeff Fenech saw what was going on and jumped in between them, thankfully calming things down. Never a dull day with Richie around!

I'd like to say a few words about Jeff. I got to meet him shortly after I was diagnosed with AIDS. Like Mike Tyson, at a time when everyone hesitated to make any physical contact, when I first met him, the first thing he did was give me a long, almighty hug, then said straight away, 'Is there anything I can do? Stay strong and talk. Don't lose contact with me now.'

And you know what – we never did. Jeff lives in Australia but is over in the US a lot for the fights and whenever he is, we still hook up to this very day. Along the way, he's helped me out financially and more than anything has been available for a talk at the end of the phone whenever I've needed him. He gets my story, keeps it real and only ever focuses on the positive side of things. I'm proud to call him a good friend.

Back to Mike and Evander. The funny thing was, I was also friends with Evander and a couple of days before the fight I decided to call him up and wish him luck. As you know, I'm a morning person and I get up early. Really early. I called the hotel he was staying at about 3am. I don't remember if it was The Mirage, Caesars Palace, whatever, but I called reception and told them who I was and asked, 'Can you put me through to Evander Holyfield, please?' And they did! I got through and this deep voice answers,

'Who the hell is this calling me at this hour?' I replied all upbeat, 'It's Paul Banke!'

Evander hung up. Fun times.

Shame the next few years weren't packed with as many great memories.

CHAPTER 25

DRUG DAMAGE

*'Addiction is a hugely complex and destructive
disease, and its impact can be simply devastating.
All too often, lives and families can be
shattered by it'*

Kate Middleton

THE same year I gatecrashed the Holyfield–Tyson press conference, I met a special lady called Connie. We met at the HIV clinic at the Cedars-Sinai Hospital, LA, where Connie was working as a volunteer. It's the biggest hospital in LA, where a lot of actors and celebrities go. From the moment I met her, we instantly clicked and I started flirting with her. This went on for a while and eventually we exchanged numbers, started hanging out and then dating.

When I first starting flirting with Connie, I remember saying, 'You might know me as a boxer. I was a world champion.' She said, 'Really? I've never heard of you!' We both started laughing, but truthfully, she had no idea who I was. It wasn't until one day in early 1997, when I took her to a press conference for Oscar De La Hoya versus Pernell Whitaker at Planet Hollywood in Beverly Hills, that she started to realize the level I boxed at.

There were loads of well-known faces there, including Roberto Duran. Boxing fans who knew me started coming up asking to take pictures and when boxers were coming over and speaking with me, I'd introduce them to her. Connie wasn't jaded, though, because she knew the whole Hollywood scene and it didn't overly impress her, and that made me like her even more. Whereas I wanted to take photos with everyone, she didn't want to be the girlfriend who's in all the photos and took a back seat.

We ended up dating for a couple of years, but it was not a perfect relationship because of where my head was at the time. We were living with my mom at first in Venice Beach. She had her little son back then, who's now a grown man and real nice guy. The problem was, at the time I was still using drugs and at the beginning I was making out I wasn't.

One time Connie found out that I'd gone to this house in Delano, California with my cousins and she didn't know that was a regular place I'd stop off at to pick up drugs. That night, Connie was thinking, 'What's taking him so long?' and decided to walk towards the freeway looking for me. The problem was she didn't know where she was going in the city and soon got lost. She ended up finding a gas station and called her parents to come and pick her up. When she told me later what had happened, she gave it to me straight. 'I don't do this. This is not the way I live.' I said, 'I'm going to stop, I'm going to stop,' but there was no way I was giving up the drugs. As much as I wanted to, I couldn't.

Then there was another incident when she found out I was scoring drugs and it happened to be the same complex in north Hollywood that her cousin lived in. Her cousin said, 'I know who your boyfriend is. He be going downstairs with one of the drug dealers.' She was like, 'What?' Connie confronted me. 'I thought you was going to get clean, but this is yet another incident. I'm not going to do this.' At the time, her son was only three years old and he'd be around us. Connie didn't do drugs and it wasn't fair for both of them to be around something like that.

The thing with Connie was, she had a very big heart. She tried to be very firm towards me, but she understood I was going through my own issues after being diagnosed with AIDS, my ex-wife wouldn't let me see my children and I wasn't working. Doing the drugs was an easy way for me to deal with not facing reality.

Thankfully, she never saw me overdose, although on one occasion she thought it was close. My mom called Connie up to let her know that I was being rushed to the hospital. Connie was thinking, 'Oh my goodness. This could be it,' but thankfully it turned out that I had food poisoning.

The problem with doing drugs in a relationship is that the dope brings paranoia. Connie was in college at the time and she had a beeper (pager) and I would beep her like crazy every day, up to ten times a day. I'd then get upset because she wouldn't respond right back to me. When we did speak, she'd say, 'Fool. I'm in class! I can't just get up. I need to go find a payphone.' I'd say, 'Then don't pick it up.' But when she didn't, I'd leave message after message. She'd then call back and say, 'What's with the voice messages? You told me not to pick them up?'

Another time, when Connie was staying at her grandmother's house in Compton, she found out from a neighbor that I was racing up and down her street, trying to find out if she was with somebody else, peeking through the windows. That happened a few times. I'd ask, 'Who you with? What you doing?' and she'd reply, 'I ain't with nobody.' She'd address it with me and would say, 'I know it's not you making you do this, it's what you're taking.'

But then other times, I was like a functional alcoholic. I'm not the kind of guy to say I had the drugs under control. I didn't. But I was clear enough to know when to speak to my loved ones when I was strung out. I'd never make a call or see anyone straight after using.

When I was with Connie, I'd have my donuts and coffee every morning and every Saturday I'd get up and go rollerblading down Venice Beach with my earphones on. I tried to get Connie to do it and she said, 'You've lost your damn mind! I don't do that.' I'd be off rollerblading while Connie would go to the park with her son.

The relationship with Connie was a rollercoaster and despite having some great fun memories, the lows and the negative episodes from my dope were too much for her. In the end, she had to leave me, which was the right thing to do, as she needed to look out for herself and her son. She remained cool with my family and thankfully, many years later, we'd reconnect.

* * *

The food poisoning episode should have acted as a wake-up call, but it didn't. I eventually did overdose. A few days before Oscar De La Hoya was getting ready to fight Oba Carr in May 1999, I did a roofing job and got paid a couple of hundred bucks. I gave my mom $50 and went and spent the rest of it on cocaine at a friend's house in Echo Park, Los Angeles. He was a homie thug and had a gun with him, and was moving dope around left and right. People were coming in and out of the house buying. I slammed cocaine about six or seven times that night. Then he and his girlfriend started fighting. She was smoking crack and I can't remember why they were arguing but he didn't want to give her any more dope because whatever he had left he wanted to sell.

She took off out of the room and had a crack pipe with her. I followed her and said, 'Can I get a hit?' 'Go ahead,' she replied. That's all I remember. Next thing I woke up on the floor, with my friend screaming on top of me as I'm saying, 'What?' My homie was mad that I'd done the crack pipe and told me I had a seizure. He took me to the hospital and said, 'Don't tell them you took drugs, just tell them you had a seizure, because if they know you OD'd on dope, you'll go to jail.' That seizure took away my taste buds for about a week.

I went to rehab after coming out of hospital. In fact, I did 13 stints in rehab, which is nothing to brag about. I'd get very good care from the clinic and it was free then, whereas now they want thousands of dollars. I'd come, then go back in and this would happen over and over again.

The effects of drugs didn't just leave me in a bad way, it also left my loved ones in pain. I tried to do my drugs away from anyone who knew me well as I was embarrassed for them to see me strung out, but a few years after the Echo Park incident, I went missing after a drugs binge and my mom came looking for me. I was in some dingy little motel near the Luxor Hotel on the Las Vegas Strip, booked in under my brother's name, and had been out for about four days. She knew my hangouts and found me. When she walked in, I was lying down on the bed and there were flies swarming around my mouth because I hadn't moved in so long.

If my own personal experiences didn't highlight why I needed to stop taking dope, then losing people close to me should have. I lost two of my friends from Azusa to drugs, Frank and Ricky, who were brothers. They were good people.

Frank died in jail from an overdose in 1995. A few months after I overdosed in Echo Park, I went back to Vegas in 2000 and called Ricky's phone. I left him a message. 'Hey Ricky! Where you at? Give me a call, man, and let's meet up.' A week later, his brother Guy called me up and said, 'Hey Paul. Ricky got shot in the head.'

RIP brothers. Gone but never forgotten.

* * *

Later that year, 2000, Mike Tyson was getting ready to fight Andrew Golota on 20 October and called just to have a chat before he got on the plane. I was with my second wife at the time at her house in Vegas and had a quick chat, then said, 'Mom. Michael wants to speak with you.' 'Michael? Who's Michael?' she says. When my mom answered the phone, he said, 'Hello Mrs Banke. This is Mike Tyson.' When mom put the phone down, she said, 'I couldn't believe how the most ferocious boxer in the world had the most beautiful soft voice. Not to mention how incredibly respectful he is.'

Same year, Mike gave me a ride home in his Mercedes as he was on his way back from the gym. Mike was sat up front with the driver while I sat at the back. I was working construction at the time and Mike asked how things were going for me, and I told him I'd started a new job paying $21.06 an hour, but that it wasn't a lot of money. He looked at me with a straight face and said, 'That is big money.' Whether it was or not, he gave me a sense of worth.

However, not everyone was a fan of Mike. I had a friend I worked with in construction called Tex and he used to constantly bad mouth him. One day, I decided to take Tex and his little son Pete, who was a huge Mike Tyson fan, to meet him at the Golden Gloves Gym working out. Mike was getting ready for a fight at the time. When we got there, all these cars were pulling up full of people. Mercedes, Hummers, then this Rolls-Royce pulled up. They were all part of Mike's entourage. Mike gets out, sees us, then comes over. He gave me a hug, then I introduced him to Tex and he gave him a hug, then he saw Pete and picked him up and gave him a big hug. He then said, 'Come in the gym with me Pete, come on.' The look on Pete and Tex's face was priceless. That Monday at work, Tex couldn't stop talking about Mike. He was now a big fan.

Despite support from good friends and family, I still continued to end up behind bars. In 2003, I was back in the Vegas jail. When I got in, the police officer said, 'You know where you're going, Mr Banke,' because I'd been there so many times. Not something to be proud of or a place to want to be familiar with. However, they'd remodelled it and were taking me to a different floor than I'd been to previously. They knew I had full-blown AIDS and decided to isolate me. Some jails did that, some didn't.

Even though I was in a cell on my own, it was really hard to sleep. If you've been in jail, you can understand this. Everybody's talking, a lot of people are shouting things like, 'Shut the fuck up, man,' while people are talking nonsense, but very few sleep. The guard kept checking on me really often and I asked him why he kept doing that. He replied, 'Because when you're in a jail cell on your own, your mind can start going crazy. I just want to check you're OK.' He wasn't wrong. Your mind does nothing but think, think, think and when you overthink, you can start to lose control.

Thankfully, my last stint in jail was February 2004 in Las Vegas. I was in for a possession of drugs charge. After that, I behaved myself. Well, maybe not totally, but I didn't get caught as much! I guess it was like a phase. I did the drugs phase, the homeless phase and the jail phase. I was now done with that side of my life, which was a positive, but that's not to say the next decade was going to be easy cruising.

CHAPTER 26

HOMETOWN HERO

'Today will never happen again. Don't waste it with a false start or no start at all'

Og Mandino

ALTHOUGH I married my second wife in Vegas on 12 August 2000, my mistress was still dope. When you start doing drugs in a relationship, it might not crash for a while but it will crash eventually. Absolutely no doubt about it. Similar to my first wife, I became paranoid and jealous all the time, and that eventually wrecked the marriage. By 2002, I was divorced again.

I stayed in Vegas for about four or five years and on 17 March 2005, I got married again to a lovely lady called Theresa. I was still strung out, but I was trying to get some normality into my life. I started training white collar fighters in downtown LA and with a straight head on, I could have made and kept some really decent money.

I had a real mix of clients. A lady attorney and this big gay guy who was also called Paul. He was cool and we got on real well. I have gay friends and you have to understand, a lot of the gay guys around Beverly Hills were loaded, but not just that, they accepted me for having the virus when many didn't. Once again, though, I couldn't stay off the dope. There's a video of me on YouTube at the time saying that I was straightening out my life, but that was bullshit. I was still strung out and ended up separating from Theresa less than a year after getting married because I was incapable of holding down a relationship.

One episode around this time I'm able to look back positively on was an unexpected phone call. I'd already separated from my wife and was living in Hollywood between my mom's apartment and homeless shelters. On this particular day in 2006, I'd just stepped off a bus when I received the call. I could see it was an LA number, but I didn't recognize it. I answered, 'Hello?' A voice replied, 'My champion! My champion!' There's only one person who called me that. I replied, 'José Sulaimán?' 'Yes Paul!' Oh my gosh. José called me when he was in hospital to check up on how I was doing. I asked him how he was and he said, 'I'm good. I'm checking to see if you need anything?' There he was recovering in hospital and he's taken the time to see how I was. You can't believe how good that call made me feel. I was high off that call for days.

Just over a couple of years after getting married, tragedy struck. Theresa died from cancer. When she passed away

I desperately wanted to cry, but I couldn't because I was so high back then. It's terrible to say, but when I got separated from my second and third wives, the pain was nothing like the first time. I was strung out and didn't give a fuck. No kids involved, no boxing on the line. If I could turn back the clocks and treat those people differently and be clean, I'd do it in a heartbeat. It was almost like I could see myself and didn't want that version of me to do what I was doing, but I couldn't stop it.

* * *

One of the few things I did try to keep consistent after getting the AIDS diagnosis was keeping in work. Obviously not permanent jobs because I couldn't hold anything down, but finding jobs day to day to bring in some cash. By the end of 2007, I was living back in Venice Beach with my mom for a few months and I used to take the city bus most mornings to go to the big stores and stand in line outside to see if there was any work on offer. Construction, painting, whatever.

There was always a number of immigrants there who didn't speak English and were desperate for work. Mexicans, Hondurans, you name it. All they could say was 'Labor, labor.' Although I didn't speak their language, I did my best to hook them up for work. I was hard up myself and a lot of the time I was queueing up I was actually living in a homeless shelter, but many of these guys didn't even have that luxury because they were either illegal or refused. These guys waited for eight hours, which was like a job in itself. I'd stay for a couple of hours and if I got ten or 20 rejections, I was done. I'd walk away tired. Not these guys.

Anyway, on the morning of 3 October 2007, I jumped on the city bus on the way to try and get some day labor on a construction project. The guys who didn't speak English sat at the back of the bus, but I didn't like sitting there because that's where all the chaos was. I didn't mind when I was younger but I was 43 by this time and sat further up the front of this packed bus.

As we pulled up to Pico Boulevard bus stop, this Chicano walked on, a well-built, big guy, no less than six feet tall and still wearing his bracelet from county jail. Instead of taking a seat, he started talking shit in Mexican to the driver, then began slapping him hard. I couldn't understand what he was saying, but all I could see was the bus driver, who was about my size and a lot older, taking a beating. I felt bad for him, so I got up, walked over fast and hit this guy once with a left hook to the jaw. Down he went.

We were still at Pico Boulevard bus stop and some security guards saw what happened and asked the driver if he was OK. They were getting ready to go for me when the driver said, 'No. He's OK, he's OK. Leave him alone. He's the one you want,' pointing at the Chicano out cold on the bus floor. The bus driver then opened the door and we pulled this guy out to the sidewalk, closed the door and left him there dazed. When I walked back on, the old ladies were screaming with joy, tapping my legs, hugging me as I went past, and the Mexicans at the back were standing up, cheering and clapping. The incident even made it into the *Free Venice Beachhead* newsletter a few days later. They said, 'Paul's courage against the thug stands in stark contrast to the sheep-like behavior that too many of us exhibit. In today's America, Paul Banke's heroism seems to be as rare as hen's teeth.'

Not sure I'd call myself a hero, but it felt good to have a high moment in my life that didn't come from a syringe. Unfortunately, those moments were still rare at the time, even though they were presented to me on a platter for the taking in the coming years.

CHAPTER 27

HALL OF SHAME

*'I was excited to join Filipino sensation Luisito
Espinosa at my induction and some of the most
legendary boxers ever to have laced a pair of gloves
who have already been inducted, including Lennox
Lewis, Gabriel Ruelas, Roger Mayweather,
Paul Banke, Ken Norton, Genaro "Chicanito"
Hernandez and the late Diego "Chico" Corrales'*

Former world champion Wayne McCullough
reflects on his WBC Legends of Boxing Museum
induction. BBC website, 7 December 2010.

I'D retired from professional boxing in December
1993 and just under 15 years later, I was still being
recognized for my efforts.

On 21 June 2008, I was inducted into the California
Boxing Hall of Fame. A day that I should have been
celebrating, remembering and sharing. Instead, I can barely
recall what happened. I'd come off the drugs a couple of
days before, but when you've been on the dope consistently
for so long, it takes a long time to get it out of your system.

I was inducted alongside the likes of Laila Ali, Michele Chong, Israel Vazquez and Jack Mosley (Shane's dad), but I don't remember any of these people on the day. All I remember was Ruben Castillo doing a long speech introducing me and that's about it. It was an opportunity for me to shine but instead I did the opposite. The same goes with the WBC Legends of Boxing Museum, which was the same year. I was among the first members to be honored into the museum in 2008. Others included the likes of Bobby Chacon, Roger Mayweather and Danny Lopez, but for the life of me I don't remember anyone on the day.

It's funny how your brain remembers certain random things, though, and one memory I do have of that year was when I was working in Vegas doing some construction work and bumped into Henry Tillman. I was on this high-rise building and was about 25 storeys up when I spotted Henry walking on the sidewalk about to get into his car and ride off. I shouted, 'Henry! Henry Tillman.' Henry's looking left, then right, then finally looks up and sees me. The second he realized it was me, he started laughing. I ran down to him and the first thing I said was, 'I can spot that walk from anywhere!'

There was only one major highlight for me in 2009. I became a proud grandfather for the first time. I now have three grandchildren, but back then I didn't fully appreciate how special that was. You can only spend time, not save it, and I spent mine badly back then.

In March 2010, the *LA Times* came over to my small one-bedroom apartment and did an interview, basically trying to share with the public where I was at with my life. I had two dogs, my birds, no car and an apartment that was so badly in need of fumigation, I had to dump all my furniture.

However, the article was making things out to be worse than they were. You have to remember that I lived on the streets, so having a few roaches in an apartment was no big deal. Not having a car wasn't a problem either because I used to get on the bus and subway in Hollywood and get to wherever I needed to. I went without a car for nearly ten years and it wasn't until 2017 that I finally got another one.

Loneliness was something else they tried to push, but again I was fine. I had my dogs and didn't feel like I was lonely. I was always in a relationship and had friends, whenever I had my dogs. If my dogs hadn't been there, then yes, I would have been very lonely. Oh – and apparently I was clean and sober. Yet again, more bullshit. I was lying through my teeth. The only thing that was truthful in the article was a note I had taped to the back of my front door that said, 'It's not he who falls that fails but he who falls and fails to rise again.'

Two years after I was inducted into the California Boxing Hall of Fame, I had the pleasure of attending Victor Valenzuela's induction in June 2010. Alongside Victor were the likes of Jerry Cheatham, Tony Cerda Jr and Sean O'Grady.

Many years later, Victor talked about the day and said, 'It was special. I was genuinely overwhelmed. It was great to see Paul and several other of my ex-boxers there. Paul was a big part of me being there.' When the Valenzuelas had their family photo to mark the occasion, they all shouted, 'Hey Paul. Get in here. You're part of the family.' That was a real boost to me.

I brought my daughter Paula with me and was so very proud to introduce her to everyone, but the truth is, the day before, I was getting high. Stupid. If you see any pictures of me, you can see my face looked terrible and I couldn't talk good because I was strung out. After everything Victor and the Valenzuela family did for me as a person and amateur boxer, this was a terrible way to repay them.

From one strung-out fighter to another. Randomly, around this time, Mark Wahlberg's movie *Fighter* had just come out. *Raging Bull* was good and I loved the Rocky movies, but *Fighter* had a different effect on me. Mark plays the part of Micky Ward, who was trained for the part by my old sparring partner and friend Freddie Roach. However, it was Micky's half-brother in the film, Dicky Eklund, played by Christian Bale, who I could really relate to, as he was a long-term suffering drug addict. I ended up doing a bit of research about Mark and I read somewhere that when he was younger, he used to put his daughter to sleep and then after, for a couple of hours, he'd watch boxing into the night. I was a big fan of Mark's anyway, then when *Fighter* came out I decided to pop him a note on Instagram and said, 'Did you ever watch me fight?' He replied, 'Yes I did.' That made my day.

Thankfully, against all the odds, like Dicky Eklund, I was about to take one of the most positive steps in my life, one that I've never looked back from since.

CHAPTER 28

CLEAN

'The pain I went through as a mother, seeing my son on drugs, was worse than the pain I saw when he took punches in the ring. However, even in and out of rehab, I never lost him. When he started to attend AA himself, I was thrilled. Over the moon, because I felt he had a chance. Am I proud? Yes. Absolutely proud'

Yolanda Miranda

ALMOST three decades on from the first time I stuck a needle in my arm, I was still addicted to dope. A number of people have helped me along my route to sobriety, but one person who gave me a little push was Mario Miranda (no relation to my mother). Mario had followed my journey from the amateurs in Azusa, through to turning pro, but I didn't get to know him properly until Louie Valenzuela introduced us at a boxing event. We kept in touch and I'm so glad we did. Then, about 2013, Mario started supporting me. When he first met me I was down and out, living on social security. He knew I didn't have money, so he would buy me some groceries and offer me some money. Sometimes he'd bring me food round and say, 'Pick what you want.' I was very appreciative but the problem was, I found it difficult to take anything. Mario would say, 'Paul. You've got to swallow your pride, bro. I'm not helping you because I think you're a down-and-out fighter, I'm helping you because I'm a compassionate man. I'm not looking for any gratitude, I'm just trying to help.' I was very suspicious at first, wondering why someone would simply be that nice, but then he started taking me to breakfast and we'd talk and I started trusting him more and more. Then I started inviting him to some boxing events and I had the pleasure of introducing him to a lot of fighters who he grew up admiring. It wasn't a lot in return for what he was doing for me, but I was glad I was able to do something that made him smile.

Mario still helps me out to this very day. He makes sure I never go hungry, but I also need to mention a few others. My girlfriend Angel is a huge help, along with Louie and Richie Rich. The list is actually a long one and although I may not have mentioned you by name, you know who you are. Thank you to all of you.

Back to Mario. As we became good friends, we talked about my personal demons and experiences of being on drugs, my character, my anger side as a result of the drugs and how my sense of humor became affected. Mario is a straight talker and at the time he asked me, 'Are you still using drugs?' I replied, 'No,' but he'd been around the addicts on the street long enough to know the bullshitters.

He could tell I was lying by the crazy things I was telling him. I'd become very suspicious and paranoid, and genuinely thought everyone had an agenda. Mario was the only one who looked at me and could see that. To be honest, the paranoia still lingers in me to this day from the drug use. It can happen real easy over the smallest things and I get snappy. I'm getting better, but the long-term effects of drugs are no joke.

Mario didn't know what drugs I was on at the time, but he'd say, 'Come on, brother. If you're going to these meetings, you've got to stay on top of things.' Mario had a hard life growing up and was wise to the ways of the world. He too ate out of trash cans but was now mentoring people with his life experiences, something I'd look to do myself later in life.

Then, in September 2014, it happened. I got clean and sober.

From the time I started slamming dope in my arms, I'd seen guys get crazy, spun out, but I'd never hallucinated like them. They'd tell me they'd seen things or that they felt people were following them and I used to think, 'Shut up, you tripping ass idiot.' Then it happened to me.

I was sitting in my apartment watching people suspiciously through my window blinds. I went to the gym one morning and thought the FBI had come to my house, checked my shit and thought they were training my dogs to go against me and report back to the FBI what I was up to. I'd also lost my phone and thought again that the FBI had taken it and were on to me. Then, when my key worker came over to take me to the food bank, I explained how scared I was about what was going on and he said, 'You OK? You want me to take you to the hospital?' I said, 'No, I'm OK,' and gave him a hug. I wasn't really hugging him, though, I was patting him down to see if he was wearing a wire. I'd lost my mind and that scared the fuck out of me.

I got down on my knees in my apartment on 22 September 2014 and asked God for help. I said, 'Please let me get through this and I promise I'm not going to go back to the drink or drugs.'

My life changed from that moment on. I was genuinely so scared I was not going to come out of it this time. I'd had so many recoveries and lived in so many different places that I thought my days were numbered. Losing my mind was a wake-up call and one I listened to like I'd never listened to anything ever before in my life.

I started going to AA meetings in Covina soon after I turned pro, mainly because my mom forced me to go. I was doing a lot of cocaine at the time and my mom realized that my boxing career was going down the pan as a result and told me to go. However, I never took the meetings seriously. It was more of a face-showing exercise. Check in, speak a bit, listen to everyone, walk out and then hit the cocaine straight after.

This time round, when I started to attend that first AA meeting on 24 September 2014, I watched people share their stories and saw how much they really cared for one another. There was a lot of love in that room. I genuinely wanted to get better and the love and trust from these people made it so much easier. Although it's *Alcoholics Anonymous*, it's open to anyone with addiction issues. I battled with drugs and alcohol as the two almost came as a pair. I cannot drink a beer. If I have one, then, boom, I'm already thinking about where I can score some dope. I knew that in order for me to stop taking drugs, the alcohol also had to go and I wasn't alone with that.

Meetings start at 6am and all kinds of people turn up. Doctors, attorneys, cops, famous people, non-famous. Addiction doesn't discriminate. The first time I walked into the room, there were these three old guys sitting there, who'd I'd go on to name the 'three wise men'. One is a retired principal, a real smart man, the second is an actor and I don't remember what the other one did in his life. Either way, when I first arrived they greeted me, made me a cup of coffee and made me feel comfortable. For the first three years, they'd prove to be so helpful. I'd sit on the bench outside with them and just listen and agree with what they were saying. They're intelligent, quiet, warm-hearted and when they speak, it makes total sense.

Since September 2014, I started attending about four, sometimes five days a week, and that hasn't changed to this present day. I've got into a positive routine. I get up, have my coffee, go to AA meetings and when I get there I hug half the people in the room. It feels good. They're like my family. I can tell my shit to these guys and they don't trip on it. We laugh and cry about what we've done and nobody judges, only supports.

Listening to others share their stories is a huge help. Sometimes we don't tell our family members or friends everything, like the stuff we did on alcohol and drugs, and how screwed up we were. If we were to tell certain friends and family, they'd look at us like, 'Damn. You crazy.' But at AA, we accept it. I always start by saying, 'Hi. I'm Paul and I'm an alcoholic. We don't look the same, but we think the same.'

The crazy thing is, everyone who knows me knows I talk a lot, but the most powerful thing I've learned in AA is to listen. They help me by simply listening to my story and I've helped many addicts by doing the same. Even outside of the meetings, I take phone calls and listen to people's stories. I'm happy to take those calls all the time because I know that not answering and listening to that person could be the breaking point of them going back to their addictions, and nobody wants that.

Since going to AA, I've had people asking me to sponsor them, but I'm not ready for that yet. Although it's similar to what I do with many people at AA already, maybe it's just the fear of the responsibility, the title of being a sponsor or the fear of failure. Either way, I'll get there one day, but not right now.

* * *

It took a lot to make it to 365 days without taking anything. When I first starting going to the AA meetings, I used to listen to these people saying that they got two years' sobriety, five, nine, whatever. I used to think, 'You lying motherfuckers! All of you.' But you know what, I've gone past four years sober and I believe them now. After I had that crazy episode hallucinating and then having Angel in my life and good people to support me, I knew I was going to recover. The temptation disappeared. To this day, you can put dope or a beer in front of me and it doesn't bother me any more. I'm cool, I'm good. I've lost that desire. I love my life now.

My first big landmark was 24 September 2015. I'd managed to stay sober and clean for a year. Louie and Mario both attended as I picked up my coin. I'm very proud to say that as we speak, I have my fourth one and the fifth is not far away. Several friends, such as Richie Rich and my girlfriend Angel, have attended with me and I'll be forever grateful to them for coming. Without the support from loved ones, staying sober would be nigh on impossible.

Quick mention and hats off to my man Richie Rich. Drug addiction ain't an easy one to lick and at the time of writing, he's 20 years free of alcohol and drugs. As Richie himself says, 'There's something about when you let a chemical into an addict's body. It's like letting all the gorillas out of the zoo running wild. They're opening up each other's cages, beating everything and tearing it up.' Richie is aware that drugs take over your life, but especially your mind. Having him there, knowing he'd beaten the addiction, gave me inspiration and still inspires me to this very day.

My message to any struggling alcoholics or drug users wanting to give up in life – don't. Go to AA. If you hang out with people who have recovered, after a while it's going to rub off on you.

CHAPTER 29

FACEBOOK FRIEND

'He is known as a major Facebook addict now.
His social media game is a big hit. He makes
everyone smile'

Michele Chong

PEOPLE ask me if I believe in God, and the answer is I think about God all the time. I know there's a God and I know that I had help from God to turn my life around after three decades of major drug abuse.

The best and the biggest thing to ever happen in my life was to get sober and when it happened, I wanted to let the world know. Ten or 15 years before, people would bump into me and say, 'Are you Paul Banke? I thought you'd died years ago.' In a way, I had. I'd technically disappeared. So now, with a clear run ahead of me, I wanted to shout out, let the world know how happy I am.

Back in 1990, when I was world champion, the media took care of sharing everything that was going on in my life.

Newspapers, television, radio, that sort of thing. About 25 years later and this thing called the internet is how everyone seems to do it. I'd heard about Facebook, but never really understood what it was about. Then a long-term friend of mine, Geraldine, introduced me to it, to show me what all the fuss was about. She helped create my profile, set up the password, post some photos and showed me how it all worked. The rest is history.

The thing about social media is that it can depress some people. They see friends getting on a flight and going to Hawaii or all around the world, new job, new car, new clothes, eating good food in a fancy restaurant. I can understand how that can get some people down when things ain't going well in your life. Back in the day, I'd get high to get over that sort of thing, but now I'm happy for those people and I'm happy for what I now have, as opposed to what I don't. Everything I have is a blessing. My girlfriend Angel, my dogs, my birds, my family, food to eat. I don't take any of it for granted.

I used to be addicted to booze and dope, but I'm now addicted to Facebook. I'm so happy in life and I probably burn a lot of people out with the number of posts and how much I tag, but I'm not intentionally trying to do that. You have to understand that if I'm posting a video of me at a barbecue, having a cup of coffee, some breakfast, a new pair of sneakers, walking my dogs, hanging out with people, it's because I never forget that there was a time when I was living homeless, eating out of trash cans.

There was a time when I wouldn't eat for days and stunk, wearing the same old clothes. People didn't want to stand or sit near me because I smelt and looked so bad. So when I now get asked by people to hang out with them, for me, that's incredible. That's why I'm posting all the time. I'm excited all the time. I'm so fucking happy just to eat, hang out with people, talk to friends, talk to everyone. Come and talk to me!

I'm not going to lie, to an extent Facebook has made me a better person and helped me deal with my insecurities and anxiety. Instead of hitting the dope when I'm a little down, now I jump on to Facebook and speak to people. I have positive options. Five thousand of them, in fact!

However, the best part about it is not me constantly posting, it's the number of people I've been able to reconnect with. Old friends, boxers, people who meant a lot to me before, people I may have pissed off for whatever reason. Facebook has allowed me to bridge those relationships back. My dad even uses Facebook and he's in his late seventies. I hardly spoke to him growing up and right the way through adulthood, but now most mornings we'll say, 'Morning son,' 'Morning dad.' That's good.

Boxing was such a huge part of my life but after the AIDS diagnosis, slowly slowly I started to lose touch. Partly because I wasn't on the scene so much and partly because when I was strung out, I didn't want people to see me in that state, which was very often. Then, when I got clean and started searching for people on Facebook and they'd connect with me, it was magical. And the best part is, I'm connecting again with boxers all over the world and I don't care what time I message or call them either! Guys I trained with, fought against in the amateurs and pros, most of them are on Facebook.

I'm also able to keep in touch regularly with friends and family I previously had to travel to see, or pick up a phone to, which would cost money. One of those close friends was Connie, who had known me during my darkest time. Around 2015, someone had written an article about me in the *LA Times* and she ended up contacting the journalist to ask how she could get in touch with me. Then, coincidentally, she received a friend request from me on Facebook at the very same time. I called her on Messenger and said, 'Connie, my sister! I love you!' She replied laughing, 'There he is! There's that guy I first met.' It was like we'd never lost touch.

I'm glad Facebook hooked me up with my old people, got me to the fights again and got me doing something with my life. When I hit 5,000 followers I was so excited, as I got a message from Mark Zuckerberg [Facebook co-founder and CEO]. I thought I'd been singled out especially and didn't realize it was an automatic message. I said to Angel, 'Mark Zuckerberg has contacted me!' We were cracking up all day as I kept bringing it up. The simple things in life now give me pleasure, but it's the important people who keep me on the right path to being able to enjoy life.

CHAPTER 30

GUARDIAN ANGEL

*'He'd worked his whole life training and dedicating
himself and when the opportunity presented itself
to become world champion, he took it. It's taken
him a long time to realize again that he's still a
champion. Sometimes, his humbleness comes from
the way he feels he's made so many mistakes in his
life, that he hasn't always been able to fully accept
and recognize what he's earned'*

Angela Stanfield

I'VE been able to connect and reconnect with some great friends over the years through Facebook, but one in particular proved to be very special.

I first met Angela Stanfield (Angel) when I was coming back from the Olympic trials and had just turned pro. She was starting college and was 23, two years older than me. We ended up dating and living with each other for about six months. The contrast in our characters worked perfectly as I took life very lightly, was always joking and laughing, whereas Angel was always the serious person at school.

We used to go out dancing a lot, but at the time I was heavily into my training, and one time when she was over at my place, I asked her to come running with me. She said, 'You've got to be kidding me.' It was 4am, which was a great time to run at! Fair play to Angel, she came out with me.

We were running up this hill just as the sun was coming up and I could see the look on her face of, 'I hate to run.' I started running backwards saying, 'Come on, Angel. You can do it!' She was out of breath saying, 'How can you talk and run? That's not normal.'

Angel knew I boxed but wasn't really aware of to what level until she had the opportunity to see me fight against Arturo Lozado at Cal Poly Gym in Pomona. It was my fifth pro fight on 7 February 1986. She came along with a few of her girlfriends, but straight after said, 'Why would anyone get into the ring to do that? Why would you allow yourself to get beat up? You're good, but your face is all bruised.' Me and Angel went out for a few more months, then split up. We ended on good terms and remained good friends.

Then one day, a few years later, I went over to her house to see her brother Hector, who was also a good friend, and I got chatting to her mom. As I was there, Angel walked out, heavily pregnant with her first daughter. I looked at her and was like, 'Wow! You're pregnant.' Angel then said all surprised, 'Hey! How's it going, Paul?' It's funny, but after all that time and everything that had happened in our lives at that point, we still had a connection. We were more than just boyfriend and girlfriend, we were friends. We were always very honest with each other, no matter what. I remember telling her mom, 'That's the good one I let go of,' and her mom said, 'You sure did.'

We then kind of drifted for about 20 years. Angel got married, I got married and we didn't really hear from each other.

Soon after I was diagnosed with the virus, Angel received a call from aunt Olga and uncle Don's daughter Vicky telling them that I had AIDS. At the time, Angel cried because she thought, like most people with the AIDS diagnosis back then, that I was dying. After she received that phone call, she didn't really expect to see me again.

In 2012, Angel's husband sadly passed away and in 2014 she decided to move closer to her parents to help them because they were both elderly. She didn't tell anybody she was in this area because she wanted to start over. Then one day she picked up a smartphone and decided to give this Facebook thing a go, even though she wasn't into social media. She looked up my name and I answered her straight away. In all honesty, I tried looking her up a number of times on Facebook, but I could never find her because I was looking for Angela Gonzalez, which is the name I knew her by back then, not realizing her name was now Stanfield.

So you can imagine how over the moon I was when she connected with me. I wrote her a note and said, 'You need to come over and have coffee with me and we'll walk the dogs.' She said, 'Sure. When?' I said, 'Come over at 5am tomorrow.' She replied, 'Some things never change!', but she came over.

It was the day before Thanksgiving 2014 and I shared my life with her since having last seen her. My addiction, homelessness, the virus, everything. I told her stories about how my addiction took me to a lot of places I didn't need to be and how I did things that I shouldn't have seen or done. I started telling her this story about how I'd found about 500 or 600 dollars at the complex I was living at in Hollywood around 2007. When I saw it, it was like, bam, straight cash. It must have belonged to one of my neighbors and before the afternoon was over, I'd spent it on drugs.

As Angel listened to my story, she grabbed me by this puffy jacket I was wearing and told me, 'I don't want you ever telling me a story like that again. You can't go back to that life. Ever.' I was taken aback. Angel then shared her life and told me about her husband passing, and cried with me as I listened. I hated seeing her in tears. I found it really tough to see that as it made me very upset.

Angel was still going through a lot of hurt having lost her husband, and when we rekindled our friendship one thing I used to say to her every morning was, 'Today's going to be a happy day. Today's going to be a good day.' Angel was in a place in her life where she needed someone to say something like that, to remind her that today was another day, a different day, but a good one. Our personalities and perhaps the time of our paths crossing again worked very well.

I'd only been sober three months when we started seeing each other again, but one thing I noticed about Angel was the way she'd help me make decisions. She'd never force anything on me because she realized that was the quick route to making me run away. Instead, she spoke to me in a way that would leave me to figure out the decision. Made it my choice.

However, every so often she'd have to have these eye-opening talks with me, where she would have to be the serious one, especially when it came to my health. For example, occasionally I'd go to the doctor because I was losing weight, which was a by-product of the AIDS virus. The official term is 'thinning', but Angel had no idea what it meant, so she did a lot of research because she's a proactive person and thought it was very important to know as much as possible about the relationship she was in. What happened was, the doctor would give me steroids to build up my muscle mass when I'd lose a lot of weight. The problem was, when I went outside of my doctor I'd get street drugs that were uncertified supplements or steroids, just because I could get them more regularly and cheaply.

Angel would go mad and say, 'What's the difference between getting drugs off the street and steroids? They're not prescribed to you by a doctor, so it's not good for you. That's not OK. If you really want to keep your sobriety like you say, and you've worked so hard on it, then you need to think about that.' Everything she said made sense. I was taking these steroids and my temper was getting worse. I'm already crazy enough naturally, but those steroids moved me up a few levels. I've always been polite, like hugging and shaking people's hands, but the 'roids were changing me. I didn't like that because that wasn't me. I now understood what 'roid' rage was all about.

Angel asked why I did the 'roids and I said, 'Because I want to be strong in the ring with the pads as I don't feel I'm strong enough at the moment.' She replied, 'You think you're going in the ring boxing again with these people, some of whom are going pro and they're hard hitters. But that's not you any more. You're not boxing them, you're training *them* to box. There's a difference. Those steroids are changing you and that's not a person I like. Now you're trying to live life and that comes with some challenges that are not going to be dealt with well with that kind of supplement.' We didn't agree about that in the beginning and I got upset with her, then we got over it. In the end, she made me see total sense.

Angel's also been great at keeping me in check with my AIDS medication. For years I've been very inconsistent with my meds, which is crazy as they help to keep me alive. When Angel found out how I was, she gave it to me straight. 'We go to see your doctor and he gives you medication. This is what you have to take and this is what keeps you well. If you're supposed to take two pills every single day, one in the morning and one at night, how hard is that? The doctor basically said to you, 'It's not a question of you getting sick, it's *when* you get sick. We want to make sure we can fight it off as much as we can and prevent anything being as bad as it could be, because your immune system is so low it will struggle to fight back.' She then said something that really hit home. 'You wanna know why my mom is worried about me? I'll tell you why. She's worried you're going to leave me behind like my first husband did and die early. Is that what you want?' I replied, 'I'm not going to die.' Again, she made total sense.

Alcoholics Anonymous changed my life but when I found Angel again, it was like I'd reached a crossroads. I'd been sober and clean before but now, at the age of 50, I kind of felt it was now or never. I'd done 30 days, 50, and five months before, but never lasted. However, Angel made it easier for me. There's no chaos about her, she's real smart and knowledgeable, and she's constantly there to remind me why I need to keep myself in check. I'm so glad I'm sober because the drugs took over my positive attitude.

* * *

Angel started going to AA meetings with me, although the first time she came along she didn't realize that she wasn't supposed to speak. She wanted to support me and shortly after the session started, she raised her hand to talk. The guy in charge said, 'You're not supposed to do that.' Even now, my friends at AA still tease her and say, 'Go ahead, Angel. Talk. Go ahead!' She always replies, 'No, no. Paul might get mad!'

Angel treats me real good. She not only helps me in life, as a person, and keeps an eye on my health, but she also sometimes helps me out when I'm low on cash for things like groceries or gas. However, I always make sure I treat her to a nice meal and that's something I've done since we started dating again in 2014.

Well, kind of. Shortly after we started seeing each other, I took her for a date at McDonald's. I was a total gentleman and even opened the door for her. We walked in and there were about four or five people in the line waiting to order and I've said, real loud to Angel, 'Go ahead! Order what you want on the menu. Extra cheese, supersize, anything. I got you.' People were looking around like, 'God damn,' while Angel was getting embarrassed. Even now, people say, 'You took her for the first date at McDonald's?' 'Yeah!' I say. That then became a regular place and every time we went in, the people at McDonald's got to know us and would give us the special treatment. 'You again!'

Our dates to McDonald's became a little joke with us and I used to say, 'When I really have a lot of money, I'm going to take you to Pollo Loco.' The romance happens at Pollo Loco, but it goes crazy when we hit Panda Express.

I did try and cook for Angel on a few occasions, so much so that I'd forgotten I'd even done so. One time I texted her and said, 'You've got to try these ribs I've made. I've marinated them in that Paul Newman sauce overnight and oh my gosh, they're the best in the world. All the girls want to marry me because of these ribs!' She brought up the story recently and I told her, 'I never said that,' and she showed me the text. Don't mess with Angel!

When I met Angel after those first few months, I realized there was a reason she came back into my life. I even said to her, 'I prayed for someone like you. A good person. Not like many of the women I'd dated before. Not that they were bad, but I just needed someone who didn't do the things I used to do before.' She replied, 'I prayed for someone like you too. Someone that would come into my life and bring joy back. I was so distraught when I lost my husband and you've brought that joy back into my life again. You brought my smile back.'

It's so easy to find out who someone is today with the internet, but a lot of kids won't know who Paul Banke is. However, when they do and hear his story, their eyes light up. You see young pros, 18, 19, 20 years old, crowding around him as he brings out his WBC belt. His belt gives them a goal to aim for.

I'm glad Paul's back in the boxing world. Many boxers, especially former world champions, walk away from the sport and don't get involved. You never hear from them again. You might see them 30 years later at a Hall of Fame event or something, but that's about it.

I train a few fighters and do personal training and he'd been saying for the last few years since he got clean about getting back into it. I was like, 'That's brilliant!' It also keeps your mind focused.

When you've boxed your whole life, you start thinking, 'What do I do now?' You get a bit depressed. Paul could have got back on the drugs again, but he hasn't. He's focused back on the boxing and the boxing's brought him back to the forefront of keeping his body and mind healthy. That's a good thing. Boxing has saved his life more or less and hopefully he can influence generations of kids who might go astray in the future.

Paul's a beautiful, humble guy. He's a former world champion and nobody can ever take that away from him. This guy has fought everyone and everything. He's a true warrior, no matter what he faces.

Wayne McCullough
WBC world bantamweight champion, 1995/96

CHAPTER 31

OLD FAITHFUL

'He left Azusa, but never forgot about us.
Always gave us tickets to his fights. When he had
something, he'd always give it. Now he don't have
much, he still gives whatever he has. And if he
hasn't got something material to give you, he gives
you laughter and smiles, which are priceless'

Louie Valenzuela

FTER the AIDS diagnosis, even though I did my best not to show that I wasn't insecure, I definitely was. People stayed away from me because of the stigma with AIDS, so that meant my social aspect of boxing changed unbelievably. It was no longer fun to be out because when I was at a boxing show or among people, many would walk away before I even went to say hello.

Then, at the age of 50, boxing helped me again. I started attending fights, attending conventions, training, all the things I previously loved so much, but now without any dope in my system. I'm so excited to attend boxing matches or shows that whenever I'm invited I always arrive super early, sometimes hours in advance, just to make sure I don't miss a moment. It annoys the hell out of Angel.

Facebook got me reconnected to the boxers and when that happened, it got me in the gyms again.

However, there are a few key people who made sure I didn't lose sight of my boxing.

The Duarte Gym is about ten minutes from me and when it first opened, it was almost like a playground. They didn't have any trainers or anything. It was more of a hangout for the kids instead of a serious, competitive gym. Louie's grandfather on his mom's side went to Duarte in 1918, a hundred years ago. It wasn't Duarte then, though. It's only gone under that name for around 60 years. Then, when Louie's brother, my amateur coach Victor, left Azusa and came to Duarte, it was like the gym came home.

The gym is special to me because I grew up alongside the Valenzuelas and know a lot of the people from the gym. When I got sober, the Duarte Gym was a natural place for me to start going back to. And when I did, I was made to feel like I'd never left.

At first I started going once a week, then I started attending the sparring at the weekends, but lately I've been going more, even just to hang out. They have a picture in the gym of me with my belts on and when me and Zack Padilla come in, we're like celebrities because everyone in that gym knows we both had world titles.

Working with the kids and up-and-coming boxers gives me a real high. The kind of high I hadn't tasted in a long time and the kind of high that doesn't leave any bad side effects whatsoever. I like working on hand speed and punches with the kids and tell them, 'When you fight, let it all out. Don't hold back.' My drills tend to be lots of combinations and lots of offense. I'm basically trying to make them fight like I used to. Most of these kids came from the other side of the tracks, as they say, but with the discipline of boxing some of them will become scientists, laborers, soldiers, doctors, anything they want really.

On a personal level, I'm back into a routine. I get up in the morning and I have that focus again. Training people not only gets me in shape but makes me want to get back in shape. I run in the mornings, hit the bags, skip some rope. When I started training again, I was like, 'Man, I've missed this shit.' I'm aware of my limitations as I have hernias and a badly torn rotator cuff, but it doesn't stop me participating. Everything slows down a little, but my timing and balance are still there and I still got them moves! I'm down the gym now almost every day early in the morning and I'm starting to lose weight. The difference is, I'm enjoying that process, which makes it even better.

Boxing gave me the opportunity to travel and I'll forever be grateful for that. There's no way a kid like me from a poor upbringing at the age of 16 would ever have had the chance to travel somewhere like New Zealand and then go on to see so many other parts of the world. Now it's my duty to let these kids in the gym know how far boxing can extend them as a person, both inside and outside the ring. More importantly, to let them know that this can only happen with a lot of hard work.

* * *

I'd just like to say something about Louie and Victor. When I turned pro and left Azusa, I never lost contact with them but I also wasn't in touch with them as much as I would have liked and that was purely down to the dope. Victor, after I turned pro, I lost touch with you for a while, but I want to say that I'll always be grateful for what you did with me as a person and a boxer during the six years of my life we were together. I wish I could have been sober and clean for your induction, but at least I am now and I thank you for everything.

With Louie, I never lost contact. I'd always call him once in a while. It might be a month, two months, sometimes even as long as a year, but I'd always somehow pop up. I knew his phone number by heart and he used to say, 'You still remember my number from high school?' and I'd say, 'Yeah. I never forgot that number.' No matter where I was at or what state I was in, I'd always call him. Louie, thank you for always being there.

I've known Louie for over 40 years and there's never been a dull moment whenever we've hooked up. We have fought, argued, laughed together and been on boxing trips, although on the last one to Vegas he got ratty with me. I go to bed real early whereas Louie is the complete opposite. When we were in Vegas, he'd get in about 4am and I'd be up calling him, asking what he's up to as I'd just woken up. He got mad at me and then I'd put on Facebook at seven in the morning, 'Me and Angel are going to breakfast, but Louie's still asleep!', just to make him look lazy.

He'd then reply a few hours later and say, 'I went to bed at four in the morning and he went to bed at 8.30pm the night before. Why would I be having breakfast at seven? We're on vacation in Vegas. Why would I not stay out late and then sleep in?' I'd then reply, knowing it would annoy him even more, 'Why you getting so mad, Lou-dawg? You OK?' The exchange went on for a while and everybody laughed at it, but nobody more than me and Louie.

I'm very grateful to him and his family for the love and support they've given me from a young kid up to the present day.

CHAPTER 32

TAKE CARE

'Know the true value of time; snatch, seize and enjoy every moment of it. No idleness, no laziness, no procrastination: never put off till tomorrow what you can do today'

Philip Stanhope, 4th Earl of Chesterfield

IN 2017, I went to the Nevada Boxing Hall of Fame with Angel and Louie to see Ray Mancini get inducted alongside the likes of Pernell Whitaker, Ricardo Lopez and Christy Martin.

Ray had a big entourage of people that were guarding him and was being rushed through. As they're going past, nobody could get to him because his security team were dragging him through the crowd, so I shouted out, 'Hey Ray. Hey Ray! It's me, Paul Banke.' Ray stopped, looked around and said, 'Where you at, Paul?' He then spotted me and said, 'Come here, Paul!' and gave me a big hug. Louie said, 'That's love for you, man.'

I didn't know Ray too well until after my career ended, but when he found out I had AIDS he did an interview with me for television to help air what I was going through and to raise awareness of the virus. He's always been a positive influence and I have nothing but respect for him as a person and world champion.

So there's Ray getting inducted into the Hall of Fame and getting ready to start his acceptance speech. However, before starting, he gave a shout-out to me. Here's the sad part. I stayed most of the evening, but I wasn't there to hear Ray's speech! We left early because I was tired and I'm really impatient. I'm getting worse in my old age. So Louie called up later to tell me what Ray had said. 'Hey Paul. You missed the best speech from Ray Mancini!' I was so pissed off, but also thankful to hear from Louie what he'd said.

Ray started his speech by saying, 'There's a few people I want to thank, but first of all, I want to say something. There's a lot of great fighters here, a lot of great champions and a lot of my friends. But [there's] one guy I want to single out and it's only because he's [been] a friend for a long time. If you know a little bit about his life, you'll know he's battled so many things, both inside the ring and outside the ring. I'm so proud and happy that he's here tonight, and he's my friend, Paul Banke. You're a true champion.'

Then there was a big round of applause.

The speech is on YouTube and it still gives me goosebumps whenever I look at it.

* * *

2014 was a great year. I became sober, cleaned up and boxing became a big part of my life again. I also got to meet some fantastic new people as a result. One of them is Alfred Godinez.

Alfred is Mexican but has been living in California since 1966. He came from the 'hood, the streets. I'd been there too, so we had some things in common. He's also been a big boxing fan all his life and started following the sport in 1969 at the Olympic Auditorium.

The auditorium was in *18th & Grand* and he used to live on 11th Street. His dad would take him to see boxers like Bobby Chacon and along the way he's seen the likes of Sugar Ray Leonard against Roberto Duran and Salvador Sanchez against Wilfredo Gomez, live.

When I was fighting, Alfred was working for a Toyota dealer and they used to give him tickets for boxing, which meant he'd attend my fights at the Inglewood Forum. Stroh's, Zaragoza, all of them. But I never met him back then.

We initially became friends on Facebook but the first time we met was at the West Coast Hall of Fame in 2014. He came over from Texas with a group of six people to see me get inducted. We started talking about the fights I was in, my story, what had happened to me over the years. Then, from there, we started crossing paths at the boxing matches. Every time I'd go to a fight at StubHub Center, Staples Center, Vegas, I would see him and we'd start talking, and that's how we became good friends.

Alfred knew my brother Steve and would often see him at his friend's house, and one day said to him, 'I'm going to take your brother to this fight and that fight.' He kept his word.

Alfred goes to all the big fights. He doesn't do little fights and he only does floor seats. When you're not fighting any more and don't have any money, and a guy takes you in an aeroplane to a world title fight, puts you up in a nice room and takes care of you, that's a special guy. He doesn't make any fuss at all, he makes it feel like it's nothing, but it's an incredible thing for me. He makes me feel like a champion all the time I'm with him, a feeling I'd forgotten for a while. I'm very grateful for that.

Alfred started off taking me to one fight, then two, then before you knew it, he'd taken me to over 20 fights. He went from an acquaintance, to a friend, to a very good friend. Alfred tells me, 'This is only the beginning. I'm taking you with me to wherever I go, champ. If I go to Vegas, you're going with me. If I go to Texas, same thing. New York is the big one I want to take you to. I've never been to Madison Square Garden. I want to take you to New York to see a fight.'

Every fight with Alfred has been great. We've had real fun, and as boxing fans we love soaking up the atmosphere on the night and talking to the other boxers and champions in attendance. However, the most memorable was when we went to see Mikey Garcia against Sergey Lipinets on 10 March 2018 at the Freeman Coliseum, San Antonio.

I'd first met Mikey in July 2016. Here's what happened. Carl Frampton and Leo Santa Cruz were having their press conference and Mikey was there because he was fighting on the undercard against Elio Rojas. This was his comeback fight after having been out of boxing for over two and a half years.

I walked up to Mikey and said, 'I'm Paul Banke. You're a great fighter. You're probably too young to remember me.' He said, 'No! I know exactly who you are. You were world champion and you sparred my brother.' That's when our friendship started. Whenever I see Mikey and Robert, they always call me 'champ' and that makes me feel awesome.

Back to the Lipinets fight. The second the tickets went on sale, Alfred called me up and said, 'Paul, get ready. I'm taking you with me. We're going to San Antonio to see Mikey Garcia.' Oh my God. When he said, 'I'm taking you,' I said, 'What?' I was so happy. I'll never forget that trip.

Mikey beat Lipinets comfortably on points, then soon after he'd done his interview in the ring, they rushed him through. As he's walking out, everyone's trying to tap him on the shoulder, hug him, take a picture, you name it. Mikey went past me, then a second later turned around, came back and gave me a hug. I turned to Alfred and said, 'Wow! I can't believe he turned and gave me a hug.' Alfred replied, 'These people recognize you. You're a world champ, too, you know?'

We followed Mikey and his team back to the changing room and I was able to get me and Alfred past security, which he loved. Mikey and Robert were really polite to him and it was priceless to see how happy Alfred was from having the chance to be in there speaking with them.

Alfred always says, 'Wherever we go, people recognize you.' Despite being a big talker, believe it or not, I get quite shy with the attention and it's not always true that I'm a known name, although Alfred did prove his point at the airport on the way back. The parking attendant was a Mexican guy and Alfred asked him, 'Do you like boxing?' He says, 'Yes.' Alfred then says, 'You know this guy right here? He was the one who beat Daniel Zaragoza.' The attendant says all excited, 'What? That's Paul Banke?' All of a sudden, there's a group of parking attendants talking to us, following us around, taking pictures with me.

Someone else who has not only helped me get back into the boxing community, but has also helped me share my story, is Jaime Cantu. Jaime grew up in LA but left when he was 16 and moved to Texas. At the time, I was starting to make my name in boxing and Jaime started following me from my amateur fights right through to my pro career. I was in a weight class he enjoyed watching, one in which his son Oscar would also go on to fight and do very well, becoming a WBC and NABF champion as well as fighting in the Olympic trials in 2012.

Growing up in LA, Jaime boxed as an amateur from the age of about 14, but never turned pro. By the time he was 17 he'd already moved to Kingsville, Texas, joined the army and had a career there for 23 years as a recruiter. He never boxed in the army but while recruiting he started wondering, 'How can we make contact with these kids in the local area?' That's when the idea for a boxing gym came up. He wanted to give the youth some direction, especially for those at risk, and he was able to use the boxing program to help them make better decisions. A few joined the military but some made better decisions in their lives. Since then, he's been involved in boxing and never looked back. Jaime also served as assistant coach at the Olympic Training Center in Colorado around 2010/11 and was in charge of developmental camps, where they'd bring up elite boxers and prep them for international competitions.

As we speak, his 12th Street Gym, also known as Kingsville Boxing, has been training kids, adults, pros and amateurs for 27 years. They've officially been registered by USA Boxing for over 22 years. Boxing is the umbrella but Jaime also does a lot of community work and even has church service classrooms, so they are covering the physical, mental and spiritual side of everyone's development. When they're in the program, he asks for a $10 a month donation, but if they can't pay it, that's fine, they're still allowed to come to the gym. He only asks for the $10 so they can take some kind of ownership of the gym and feel they are part of the community. Jaime understands that helping our fellow man is very important.

Anyway, here's how me and Jaime connected. About four years ago, through Facebook, he saw a post about myself and thought, 'Oh my God! Whatever happened to Paul

Banke?' We connected and started going back and forth in conversation and Jaime started seeing what had happened in my life and what I was doing now. We ended up talking on the phone and he said, 'You've got a story to tell, man. What if we brought you to Kingsville and you talk to the kids? We can get you sponsored to come out to talk about drug and HIV awareness, and your story as world champion. You could make a presentation. What do you think?' I replied, 'OK,' but I didn't know what to expect. I'd never done something like this before and I wasn't confident with public speaking, but I agreed nonetheless.

So, on 10 December 2016 I went over to Kingsville. About 60 people turned up to hear me speak, which is far more than I'd imagined. What I didn't realize was that Jaime had told everyone who used the gym that they were required to be there. He also briefed them in advance that they had to do homework and find out a little bit about me. Each person had to have a question and no one could ask the same one. Jaime runs a military-style program.

When they started firing the questions over, my first thoughts were, 'Oh my God. I feel like I'm being interrogated.' They all came at me at different angles. Family life, drugs, AIDS, poverty, homelessness, the streets, boxing. It was tough at times to talk about it, especially when one kid asked what it was like having my kids taken away and not being able to see them. I answered everything and it really helped to get a lot of things off my chest.

I wasn't sure how I did. I was very nervous and didn't want to embarrass myself or let Jaime, Oscar or the kids down, but Jaime said something after that made me feel great. 'Paul, you were incredible. A real live world champion, who came from poverty, made it to the top, fell back down and made it back up once again. You need to get out there and spread the message more. We've got a lot more work to do with you.' I'll always appreciate being given the chance to share my story and for Jaime, his family and students to have taken me into their gym with such warmth. The video of the day is on YouTube and is called, 'Down, but not out,' and was heavily supported by the WBC. It's worth a look if you have a chance.

Now's probably a good time for me to talk about how the WBC have been supportive of me for three full decades. Ever since I became WBC super bantamweight champion of the world on 23 April 1990, the Sulaimáns, José, Mauricio and Pépé, never turned their back on me.

Once I stopped boxing, the late José Sulaimán would come and visit me in Los Angeles or make a point of meeting me if I was attending the fights in Vegas. After I was diagnosed with full-blown AIDS in 1995, many people didn't want to know me any more, but the WBC did. José called me all the time. It was as if he was more determined than ever to see me.

He wasn't asking out of sympathy, but out of concern. He'd always tell me, 'You're a WBC champion and you have the heart to get through this,' at a time when all I heard was, 'Poor Paul, poor Paul.'

The last time I saw José Sulaimán was in April 2013. I was with Richie Rich and we were leaving the arena in Ontario after the Chris Arreola versus Bermane Stiverne fight. By this stage, José was in a wheelchair and didn't look very coherent at all. Richie was walking in front of me and said to José, 'Paul Banke is with me.' José got a little teary eyed and said it, 'My champion, my champion,' which got both me and Richie emotional. I can't say enough good things about the Sulaimán family. The way they've taken care of fighters through the WBC, but more the things they've done without the cameras watching. From me personally, thank you.

Every year since José passed on 16 January 2014, I've attended a memorial service for him. I miss that guy. He showed me a lot of love. Thankfully, his son Mauricio took over from where his father left off and is doing an incredible job. Mauricio told me recently, 'The WBC's only reason for existence is the boxers, and the WBC will always be there, before, during and more importantly after the championship years.'

A few years down the line the WBC's charitable arm, World Boxing Cares, decided to support me with a pension and even helped get me a car in 2017. I'm truly humbled. The WBC has also, very importantly, allowed me to keep in touch with many great boxers and champions through their various events and conventions.

One event in particular comes to mind, the WBC convention in Las Vegas in 2011. The place was packed with champions. Mike Tyson, Evander Holyfield, Vito Antuofermo, Floyd Mayweather Jr, Marvin Hagler, you name it. However, the one champion who turned up, which came as a great surprise, was my old rival Daniel Zaragoza and he was there with his son, Daniel Jr.

It was the first time I'd met his son and he was a lovely, good-looking kid who spoke beautiful English. When Daniel Sr saw me, he shouted, 'Hey, Paul Banke!' I went over and gave him a big hug. He's my brother. I love Daniel. Then Jr says all eager, 'Paul, let me tell you this funny story.'

He said that when he was smaller, he had disobeyed his dad's instruction one day and his dad started chasing him around the house. He realized he was angry with him, so he kept running, trying to stay ahead of him. All of a sudden, he looked behind his shoulder and yelled at his dad, 'You better stop or I'm calling Paul Banke on you!' I think when Daniel Sr caught up with him, he probably got more of a spanking for threatening that! Jokes apart, it was great to see my old friend again and meet his son.

* * *

Boxing is back in my life and that's very important to me. When I see other boxers, I light up again. I'm sure I irritate Angel when we're at events or shows and I say all enthusiastic, 'Look, look, there's so and so. Do you know him?' Angel doesn't really know the boxing world that well, but she gets energy off seeing me happy.

I've told Angel everything that's happened in my life and when I first told her that finishing my boxing career early left me with a sense of not being able to accomplish everything I wanted, she said, 'There's many stages of life and various accomplishments we achieve at those different stages. Your boxing is the springboard to whatever you do next. You're a great mentor to other people. Young kids especially look up to you. I love seeing your face when they say, 'Did I do that right, coach? Is that OK, coach?'

I don't see things the way Angel does, so to hear that gives me that little bit more of a push to share what I've learned with anyone who wants to lace up a pair of gloves.

Just a shame I didn't do that with my kids.

CHAPTER 33

FRESH START

*'Since going clean, he's completely different and it's
really great seeing how different he is. He is more
outgoing. He wants to see people, talk to people.
Before, I kind of felt he wanted to shelter himself
away. Now he wants to cope with society and has
become confident doing so. He has overcome so
much and he's still alive, and with as little as he
has, he feels truly blessed'*

Paula Munson, Paul Banke's daughter

THE biggest regret about using drugs was the years
I lost as a husband, father and friend. My memories
of my kids when they were little are a handful, as
they grew up with their mom, while I was out partying,
pleasing myself, being selfish.

One of the few memories I have is going over to my first
wife's house, taking them out to the park and playing with
them. I also enjoyed spending time with them at Santa
Monica Pier on Venice Beach. My daughter Paula was quite

a strong-minded character as a kid and one time decided she wanted to walk all the way to the pier from my mom's apartment. I said, 'No. It's too far,' but she insisted, 'No, I want to do it.' 'Alright,' I replied. We walked the length of the Venice Beach Boardwalk, which was about a mile and a half, past all the shops, street vendors and performers. When we got there, I said, 'You want to walk back home now?' She replied, 'No, we can take the bus!'

One thing I remember about walking down Venice with my kids was people stopping to come over and say, 'Hey! It's Paul Banke! The champ!' I don't mention this for my own ego, I mention it because my kids didn't really understand what it was all about and that was my fault. I wasn't around for them to be involved with my boxing or understand my accomplishments. They knew I'd boxed, but didn't get what being a world champion was all about. They were more intrigued about why everybody knew me walking down the beachfront. To this day, my daughter Paula maintains she still hasn't watched a single one of my fights all the way through.

I have fond memories of trying to teach my two sons how to box when they were very little. They loved shadow boxing and jumping around, but when it came down to it for them to actually do it as a sport, it wasn't for them. The boxing wasn't the great part of the memory, it was just spending quality time with them that I'll always treasure. I wish I could have done more of it.

Something else I wasn't able to share back then with my kids was my sense of humor. Due to the drugs, I had a different outlook on life and wasn't very happy. I also had to deal with the situation with my wife, their mom, as we didn't get along, so that can't have been good for them to watch. In addition, family and friends of family would also say to my kids, 'Don't kiss him on the lips. He has AIDS.' That didn't help.

Then, when I went off the rails with the dope in the mid to late 90s through to the early 2000s, I only saw my kids a few times. They came and stayed with me and my second wife in Vegas occasionally, but again, it was hit and miss with the state I was in. When I married my third wife Theresa in Hollywood in 2005, my daughter Paula came to the ceremony. My sister drove them up. Richie Rich was also there, as was the magician, singer and songwriter Raphael Saadiq. That was when I started to see my kids more often, but unfortunately, I was still on the drugs.

Roll the clock forward to 2014 and my family are more important than they've ever been because I'm sober to appreciate them. I remember the first Christmas I spent with Angel, she put up a tree at my place as I'd never done that before. I was never around my family, so what was the point of me getting into the spirit? Angel told me, 'You've got the opportunity to be a part of your children's lives again by being a grandpa. It's time for you to be around your grandchildren.'

Now I appreciate every little thing my family involve me in, good or bad. I'm so happy that I'm able to see my grandkids at my daughter's house in Rancho Cucamonga.

It's funny because when they were younger, they weren't old enough to know who I was. When I'd go to see my daughter Paula, I'd say to her kids, 'Come to Tata, come to Tata.' They didn't understand that I was saying come to their grandad – they actually thought my name was Tata! Now they know who I am and that fills me with joy.

That first Christmas with Angel was memorable, which is more than I can say for our first New Year's celebration that same year. We were watching the television at my house when I fell asleep on the couch. Angel stayed up watching the New York festivities and just before the ball dropped, she woke me up and said, 'Babe! Happy New Year!' I think she was expecting me to roll over and give her a Happy New Year's kiss, but I was still half asleep and kissed the dogs first! Angel said, 'I should've known better!'

I was young when my dad used to take me to watch the fights at the Great Western Forum, Inglewood. I remember Paul's trilogy against Daniel Zaragoza. They were fight-of-the-year type of fights. He was a great fighter, great athlete, would always be in tremendous condition and would never back down. When he stopped Zaragoza in their second fight to become world champion, it was an incredible achievement.

Being a young fighter, growing up in boxing gyms and knowing southern Californian fighters, it was always great to see when someone like Paul made it. When I finally met him, we became good friends. Then, in 1992, when I turned pro, we started sparring together in Big Bear. Paul was coming to the end of his career, but they were still very tough sparring sessions.

How would a peak Paul Banke do now? A fighter like Paul Banke, who never gives up, never gets tired, is always going to be in very exciting fights. I don't even know if we have one like him right now. Those type of styles are always going to be crowd-pleasers. Fifty years ago, 100 years ago, or 50 years from now, people are always going to enjoy those type of styles and I think he would have done well in any era.

Those type of fighters who start in the first round strong and finish round 12 the same way, they are going to be good against any talented fighters. That was Paul Banke.

Robert Garcia
IBF junior lightweight champion 1998/99 and trainer of world champions

CHAPTER 34

EXPERIENCE, STRENGTH AND HOPE

*'If anybody's had a real bad day, just call
Paul Banke. He will get you out of a rut in
a minute. He's a boatload of positive energy.
A 100,000lbs of happy'*

Ruben Castillo

I MIGHT not have been in a good place in 2008 to remember my inductions, but thankfully, on 15 October 2017 at the Garland Hotel event center in north Hollywood, I remembered everything when I was inducted into the West Coast Boxing Hall of Fame. I was honored to be inducted alongside my good friend Paul Vaden and a host of others, including Frankie Duarte, Oscar Albarado and Alberto Davila.

I actually knew about my induction a year before when Rick Farris called me up, but I had to keep it a secret for a whole year. I'd been inducted twice before in 2008, but this was the only one I attended totally clean and sober, and I was able to appreciate it so much more.

A few days before the awards, Angel asked me, 'What are you going to say? You can't just make it up.' 'I know what I'm going to say,' I replied semi-confidently. 'You need to practise it, Paul, because you'll get nervous and won't know what to say.' 'I'll be fine!' I replied.

On the night itself I started to get real nervous but as I walked in, there was a painting of me by the famous artist Jun Aquino and that was a very special moment. That stopped me in my tracks. Soon after, the nerves kicked in again. I wouldn't sit down and kept going round to everybody and talking with them. When it finally came to the time to start announcing people and we had to sit down, I kept turning to Angel asking, 'Am I next?' Finally, someone came over and said, 'You're next.' Now I was really nervous.

They announced my name, showed a clip of the Zaragoza fight and then I was asked to come up on stage by the MC, Jim Fitzgerald. The first thing I said because of my nerves was, 'Hello. My name's Paul and I'm an alcoholic.' Everybody loved that. They started clapping, laughing, cheering and gave me a standing ovation. That helped me to relax because I could feel the love in the room. I started thanking people who had helped me along the way and helped me become the person I was in boxing, instead of talking about my career. I couldn't look over at Angel because she kept tearing up, and that would have got me emotional.

At the end I received another standing ovation, which I don't even remember, because I was so caught up in the moment and how special the whole evening was. I didn't write my speech down, so I couldn't practise it. I wish I had because I should have said a few more things and thanked a few more people. It came off the head and the heart. I was and still am appreciative of everyone who turned up on that day, including my mom, sister, aunts and good friends, many of whom travelled some distance to be there. Top writer Michele Chong attended and wrote a great piece about the day. My good friends Jaime and Oscar Cantu came all the way from Texas, and Mario Miranda, Carlos Palomino, Ronnie Essett and many others were also there. I'm sorry if I've missed anyone out!

The induction in October 2017 was truly a blessing, especially as I thought I'd blown it with my appearances in 2008. However, it seems my life, sobriety and boxing makes for good reading and listening, and I've been nominated for the 'Experience, Strength and Hope Award' for 2020. Previous nominees and winners have included Buzz Aldrin and Robert Downey Jr, so I'm genuinely humbled to even be mentioned alongside such names.

I've known Paul Banke since he was 12 years old and I was nine. During that time, he was boxing out of Phoenix, Arizona under the very capable tutelage of Mr Bill Borchert.

Bill was friends with my coach Robert Coons and we used to go to their gym to work out, and would stay at Bill and Nettie's house. His wife Nettie would always make a mean breakfast. They were just beautiful people and hosts. The thing about them, even though they were from Phoenix, they always rooted for our guys out of San Diego. They were helpful to us.

Although I was only nine at the time, I could easily see Paul's abilities as a southpaw boxer and consequently observed him like a student in class. He was immediately likeable and supportive of my own efforts as an up-and-coming amateur boxer, but in a very kind and respectful manner. He'd watch me when I was working with Robert Coons and then say after, 'When you grow up, you'll become world champion.' When someone who's older and better than you takes the time to look at you, that's a compliment in itself. As we got older as amateurs and eventually as pros, that never changed from Paul. Never. He was always supportive. To this very day.

As he transitioned to represent the stellar Azusa Boxing Club, I continued to follow Paul's ascension before the national and international stages of amateur boxing. As his journey escalated to the professional ranks, so did his capabilities. On 23 April 1990, I'll never forget watching Paul on Prime Ticket Television remain engaged and relentless against a very game and determined champion in Daniel Zaragoza. Finally, after nine rounds, referee John Thomas agreed Zaragoza had absorbed enough punishment and halted the fight. My friend was now super bantamweight champion of the world! I can't properly describe how special the feeling is to see your friend from childhood reach a destination such as this. He was now engraved in a rare fraternity.

Despite his new-found success, Paul remained very supportive of me, but he also became distracted and lured by negative offerings and temptations. At the time, I was on the US team as an amateur and I'd read and heard things about Paul, things I didn't want to buy into or believe. He got caught up in the limelight, in the shine of him being champion of the world, caught up in the celebrity status and also caught up with who wanted to be around him. He got consumed by that and sometimes when that happens, people lose that purpose, that reason for why and what got them there.

He'd forgotten about the foundation of what made him that elite boxer. He got caught up in the celebrity side of his personality and kind of lost track of the responsibility that came with becoming a world champion. He started hanging around with the wrong people. Once you get to that level, you start getting more 'yes' people than ever before, whereas what you really need is people to be straight with you and say no, or give you some straight talking if you're stepping out of line. That started to consume him. He wasn't that person I saw grow up when he was 12 years old.

Despite being caught up in the celebrity thing, one thing I can personally say about Paul, he never played the celebrity with me. Never acted big time around me. If he saw me at an event, I'd never have to go to him, he'd always come to me. He always made me feel like I was the important one. Always made me feel special, still does. Paul never became a jerk with stardom, he just forgot where he came from and what got him there.

Sadly, Paul would lose his world title a matter of months after winning it. Even worse, for two decades he lost himself completely. By the end of 1993, his tenure as a boxer had expired. His formidable opponents now came in the form of partying, drugs, alcohol and poverty. Honestly, he became a washed-up version of himself. Then came that news. He had AIDS. The moment I heard, that news hit me hard. My first thought, to be honest with you, was, 'He's going to die.' I was hurt by the thought of that. Very hurt. I was mentally having to prepare myself for that and that's not something that comes easy.

* * *

I lost touch with him until recently, so thank God for social media. We live in a world where everyone is so busy, that you lose touch with people, some who mean a lot to you. Around the time he went clean is when I had the pleasure of reconnecting with my good friend.

On 24 September 2014, Paul became sober to alcohol and began crafting his comeback to respectability. He reached deep into his inventory to recapture the tools and instincts that made him that fighter and champion. He accepted accountability for his mistakes and exerted action to become 'The Real' Paul

Banke again. We're all better for it. Paul has an infectious personality that's authentic to the core. He doesn't have the ability to be phony. I say that as a compliment and episodes of positive light eventually resumed back in his direction.

On 15 October 2017, in north Hollywood, it did my heart proud to be in attendance to witness him being inducted into the West Coast Boxing Hall of Fame. In fact, we both got inducted that same day, which was pretty special. It was a really well put together luncheon, showing the highlights of his career. As he was watching and people were applauding, it hit him. He had to turn his back as the emotion affected him.

When he spoke, it was heartfelt. A real speech. I'll be honest – I thought Paul would have been inducted posthumously. Not being here. Watching him getting emotional got me emotional. I observed a man considerably moved by life – his life. I couldn't help but reflect on the totality of his script and how he's rediscovered himself and his purpose.

A lot of people talk about going clean, but I always knew, when Paul spoke to me back in 2014, there was no filter. He'd tell it to me straight. He'd never fake it with me, that's how close we are. He knows that I'm not going to judge him. If he's slipped up, which he hasn't, he'd tell me. I wouldn't look away from him, I'd look at how I could support him and help him through it, because he keeps it real with me. We have deep conversations, things I'll take to the grave with me.

The thing is, although Paul is older than me, for the most part I'll always be that nine-year-old and him that 12-year-old. However, in recent years, that role kind of reversed significantly. That doesn't make me any better or any worse, but I remind him of who he is, what he's been through and why he's been through it. I will not let anyone talk bad of him, verbal or written. This guy's a world champion! There's not a white-out or eraser that can remove what he's accomplished and, most importantly, how he improved himself back to respectability as a human being. He could have easily stayed down but he didn't and I remind him of those things. It's like boxing – you have good rounds, bad rounds and crappy rounds.

Summing Paul up? He has a storybook of events in his life that you wouldn't wish on people because you have to be a fighter to endure it, and that's what Paul's been. When you break him down, he's basically that person in that fight against Zaragoza who won the world title. That's who he's been in life. He's been triumphant and now he's walking in triumph because he's still here.

That's the mark of a real champion in life. Yes, Paul Banke has lost some 10-8 rounds in periods of his life. He's been dazed and knocked down, but the champion that resides in him refuses to let life count him out.

Paul 'The Ultimate' Vaden
IBF junior middleweight champion, 1995

CHAPTER 35

POSITIVE

'I thought he was a champion when he won the WBC world title. I thought he had achieved greatness. But to watch him deal with a full-blown sentence of AIDS and decide, "You know what. I'm going to champion my life. I'm going to champion what I have left to give and give up drugs and start training fighters and be the best I can be with the situation I'm in." I can't even describe how proud I am of him'

Tim Munz, Paul's brother

WHEN I was diagnosed with AIDS, I couldn't sleep and used to stare out of the window, scared, just wondering what was going to happen. I'm more comfortable now. But I still have to remember that I have the virus and that requires me to live a certain way. However, the main thing is that I live and when I say live, I don't just mean for survival, I mean for a purpose. For happiness, mine, other people's, everyone's, and to share the lessons my life has given me through boxing, addiction and AIDS. I'm no expert, but if any of my stories can inspire just one kid to lace up a pair of gloves, steer clear of drugs and be aware of the AIDS virus, then I've achieved more than I'd ever set out to in life.

I sometimes hear people saying that getting the AIDS virus ain't no big thing any more because there's drugs out there that help you live a normal life. It ain't like that. The drugs will help you, but you're still vulnerable. In the early 1980s, there were only a few thousand reported cases of AIDS in the US, but by the time I'd been diagnosed in 1995, that figure was around 500,000. By the year 2000 this was over 750,000 and by 2017 an estimated 1.1 million people were living with the disease in the US and an estimated 40 million people worldwide.

Here's a headline for you from the *Huffington Post* on 12 September 2017. 'Thousands of Americans still die of AIDS every year.' Around 20 a day. AIDS is not rare. Awareness and precaution is still essential. The figures have risen partly due to an increase and partly due to people getting tested more frequently. There's probably thousands, if not millions, of people out there who have the virus and don't even know it.

For some, an AIDS diagnosis can come about by accident. Having a routine blood test for something else, whether it be for an ailment, blood transfusion or for insurance purposes, whatever. The virus infects the body and sometimes gives off a signal that leads you to the doctor. Without some of these accidental visits to the doctors, many would have had a very late diagnosis, and a much shorter life. Many would have died without knowing, which also means many would be infected without knowing. With me, stealing a car got me my blood test.

So, what I'm saying is, if you've had unprotected sex, shared a needle or anything else that puts you at risk, get checked. Drugs and AIDS are similar in so much as they don't discriminate with race, colour, religion, age or gender. Either way, you'll overcome the fear of the unknown.

If you have the virus, start taking the medicine straight away. The medication can help you live longer and reduces the chance of HIV being passed on because the T cell count gets increased. Yes, sometimes there are side effects from the medication. I get the runs once in a while but if that's what I've got to deal with to be alive, I can cope with that. Thank God my immune system is still strong and maybe boxing helped strengthen my body over the years. Who knows? I'm just grateful for still being here.

World AIDS Day is on 1 December and has been held every year since 1988. The last few years I've participated in the AIDS Walk in California to help raise awareness, but the problem is I never seem to complete it. There's so many people there and ever since I've gone clean, I've started to become claustrophobic.

It takes about five minutes to walk a few feet because you're crammed in with so many people taking little steps, until the pace picks up, and that gets me anxious. Not great, especially as I've been the guest of honor on the last couple of occasions.

* * *

One thing I never had in my life when I was strung out was consistency. I've always been moving. But now I've been living in my current place since 2013 and that's stability I never had. In fact, I'm so stable I don't want to move too far from my apartment because of my responsibilities. I love having friends, family and boxing close by, but I've also got my animals, who I love dearly. I get anxious if I have to leave my three 'world-famous' pitbulls for more than five or six hours. Any more than that and they pee all over the carpet. I've lost count of how many times I've had to replace the carpets. By the way, they're not pitbulls, they're spaniels, but they don't know that. Also, I call them world famous because they've appeared on Facebook thousands of times!

My dogs mean so much to me and if I hear anyone talk bad about them, I get offended. I can talk to my dogs, they are like therapy to me. They don't talk back, they understand my speech and they always show me love.

I have a much more comfortable and consistent life these days, but I'm also aware that many people on the streets don't. When I reconnected with Angel, I'd show her places where I used to hang and do my drugs, and we'd bump into guys I knew. There's this one old guy called Charlie I used to hang out with on the streets of Pasadena once in a while, and when I see him now I give him a couple of bucks. He's still my friend and you should never turn your back on your friends or people who are in a situation you once were.

Here's another example. Me, Louie and Angel went to Vegas on the *Cinco De Mayo* weekend in 2018 for what should have been the second GGG versus Canelo fight. The contest fell through but seeing that Angel had booked a condo, we decided to still go and have a break away. We stopped at a Subway to get something to eat just as we got to Vegas, and there was a group of about six or seven homeless people outside. I've been homeless myself and have been around enough people to tell these guys were hungry and strung out. It was sad.

We went inside and started eating, but I couldn't stop looking at the homeless group outside. There was one particular young girl who looked like she was hurting the most. I stopped eating, stood up, took my sub with me and walked out, as Louie said to Angel, 'What's he doing?'

There was a guy with this girl, I don't know if he was her pimp or whatever, but I went straight in there. I know my shit on the streets. The guy looked at me like, 'Who the hell are you?' but I ignored him and said to the girl, 'You OK? You want this sub?' She looked at me, smiled and said, 'Oh thank you. Thank you.'

I walked back into Subway and said to Louie and Angel, 'I know what it is like to be homeless.' Without saying a word, Angel and Louie smiled, nodded, picked up the second half of their subs, passed them to me and said, 'Take them out there and give them to her.'

One thing I've learned since being sober is that I'm now in a position to help others and when those opportunities come up, I'm honored because that vulnerable person was me a few years ago. Over the summer of 2018, my nephew stayed with me for three days. His mom was saying he'd been struggling to get off the dope and felt that he was making excuses every time he was trying. She'd run out of ideas to help. I said, 'It's not excuses, he's hurting. He's struggling and he's getting high as a result. I understand those excuses. He's getting high because he doesn't want to face reality. The high takes the pain away a little bit, but the problems are still there. They remain after the comedowns.'

I took him to AA and spoke with him a lot over those days, introduced him to people and helped him to feel he wasn't on his own. I can't stop him making decisions, I can only advise. However, if my advice helps, that's worth every second spent with him. At the time of writing, he was doing good. He's working and living at home with his mom and that makes me very happy.

When I went to parties, alcohol was accepted. However, drugs were also accepted. Well, that's not OK. It shouldn't be. It's wasn't a good thing then and it's not a good thing now. Doing drugs, I missed out on seeing my kids growing up in front of me. I'll never get that back. I missed out on my best years as a boxer and became broke and homeless. I learned the hard way. Hopefully, my story can prevent others from making the same mistakes.

As the late and much-missed Johnny Tapia once said about taking drugs, 'First time is a mistake, second time is a habit.' He was so right. Don't ever let it become a habit.

* * *

When I'm at an event now and there's 40, 50, 60 people in a room, I'll shake everybody's hand. I appreciate that handshake. It means a lot to me. And when someone comes over and says, 'Hey, Paul Banke. World champion! I remember you.' You can't beat that feeling. Certainly beats the comments I used to get in the late 1990s. 'Paul Banke? You're still alive?'

Let me say this, though. I'm very aware of how close I was to being dead or an addict for life. I don't take anything for granted. Everything is a blessing. Above my door, I've written, '9-24-14. *Turned my life around. I got clean, sober and my life got better.*' That's my constant reminder to never touch another drug or sip another alcoholic drink. I know what happens if I don't stick to that plan.

Boxing earned me some good money and I blew it all. But I'm richer now than ever. I open the post and I get my cheque from the State. I'm broke and I know it. It's hard but it doesn't matter if you're an attorney, a cop, a judge or whatever, everybody's struggling somehow. Everybody has a fight in life. We've got to pay bills, we've got people to look after, and we've got our own issues, both mentally and physically.

The big difference for me now is that I'm surrounded by positivity. I have my girlfriend, my family, my friends, my birds and my dogs. I've got a halo of love around me and that's why I'm the luckiest guy on the planet.